THE THESSALONIAN CORRESPONDENCE

Foundations and Facets

PUBLISHED VOLUMES

R. Alan Culpepper, *Anatomy of the Fourth Gospel*
Fred O. Francis and J. Paul Sampley, eds., *Pauline Parallels*
Robert W. Funk, ed., *New Gospel Parallels: Volume One, The Synoptic Gospels*
Robert W. Funk, ed., *New Gospel Parallels: Volume Two, John and the Other Gospels*
John Dominic Crossan, ed., *Sayings Parallels: A Workbook for the Jesus Tradition*
John L. White, *Light from Ancient Letters*
Robert Jewett, *The Thessalonian Correspondence*
Robert C. Tannehill, *The Narrative Unity of Luke-Acts*

THE THESSALONIAN CORRESPONDENCE
Pauline Rhetoric and Millenarian Piety

ROBERT JEWETT

Fortress Press
Philadelphia

Biblical quotations are the author's own translation.

Copyright © 1986 by Fortress Press

Library of Congress Cataloging in Publication Data

Jewett, Robert.
    The Thessalonian correspondence.

    (Foundations and facets. New Testament)
    Bibliography: p.
    Includes index.
    I. Bible. N.T. Thessalonians—Criticism, interpretation, etc. 2. Bible. N.T. Thessalonians—Language, style. 3. Millennialism—History of doctrines—Early church, ca. 30–600. I. Title. II. Series.
BS2725.2.J48   1986   227'.8106   86–45204
ISBN 0-8006-2111-5

TYPESET ON AN IBYCUS SYSTEM AT POLEBRIDGE PRESS

2540B86   Printed in the United States of America   1–2111

Contents

Foreword to the Series   ix

Preface   xi

Introduction   xiii

1. The Problem of Authenticity   1

    The Contours of the Early Discussion   3
    Wrede and His Successors   5
    From Trilling to the Present   10
    Conclusions   16

2. The Issues of Sequence and Recipients   19

    Theories of Separate Recipients   21
    Theories of Reversed Sequence   24
    Reasons for the Canonical Sequence   26
    Conclusion   30

3. The Question of Literary Integrity   31

    Schmithals' Redactional Hypothesis   33
    The Question of the Interpolation of 1 Thessalonians 2:13–16
      and 5:1–11   36
    Elaborate Theories that Involve Redaction and Multiple
      Interpolation   42
    Conclusions   46

4. The Question of Chronology   47

    The Problem of Correlation with Acts   49
    The Challenge of the Knox Chronology   53
    The Calculation of the Dates   59

5. The Rhetoric of the Thessalonian Letters   61

    An Approach to Epistolary Rhetoric   63
    Non-rhetorical Approaches to 1 Thessalonians   68
    The Rhetoric of 1 Thessalonians   71
    Non-rhetorical Approaches to 2 Thessalonians   78
    The Rhetoric of 2 Thessalonians   81

6. The Situation in the Thessalonian Congregation:
    Inferences from the Literary Evidence   89

    The Problem of Persecution   93
    The Response to the Death of Church Members   94
    The Question of Preparedness for the Parousia   96
    The Conflict over Ecstatic Manifestations   100
    The Criticism of Pauline Leadership   102
    The Problem of the Ἄτακτοι   104
    The Challenge to Sexual Ethics   105
    The Problem of the Anthropological Trichotomy   107
    Concluding Reflections   108

7. The Setting in Thessalonica:
    Historical and Cultural Evidence   111

    Acts 17 as the Traditional Framework   114
    Social and Economic Circumstances   118
    The Political Situation   123
    The Religious Climate   126

8. Previous Models of the Thessalonian Congregation   133

    Traditional Models   136
    The Enthusiastic Model   142
    The Gnostic Model   147
    The Divine Man Model   149

9. The Millenarian Model   159

    The Comparative Use of the Millenarian Model   162
    Cultural Conditions Conducive to Millenarism   165
    Millenarian Symbols and Beliefs in Thessalonica   168
    Millenarian Practices in Thessalonica   172
    Conclusion: Millenarian Radicalism in Thessalonica   176

10. The Reception of 1 Thessalonians and the Provenance
 of 2 Thessalonians 179

 Approaches to the Previous Letter 181
 Passages Susceptible to Misunderstanding 186
 The Motivation for Writing 2 Thessalonians 191

Bibliography 193

 Exegetical and Historical Studies of 1 and 2 Thessalonians 193
 Rhetorical and Linguistic Studies 201
 Social-Scientific Studies 203
 Miscellaneous Historical, Cultural and Grammatical Studies 206

Charts 215

 1. Outlines of 1 Thessalonians Using Thematic Analysis 216
 2. Outlines of 1 Thessalonians Using Epistolary Analysis 220
 3. Comparison with other Rhetorical Analyses of 1
  Thessalonians 221
 4. Outlines of 2 Thessalonians Using Thematic Analysis 222
 5. Outlines of 2 Thessalonians Using Epistolary Analysis 224
 6. Outlines of 2 Thessalonians Using Rhetorical Analysis 225

Index of Passages 227

Index of Subjects 232

Index of Modern Authors 236

Foundations & Facets: New Testament has two major divisions as indicated by the title.

Much of the more creative biblical scholarship on the contemporary scene is devoted to *Facets* of biblical texts: to units of the text smaller than canonical books, or to aspects of the New Testament that ignore the boundaries of books and canon. In one sense, *Facets* refers to any textual unit or group of units that does not coincide with the boundaries of canonical books. In another sense, *Facets* refers to aspects of the biblical materials that are being addressed by newly emerging biblical disciplines: literary criticism and its partner, narratology, and the social sciences in various guises. These two senses of *Facets* produce the second major division of the series with its two subdivisions: Literary Facets and Social Facets.

The creative and innovative impulses in current scholarship are also linked to emerging new methods in biblical criticism or to the reconception of old ones. In addition, the collections of primary comparative material made early in this century cry out to be replaced by new collections, at once more comprehensive and more scientifically structured. These two needs have shaped the first division of the series: *Foundations*. And *Foundations* are of two types: Reference works and Texts for Comparison.

Together, the two divisions of *Foundations & Facets* will form the basis for the next phase of biblical scholarship.

Polebridge Press
Riverbend 1986

Robert W. Funk, editor

Preface

This book has its roots in Tübingen during 1960–64 when I was doing research into the congregational situations implicit in Paul's letters. A preliminary draft of the project appeared in the 1972 *Book of Seminar Papers* published by the Society of Biblical Literature. The decision to revise and expand that draft had several motivations beyond a long-standing interest in the peculiarities of the Thessalonian letters. The first was my desire to explore the method of incorporating rhetorical and social-scientific research into the analysis of an early Christian congregation. This required extensive reading and reflection outside of the arenas of my previous interests. The second was to update my command of the relevant cultural and exegetical literature in conjunction with directing a doctoral dissertation on the rhetoric of 2 Thessalonians by Frank Witt Hughes, which was completed in 1984. The third motivation was quite mundane—to gain experience in creating a technical monograph using a word processor, in preparation for a much larger project that was already well underway: a commentary on Paul's letter to the Romans in the Hermeneia Series. After working on the revision in the summers of 1984 and 85, I was granted a sabbatical leave by Garrett-Evangelical Theological Seminary in 1986 that enabled me to bring the project to completion, for which I am very grateful.

Appreciation is owed to a great many persons who have aided this project in various ways. Conversations with J. Christiaan Beker, Hans Dieter Betz, Karl P. Donfried, John H. Elliott, Thomas Farrell, David Hellholm, Michael Leff, Bruce Malina, Robin Scroggs and Wilhelm Wuellner helped to guide my explorations of rhetorical and social-scientific perspectives. I was aided by critical readings of drafts of this project by Frederick Danker, Frank Witt Hughes and Richard I. Pervo as well as by the helpful comments of anonymous readers recruited by John Hollar of Fortress Press. Charlene Matejovsky, Tami Haaland and Robert Funk of Polebridge Press provided expert guidance in editorial questions, while Walter Cason, Joe Connelly, Don Gardner, Paul Jewett, Gregory Ney, Bill Russell and the support staffs for University MicroComputers and Satellite Software International provided essential help in technical aspects of word processing. I am indebted to graduate students at Garrett-Evangelical Theological Seminary for assistance in proofreading: Martha

L. Blumer, Jeffrey A. Crapson, Jeffrey L. Henderson and David E. Knorr. Finally, I would like to express appreciation to the library staffs, who aided this research in the various stages of its development, at the Universität Tübingen, the Graduate Theological Union in Berkeley, Morningside College, the Iliff School of Theology, the North American Baptist Theological Seminary and most important of all, the United Library of Garrett-Evangelical and Seabury-Western Theological Seminaries in cooperation with the other libraries of the Association of Chicago Theological Schools.

Robert Jewett

The Thessalonian correspondence presents a complex and interlocking series of dilemmas to the interpreter. Ordinarily viewed as the earliest of Paul's letters, this material offers a unique perspective on the apostle's relationship with a troubled congregation. Each of the letters seems to reflect a quite different relationship to the audience, thus presenting the interpreter with baffling questions concerning their relationship to each other and the rapidly shifting congregational situation that could have evoked them. Many different kinds of solutions have been suggested to answer these questions, ranging from theories of inauthenticity, partition and sequence to differing identifications of the audience.

This study offers a combination of traditional historical-critical research, rhetorical analysis, and a comparative use of social-scientific theorizing in an effort to resolve the dilemma of the Thessalonian correspondence. It concentrates on discovering the interaction between the writer and the audience as the key to this dilemma. My thesis is that Paul was faced with a situation of millenarian radicalism in Thessalonica, presenting a unique profile not matched elsewhere in early Christianity. While other Pauline churches were millenarian in the general sense, believing that they were part of a dawning new age and that the end of history would occur in the near future, only in Thessalonica do we encounter a group that proclaimed the actual arrival of the millennium and then proceeded to act on that assumption. The distinctive political and religious background of Thessalonica and the unusually narrow profile of the congregation led to this millenarian construal of Paul's apocalyptic gospel, evoking the emergence of radicals who behaved as if the new age were already in effect for them.

The crisis that required Paul's intervention through the Thessalonian correspondence was a sudden deflation of the millenarian faith. It was caused by the onset of persecution and the death of congregational members, events that were thought to be incommensurate with the arrival of the golden age. But Paul's first letter produced the opposite of its intended effect. To his amazement and irritation the millenarian excitement radicalized even further after the arrival of 1 Thessalonians. The ecstatic announcement was made that the Day of the Lord had come, with Paul's teaching and letter being adduced as proof. In response to this appalling misconstrual of his theology and leadership, Paul sent the sharply phrased 2 Thessalonian letter to set the record straight and bring the situation under control. The distinctive rhetoric of each letter thus reflects a rapidly shifting congregational situation marked by elements of unparalleled radicalism.

My approach in this study is experimental and interdisciplinary. I view the various hypotheses that have been developed to resolve the Thessalonian dilemma as experiments that can be tested by the standard application of the historical-critical method. In the process of working through these alternatives, the shape of the problem becomes clear and the reliable evidence is brought to awareness. The first four chapters deal with these preliminary questions, evaluating previous hypotheses with the aim of providing a firm basis for the subsequent study. Since scholars are divided on the question of which evidence to use and how to use it, it is essential to settle these preliminary questions before proceding. For those who are unwilling to enter into a discussion of the audience situation in Thessalonica, these chapters may at least provide a comprehensive review of introductory issues relevant to any study of 1 and 2 Thessalonians.

The study moves next to the task of rhetorical analysis to provide methodical control of future exegetical inferences as well as to provide a more precise grasp of the relationship between the writer and the recipients in each letter. On the basis of this analysis, the literary evidence within 1 and 2 Thessalonians is analyzed to determine the shape of the congregational situation from the perspective of the writer. Inferences are drawn from the language and logic of Paul's arguments concerning the specific problems reported to him about the Thessalonian church. While I rely as far as possible on the history of research as well as the current stage of scholarly discussion, it is unlikely that everyone will agree with all of these inferences, which are crucial for the reconstruction of the audience situation. An important principle in my experimental method, however, is that no particular audience model or historical setting is allowed to influence these inferences from the literary evidence. By completing this discussion before taking up the question of the appropriate model of the audience, a measure of impartiality is sought in the assessment of the primary evidence.

In light of the literary evidence, I turn in chapter 7 to the unique social and historical situation in the city of Thessalonica. The makeup of the congregation predominately of lower-class Greek handworkers is correlated with evidence of the relative deprivation this group was experiencing under Roman rule. In particular the evidence about the civic cult and the prominent Cabiric mystery religion is shown to have a high degree of relevance in explaining the rise of the peculiar difficulties in the Thessalonian church. With the historical and literary data assembled, the next two chapters deal with the selection and evaluation of specific models for the Thessalonian congregation. Despite my personal share of antipathy for apocalyptic theology and my previous commitment to an alternative audience theory, I conclude that the millenarian model best explains the the exegetical inferences and the historical evidence. In the final chapter the hypothesis about a shaken millenarian radicalism is applied to the question of the puzzling references in 2 Thessalonians to a previous letter, to the appearance of forgery, and to the motivation for writing the second letter. In this final chapter the evidence is set forth concerning a massive misunderstanding of Paul's apocalyptic proclamation, leading to a radicalizing of the millenarian excitement. The study closes with the suggestion that a proper grasp of the audience situation clarifies the peculiar shape of both letters as well as their relation to each other.

Chapter One

THE PROBLEM OF AUTHENTICITY

The discussion concerning the authenticity of the Thessalonian correspondence has concentrated primarily on the second letter. While the early discussion involved both letters, a widely shared consensus has emerged in twentieth-century scholarship that 1 Thessalonians is an indisputably authentic letter, reflecting the earliest phase of Pauline writing. Problematic portions of the first letter are occasionally ascribed to an interpolator,[1] but no one in the current scholarly debate doubts its authenticity. The picture is very different with the second letter. While all but four of the recent commentaries on 2 Thessalonians maintain the traditional view of Pauline authorship, a substantial shift in critical opinion among leading New Testament scholars has been visible since the publication of Wolfgang Trilling's monograph contesting its authenticity in 1972.[2]

Since it provides orientation to the entire problem of the Thessalonian correspondence, I would like to provide a survey of this discussion. While more extensive accounts are available elsewhere,[3] my aims are to evaluate the major contributions and to provide a framework for describing the shape of the Thessalonian situation.

1. THE CONTOURS OF THE EARLY DISCUSSION

At the very beginning of the exegetical discussion of the Thessalonian problem, the puzzle of the relationship between the two letters was manifest. Hugo Grotius attempted to resolve the anomaly of the signature in 2 Thess 3:17 by suggesting a revision of the canonical order,[4] but subsequent critics like J. E. C. Schmidt[5] and F. H. Kern[6] used some of the

---

[1] Cf. the discussion in chap. 3 below.
[2] Trilling, *Untersuchungen*.
[3] Cf. Trilling, *Untersuchungen*, 1–45; Rigaux, *Thessaloniciens*, 112–52; for a history that provides extensive translations of early contributions to the debate, cf. Hughes, *Second Thessalonians*, chap. 1.
[4] Hugo Grotius, *Operum Theologicorum* 2.2.948; translation of relevant portions in Hughes, *Second Thessalonians*, 5–7.
[5] Schmidt, "Vermuthungen über den beyden Briefe"; reprinted by Trilling, *Untersuchungen*, 159–61.
[6] Kern, "Ueber 2. Thess 2, 1–12," 208f.

same evidence to question the authenticity of 2 Thessalonians. As the critical principles of the Tübingen school developed, the skepticism spread to 1 Thessalonians as well. Grounds for such a critique were not difficult to find. Ferdinand Christian Baur pointed out the lack of anti-Judaistic polemic in both letters and noted that the central Pauline doctrines such as justification by faith were missing as well. He saw in both letters an expression of typical Jewish apocalyptic thought, which in the second generation after Paul sought to answer the problem of the postponed parousia.[7] Since the followers of Baur turned attention to Paul's conversion as the fountainhead of his opposition to the Jewish law and the formulation of justification by faith, the very existence of 1 and 2 Thessalonians seemed anomalous. For instance, Carl Holsten recognized that if these two letters stemmed from an early period in Paul's life they would shatter this development scheme. Consequently neither 1 nor 2 Thessalonians could be viewed as authentic.[8]

Scholarly responses to the skeptical conclusions of Baur and his followers succeeded more fully in restoring the credibility of the first than the second letter. C. L. W. Grimm worked out an extensive defense of the Pauline authorship of 1 Thessalonians, but conceded that 2 Thessalonians might be deutero-Pauline.[9] Richard Adelbert Lipsius provided a similar defense of 1 Thessalonians,[10] presenting arguments that were further developed by Adolf Hilgenfeld who maintained the Pauline authorship of 1 Thessalonians but denied it for 2 Thessalonians.[11] Hilgenfeld contended that the first letter fit the situation of Paul's early ministry, before the issues concerning law and circumcision had arisen; the second letter, on the other hand, reflected the circumstances of a much later time when catholic circles were attempting to claim Pauline authority for new eschatological teachings. Scholars such as Lünemann, Bornemann, Jülicher, Milligan, Moffatt and Zahn responded to these contentions with detailed defenses of the Pauline authorship of both letters,[12] while Holtzmann applied the newly developing methods of literary criticism to the question of the relation between 1 and 2 Thessalonians.[13] He argued that

---

[7] Baur, "Die beiden Briefe an die Thessalonicher."

[8] Holsten, *Das Evangelium des Paulus* 2:4.

[9] Grimm, "Die Echtheit der Briefe," 753–813; his critique dealt with the 1845 German edition of Baur, *Paul, the Apostle.*

[10] Lipsius, "Ueber Zweck und Veranlassung."

[11] Hilgenfeld, "Die beiden Briefe an die Thessalonicher."

[12] Lünemann, *Thessalonians,* 10–15, 173–82; Bornemann, *Die Thessalonicherbriefe,* 498ff.; Jülicher, *Einleitung in das Neue Testament,* 43, 46ff.; Milligan, *Thessalonians,* lxxvi–xcii; Moffatt, *Thessalonians,* 11–20; Zahn, *Introduction to the New Testament* 1:153ff. A less technical response to a portion of the debate on authenticity is provided by Askwith, *An Introduction to the Thessalonian Epistles,* 29–52, 76–105.

[13] Holtzmann, "Zum zweiten Thessalonicherbrief," 97–108.

2 Thessalonians was a peculiar combination of condensation and correction of 1 Thessalonians. While most of 2 Thessalonians was a paraphrase and summary of 1 Thessalonians, new features were seen by Holtzmann in the apocalyptic clarifications (2 Thess 1:5–12; 2:1–12) and in a few personal features (2 Thess 2:15; 3:2, 13, 14, 17). These new materials in 2 Thessalonians were notable in Holtzmann's view for their lack of confidence that Paul and his readers would live to experience the parousia.[14] He therefore placed the letter in the generation after Paul as a pseudonymous effort to correct the unbearable apocalyptic expectation generated by 1 Thess 4:13–18 and 5:1–11.

Whether one is prepared to accept Holtzmann's resolution or not, he identified the essential feature of 2 Thessalonians that must be explained in any viable reconstruction. Here is his description of the task of accounting for the peculiarity of 2 Thessalonians: "A hypothesis explaining the puzzle of 2 Thessalonians must above all explain its replacement character."[15] I believe this is one of the most valuable exegetical insights about the Thessalonian problem to come out of this early phase of the debate.

2. WREDE AND HIS SUCCESSORS

The widely acknowledged watershed in the discussion of the authenticity of the Thessalonian correspondence was provided by William Wrede in 1903.[16] Placing the arguments concerning eschatology and the suspicion of forgery in 2 Thess 3:17 in a secondary position, Wrede concentrated on the literary relationship between the two letters. Assuming the Pauline authorship of 1 Thessalonians, he displayed the literary relations with 2 Thessalonians in synoptic columns. While there are few examples of precisely the same wording, the topics in the two letters are covered in the same sequence and the themes of the first letter are reflected with light variations in the second. Wrede stressed that the most striking feature of these parallels is their massive scale, more extensive than in the rest of the Pauline letters all together.[17] Unless one is prepared to assume that such parallels were accidental or that Paul would have slavishly followed his earlier letter for some unknown reason, the likely alternative for Wrede was that of forgery.[18]

Wrede made a serious attempt to reconstruct a situation in which the

---

[14] For a similar perspective, cf. Hollmann, "Die Unechtheit," 28–38.
[15] Holtzmann, "Zum zweiten Thessalonicherbrief," 105.
[16] Wrede, *Die Echtheit.*
[17] *Die Echtheit,* 14.
[18] *Die Echtheit,* 32ff.

forgery of 2 Thessalonians might have occurred in the period between Paul's death and the first citation of the letter by Polycarp in the second century. He clearly recognized the heavy odds against an early falsification and thus set the date around C.E. 100–110.[19] This required Wrede to deny that the reference to the temple in 2 Thess 2:4 implied that the Jerusalem structure was still standing at the time the letter was written. The quest for exegetical confirmation at this point was unsuccessful.[20] The situation Wrede constructed was one in which some Christians had come to believe that the parousia had already occurred (2 Thess 2:2), basing their view on an interpretation of 1 Thess 5:1–11.[21] The forger opposed this doctrine with the argument that Paul never wrote 1 Thessalonians, that it was in fact a falsification of Paul's true views. This explains why in the second letter there is a denunciation of an epistle purporting to be Pauline (2 Thess 2:2; 3:17).[22] In the forger's view, the parousia could not be present because the signs of the last days had not year appeared (2 Thess 2:3–12).

Wrede's portrayal of the extraordinary difficulties in working out a satisfactory forgery solution set a high standard for anyone wishing to follow this path. In the first place, there is scarcely enough time between Paul's death and C.E. 100 for a forgery to gain credence,[23] especially if it must do so at the price of challenging the authenticity of a well known and accepted letter. Indeed, if the precise wording of 2 Thess 3:17 is to be interpreted in light of a forgery hypothesis, it calls into question the authenticity of every Pauline letter not bearing the "mark" of Paul's signature at the end. This would have been a highly risky method of supporting the acceptance of the forgery, a factor that erodes the plausibility of every forgery hypothesis developed since Wrede's time.

A second problem was that Wrede was not able to find proof of a struggle around C.E. 100 concerning an overly intense eschatological expectation which 2 Thessalonians might be countering. It appears in fact that the intense expectation of the parousia typical for Paul's lifetime tended to slacken after his death or be transformed into Gnosticism (Cf. 2 Tim 2:18).[24] This was a serious shortcoming for the Wrede hypothesis, because a forgery theory is credible only if it succeeds in placing a document in a period that corresponds with the views and issues revealed therein.

---

[19] *Die Echtheit*, 95.
[20] *Die Echtheit*, 96ff.
[21] *Die Echtheit*, 67.
[22] *Die Echtheit*, 54ff.
[23] Cf. Dobschütz, *Die Thessalonicher-Briefe*, 36.
[24] Cf. Robinson, *Jesus and His Coming*, 117; Strobel, *Untersuchungen zum eschatologischen Verzögerungsproblem*, 111ff.; Moore, *The Parousia in the New Testament*.

William Wrede's monograph quickly assumed a central role in the debate concerning the Thessalonian correspondence. His views were accepted and augmented by Hollmann, who summarized the four main arguments against the Pauline authorship of 2 Thessalonians that continue to the present: (1) the dependent literary relation between the two letters; (2) the contradictions between 2 Thess 2:1-12 and 1 Thess 5:1-11; (3) the lack of personal references in 2 Thessalonians; and (4) the references to forgery in 2 Thess 2:2 and 3:17.[25] Wrede was strongly attacked in studies by Josef Wrzol[26] and J. Graafen,[27] but their conservative bias and uncritical construction of audience theories undermined their credibility.[28] Wrzol attempted to explain the literary dependency of 2 Thessalonians on grounds that the situation developing after the reception of 1 Thessalonians required Paul to clarify and bring to completion his poorly composed first letter; Graafen offered a less plausible explanation that Paul wrote the second letter to convey thoughts that had arisen in his mind after dispatching the first letter. Several decades later J. Stepien refined the Wrzol approach to some degree by positing a three month gap between 1 and 2 Thessalonians, during which time Paul received information about the intensification of prophetic delusions about the end of the world being present as well as about the further activities of the ἄτακτοι (2 Thess 3:6–13).[29]

Several scholars have created forgery hypotheses in the wake of Wrede's, but for the most part they fall considerably below the level of plausibility that he established. Charles Masson reiterated the traditional arguments against Pauline authorship of 2 Thessalonians, but advanced no new hypothesis about the circumstances of the forgery.[30] Herbert Braun argued that Pauline authorship for 2 Thessalonians was excluded by a "tendency towards postapostolic moralism."[31] Regarding 2 Thess 1:4-10, Braun asserted that Paul never thought of a retribution against persecutors of the church but only for those who reject the gospel, not grasping Paul's apocalyptic argument that in persecuting the church, the gospel was being rejected (cf. especially 2 Thess 1: 6–8). Braun asserted

---

[25] Hollmann, "Die Unechtheit," 38.
[26] Wrzol, "Sprechen 2 Thess. 2,3 und 3,17 gegen paulinischen Ursprung," 271–89; *Die Echtheit des zweiten Thessalonicherbriefs.*
[27] Graafen, *Die Echtheit des 2. Thessalonicherbriefs.*
[28] Cf. Trilling, *Untersuchungen,* 21–28.
[29] Trilling, *Untersuchungen,* 28–30, provides a summary and selected translations of the Polish studies by Stepien, "Pawlowy charakter"; "Problem"; "Autentyczność listów do Thessaloniczan"; "Eschatologia w. Pawla."
[30] Masson, *Thessaloniciens,* 9–13.
[31] Braun, "Zur nachpaulinischen Herkunft."

that the parousia was postponed to a distant future in 2 Thessalonians,[32] without explaining 2 Thess 1:7 which clearly speaks against such a conclusion. And he placed 2 Thessalonians in the period C.E. 107–17, giving no indication that he had considered the difficulties that Wrede confronted. Completely lacking in evidence was his assertion that ἄξιος, ἀλήθεια, and ὑπακούω are non-Pauline.[33] With arguments such as this, it is not surprising that Braun's thesis has repeatedly been refuted.[34]

A novel but equally implausible forgery theory was presented by P. Day in 1963.[35] He notes that while 1 Thessalonians appears to consider the ministry worthy of support, there is an insistence in 2 Thess 3:6–15 that ministers must work just like anyone else. Day suggests therefore that the second letter was written to oppose the establishment of a paid clergy. The forgery was allegedly written sometime between C.E. 52–70, which seems far too early for such a forgery to gain credence. But the major difficulty is that neither letter to the Thessalonians refers explicitly to problems caused by an emerging ecclesiastical hierarchy. The technical terms for early Christian leaders are missing in Thessalonians and there are no references to the support of widows or itinerants. It is therefore understandable that no other scholar, so far as I can tell, has expressed support for Day's hypothesis.

Willi Marxsen's forgery hypothesis is suitable for concluding this discussion of developments between Wrede and Trilling, because it incorporated several sound exegetical observations that must be accounted for in any solution to the Thessalonian problem.[36] He began with the observation that some members of the congregation really did believe that the Day of the Lord had come (2 Thess 2:2), suggesting that this would only be possible with a gnostic or enthusiastic misunderstanding of eschatology. He noted that if Paul wrote both letters he would have to do so within a very short length of time in order to account for the similarities in argument and vocabulary. He concluded that two entirely different congregational situations are reflected in 1 and 2 Thessalonians because the short length of time between letters eliminates the possibility of development between such extremes. This claim, however, lacks one crucial

---

[32] "Zur nachpaulinischen Herkunft," 155.

[33] Cf. the excellent section in Strobel, *Untersuchungen zum eschatologischen Verzögerungsproblem*, 194ff., in which he shows 2 Thessalonians' use of some of these terms to be correlative with Romans 1–2.

[34] Cf. Kümmel, *Introduction to the New Testament*, 188; Michaelis, *Einleitung in das Neue Testament*, 231; Rigaux, *Thessaloniciens*, 130f.; Reicke, "Thessalonicherbriefe."

[35] Day, "The Practical Purpose."

[36] Marxsen, *Introduction to the New Testament*, 42ff.; a more recent version of his hypothesis that takes account of the work of Trilling may be found in *Der zweite Thessalonicherbrief*, 15–56. A less useful forgery hypothesis was presented by Peterson, *Second Thessalonians*.

component. In order to gauge the differences between two situations or the tempo of development from one extreme to another, one must first have a firm starting point, in this case a clear picture of the congregational situation reflected in 1 Thessalonians. This Marxsen did not develop in his *Introduction to the New Testament*. If he had taken advantage of Lütgert's study of enthusiasm in Thessalonica, he might have seen some essential continuities between 1 and 2 Thessalonians, and in particular the basis for the virtually gnostic belief that the end had come.[37]

Marxsen goes on to list four indications of alleged non-Pauline materials in 2 Thessalonians, arguing that they indicate an anti-gnostic provenance shortly after c.e. 70. None of these is very convincing. (1) That the apocalyptic plan in 2 Thess 2:1–12 is fundamentally irreconcilable with the plain eschatological expectation in 1 Thess 4:13–5:11, as Marxsen contends, is likely more true for modern than for apocalyptic thinkers like Paul. If the mere inclusion of an apocalyptic plan is suspect, would Marxsen also place Romans 9–11 in the non-Pauline category?[38] (2) That the eschatology in 1 Thessalonians has a present in contrast to the future orientation of 2 Thess 1:9f. is a generalization that fails to take account of Paul's description of the Thessalonians' past and present experiences in 2 Thess 1:6–8 as signs of eschatological fulfillment. Furthermore, in 2 Thess 2:13–14 one encounters the typical Pauline juxtaposition between present and future eschatology: ". . . because God chose you from the beginning to be saved, through sanctification by the Spirit, and belief in the truth. To this he called you through our gospel, so that you may obtain the glory of our Lord Jesus Christ." (3) Marxsen's contention that the appeal to apostolic authority in 2 Thess 2:15 is non-Pauline does not take account of the similar references in 1 Thess 1:6 to the congregation becoming "imitators of us," or to the definitive apostolic proclamation (1 Thess 2:1–8) and behavior (1 Thess 2:9–12). Paul spoke in the first letter of the Thessalonians acceptance of his message as from God (1 Thess 2:13) and he describes in detail the apostolic ethic they had received (1 Thess 4:1–2, 6–8; 5:1–2).[39] Thus it is hard to accept Marxsen's conclusion that "this emphasis on apostolic authority is a post Pauline motif."[40] (4) Finally, Marxsen argues that the references to a previous letter and to the authenticating signature in 2 Thess 3:17 presuppose a situation after Paul's lifetime. Since Marxsen does not provide an ade-

---

[37] There is no sign that Marxsen had encountered the Lütgert study even in the 1 Thessalonian commentary that appeared fifteen years after the original edition of his introduction; cf. Marxsen, *Der erste Brief*, 16–25.

[38] Cf. Müller, *Gottes Gerechtigkeit*, 77ff.; also Munck, *Christ and Israel*, 131ff.

[39] Cf. Stanley, "Become Imitators of Me."

[40] Marxsen, *Introduction to the New Testament*, 43.

quate rationale for the forger to jeopardize his project by attacking the
authenticity of so many other Pauline letters by the formulation of 2
Thess 3:17, his argument carries weight only if one has eliminated the
possibility that Paul may have had reason to infer from a misunderstanding of his first letter that there must have been a forgery.

A substantial barrier to the plausibility of Marxsen's forgery theory is
the suggested date in the early c.e. 70's. As Wrede recognized, this lacks
historical credibility in the case of a forgery directed to a congregation that
already received one letter, particularly when the forgery presumably
bears within it the claim that the first letter was non-Pauline. Would the
forger not presume that the original letter was still available in the
Thessalonian congregation after an interval of only twenty years? Not
only would the original signature of Paul be likely to be checked, but
would there not also be a significant number of congregational members
still alive who could recall the circumstances and content of the original
letter?

3. From Trilling to the Present

Wolfgang Trilling's investigation of 2 Thessalonians published in 1972
was the preliminary phase of his commentary that appeared in 1980.[41]
After a thorough sifting of the previous research, Trilling begins his
investigation with the following consensus: 1 Thessalonians is an authentic Pauline letter written before 2 Thessalonians; neither the eschatology
of 2 Thessalonians nor the references to a previous letter provide conclusive arguments against the authenticity of the letter; and the major
problem in the understanding of the distinctiveness of 2 Thessalonians is
the unique relationship between 1 and 2 Thessalonians.[42] His central
contention is that the sum of various arguments is required to make a
plausible case for or against authenticity.[43] Trilling then devotes three
major chapters to aspects of the evidence to make a cumulative case in
favor of forgery.

The stylistic and linguistic evidence is somewhat ambiguous, as Trilling acknowledges. Setting aside the lexicographic evidence as ambivalent,
when in fact it points rather conclusively to the same author of both
letters,[44] Trilling moves on to discuss stylistic expressions and phrases

---

[41] Trilling, *Untersuchungen*; Trilling, *Der zweite Brief.* Trilling's conclusions are summarized
in "Literarische Paulusimitation."

[42] Trilling, *Der zweite Brief,* 23.

[43] Trilling, *Untersuchungen,* 45.

[44] The proportion of words peculiar to 2 Thessalonians is no higher than in 1 Thessalonians,

that had been identified in previous studies by Bornemann, Dobschütz and Rigaux. Concerning the seventeen examples of phrases not found elsewhere in the New Testament, Trilling concedes that comparable peculiarities are found in each Pauline letter.[45] While both 1 and 2 Thessalonians contain typical Pauline chiasms and parallelisms, the second letter contains few antithetic formulations and threefold or twofold listings of parallel elements. Trilling concludes that although these stylistic features "alone allow no judgment about the authenticity or inauthenticity of 2 Thessalonians, they speak more in favor of inauthenticity."[46] Since he provides no exhaustive study of such features in other Pauline letters, we have no way of knowing whether variations in frequency are visible elsewhere, so it would appear that such marginal evidence carries weight only for someone who has already decided against Pauline authorship. This kind of negative predisposition seems implicit in Trilling's often repeated claim that only the cumulative weight of evidence can decide the case, because marginal evidence does not add up to superior levels of certainty.

A similar ambiguity is found in his listing of expressions of fullness, repetitions of the term "all," unusual substantive and adjectival expressions, and the repeated use of key terms and expressions, all of which have parallels in other Pauline letters. Trilling correctly infers from this evidence that the author of 2 Thessalonians prefers clear, pointed and unmistakable clarifications to gracious form and flexible expression,[47] but that may simply reflect the peculiar circumstances evoking the writing of 2 Thessalonians. These are precisely the characteristics one would expect in a letter written to refute misunderstandings drawn from a previous letter; unless one eliminates this kind of provenance at the outset, the stylistic arguments against authenticity are inconclusive.

The official, solemn and impersonal tone of 2 Thessalonians conveyed by the stylistic features noted above is, in my opinion, undeniable.[48] There is also a paucity of rhetorical questions and sharply formulated imperative expressions such as are typical for some other Pauline letters. The difficulty is in drawing appropriate conclusions from such data; since Trilling

---

and is proportionately lower than in the other Pauline letters, as Morgenthaler shows in *Statistik des neutestamentlichen Wortschatzes*, 38. The vocabulary of 2 Thessalonians is thoroughly Pauline, as Dobschütz showed in *Die Thessalonicher-Briefe*, 37ff; cf. also Frame, *Thessalonians*, 45ff.

[45] Trilling, *Untersuchungen*, 50.

[46] Trilling, *Untersuchungen*, 57.

[47] Trilling, *Untersuchungen*, 63.

[48] I. Howard Marshall argues against this insight in *1 and 2 Thessalonians*, 34, contending that "it is surely time that the myth of the cold tone of the letter was exploded." But whatever term one uses to describe it, there are substantial differences between 2 Thessalonians and the other Pauline letters that ought not to be downplayed.

rejects any situational explanations, the elements of differentiation drive him to the conclusion of inauthenticity. But can one apply such a method elsewhere in the Pauline corpus? There is a much more hostile tone in Galatians than in Philippians; there is an unparalleled use of diatribe forms in Romans; there is a unique use of the form and style of the fool's speech in 2 Corinthians 10–13; the style of moral exhortation in Philemon is indirect and diplomatic, but in 1 Corinthians 5 it is direct and blunt; the style of 1 Corinthians 13 is poetic and florid, while that in Romans 16 is repetitive and low key; in Romans 1–3 we find the style of the Greek philosophical essay but in Romans 9–11 the style of the Hebraic midrash. By using the same arguments that Trilling employs, one could declare each of these sections or writings inauthentic. What modern Pauline scholarship in fact has discovered is that Paul's style and vocabulary are brilliantly situational; the variations are comprehensible when one takes the unique circumstances of each letter into account.[49] Trilling's conclusions are compelling only for those who refuse to acknowledge the necessity of the same kind of situational exegesis for 2 Thessalonians as is required for the rest of the Pauline letters.[50]

The next chapter of Trilling's study deals with the form criticism, concluding decisively that 2 Thessalonians is a "didactic and exhortative tract" not directed to any specific congregation, whose author "with high probability is not the Apostle Paul."[51] For the most part this argument consists of stylistic and argumentative details discussed earlier. Comparisons are repeatedly made with 1 Thessalonians to show that the two writings are too different to come from the same author. Trilling's assumption throughout this chapter is that 1 Thessalonians is the norm from which any deviation constitutes proof of inauthenticity. It is an argument that would produce disastrous consequences for the Corinthian correspondence even for those who do not accept a division hypothesis. When one considers style, relation to audience, subject matter and tone, the differences between sections of 1 and 2 Corinthians are far more striking than those Trilling discusses. While his observations about the tone, the argument and the contents of 2 Thessalonians are accurate, the fact that parallels for every single feature can be found elsewhere in the Pauline corpus undermines the effectiveness of his argument. It is com-

---

[49] Cf. Beker, *Paul the Apostle,* who discusses the coordination of "contingency and coherence" in Pauline theology. A decade earlier, in *Paul's Anthropological Terms,* I showed the variance in Pauline terminology was due to situational differences.

[50] It is noteworthy that Trilling cites Dobschütz's situational explanation of stylistic differences as an example of unmethodical guesswork, without acknowledging that such explanations are required for every Pauline letter; *Untersuchungen,* 63.

[51] *Untersuchungen,* 108.

pelling only on the assumption that a single mode of discourse is constitutive for Pauline letters, which is completely untenable.

Trilling's third line of argument deals with the theology of 2 Thessalonians, which is viewed as a faded form of Jewish-Christian authoritarianism that promotes a post-Pauline apocalypticism.[52] A major methodical weakness in this argument is that comparisons are constantly made with the later Pauline letters that contain doctrinal material that is missing also in 1 Thessalonians. If one took Trilling's argument with full seriousness, his earlier case for the Pauline authorship of 1 Thessalonians would collapse. That "gospel" is used in 2 Thess 1:8 without the theological sophistication of Romans and 2 Corinthians is an accurate perception,[53] but the same is true for 1 Thess 1:5; 2:2, 4, 8, 9; and 3:2. That Paul fuses his witness to the Thessalonians with the gospel is surely not an indication of post-Pauline authoritarianism, because it is visible in 1 Thess 1:5-10 and 2:1-9. That the call to adherence to the Pauline "traditions" in 2 Thess 2:15 is inconsistent with Pauline usage in some other locations is indisputable, but it is basically congruent with 1 Thess 2:13; 4:1-2, 9, and 5:1. And that Paul uses his own behavior as a model for congregational ethics in 2 Thess 3:6-12 is scarcely a sign of a post-Pauline evolution,[54] since he does the same in 1 Thess 1:6 and 2:9-12. Not only does this line of argument erode the credibility of Trilling's earlier contention of the authenticity of 1 Thessalonians, but it also presupposes a static consistency between Paul's letters that is indefensible.

Trilling goes on to argue that the apocalyptic orientation of 2 Thessalonians eliminates the typical Pauline orientation of joy and expectation. This is an fragile argument, because Galatians is also conspicuous for its joyless tone. Furthermore, the argumentative function of 2 Thess 1:5-10 is to heighten the anticipation of a glorious triumph over evildoers who are currently harrassing the congregation, which clearly involves a kind of malicious, apocalyptic joy.[55] It may not be as morally unobjectionable as Trilling would like, but it is part of Paul's apocalyptic repertoire as one can see from 1 Thess 2:14-17.[56] Similarly, it is clear that the

---

[52] *Untersuchungen*, 132. Trilling elaborates this assessment in "Literarische Paulusimitation," 153f., suggesting that the perspective of 2 Thessalonians was even more distant than the Pastorals from the historical Paul. The presence of salvation is more faint than in Pauline theology, while the concentration on the future is more intense.

[53] Trilling, *Untersuchungen*, 110-14.

[54] *Untersuchungen*, 118-21.

[55] Cf. Bassler, "The Enigmatic Sign," 500-506; cf. also Marshall, *1 and 2 Thessalonians*, who acknowledges the difficulty this passage poses to "modern Christians and humanists" (p. 174) but denies that Paul is really "gloating" over the annihilation of the wicked (p. 179).

[56] Lührmann, whom Trilling cites in his discussion of eschatology, also appears to overlook these traditional elements in Paul's perspective; cf. Lührmann, *Das Offenbarungsverständnis*, 109-12.

picture of God and Christ in 2 Thessalonians is more exclusively apocalyptic in its orientation than is the case for later Pauline letters,[57] but the same could be said for 1 Thess 1:9–10; 2:15–17; 3:11–13; 4:13–5:9 and 5:23f.

A more problematic issue is Trilling's treatment of 2 Thess 2:2. Acknowledging that the past tense verb used in this sentence eliminates translations like "the day of the Lord is imminent," he nevertheless insists that the only possible meaning is that "we stand directly on the threshold of the final events."[58] This appears to be a serious contravening of the clear sense of this citation, motivated by Trilling's desire to eliminate the possibility of gnostic, enthusiastic or any other misconstruals of eschatology. By reading the evidence in this distorted way, he arrives at the conclusion that "it is not necessary to find a particular situation" for 2 Thess 2:2 because it simply reflects traditional apocalyptic warnings of a post-Pauline period.[59] But since we have no other parallels to such warnings in apocalyptic literature, this point constitutes the weakest point in Trilling's construction. The charge of situational vagueness that he uses to argue that 2 Thessalonians is a tract instead of a letter rests in fact on Trilling's refusal to acknowledge the precise bearing of the details in places like 2 Thess 2:2.

In the decade since the appearance of Wolfgang Trilling's investigation, advocates of the forgery hypothesis have remained largely within the framework he provided. Gerhard Krodel wrote his brief commentary on 2 Thessalonians using this framework, following Trilling in stressing the cumulative weight of the evidence: "Equally important are such literary matters as resemblance in *structure, verbal parallels, non-Pauline stylistic elements, and lack of concrete personal data.* If these items are viewed separately, in isolation from each other, one might be tempted to dismiss them. Viewed together they become a strong argument for assuming the pseudonymity of 2 Thessalonians."[60] Actually there is a serious logical misconception in this idea of the cumulative weight of evidence, because the degree of plausibility with which the general conclusion can be advanced decreases with each new piece of marginal evidence. And as we have seen above, the margin of credibility for the various types of evidence that Trilling had advanced is quite low.

Appearing so closely upon the heels of Trilling's initial investigation that no influence is discernable, the dissertation by Franz Laub weighs the pros and cons and concludes, primarily on the basis of differences in

---

[57] Trilling, *Untersuchungen*, 128–32.

[58] Trilling cites Wrede on this point in *Untersuchungen*, 124.

[59] *Untersuchungen*, 126.

[60] Krodel, *2 Thessalonians*, 77; italics in original.

eschatology, that 2 Thessalonians was a forgery.[61] But in the debate that followed, Trilling's arguments concerning alleged disparities in content and historical circumstance formed the center of the discussion. His arguments are repeated in the commentary by Gerhard Friedrich,[62] and in the introductions by Philipp Vielhauer[63] and Helmut Koester.[64] Andreas Lindemann assumes the cogency of the Trilling investigation in his attempt to explain why 2 Thess 2:2 and 3:17 cast doubt on an earlier phase of correspondence as a forgery.[65] He concludes that the author of 2 Thessalonians, writing toward the end of the first century, sought to discredit the authenticity of 1 Thessalonians in order "to refute its eschatological teaching" about the close proximity of the parousia.[66] In his commentary of 1982, Willi Marxsen assumes the correctness of Trilling's conclusions but builds his case for inauthenticity on the foundations of his own earlier study.[67] The only advocate of pseudonymity in the past decade who appears to have been uninfluenced by Trilling was John A. Bailey, who contended that 2 Thessalonians was written in the last decade of the first century to counter Gnostics' claims that their "resurrection" had already taken place.[68]

Despite his extensive effort to refute Trilling's work, it is fair to say that I. Howard Marshall's assessment of the state of scholarship is still accurate: since the early 1970's "the tide of critical opinion has shifted decisively in favour of inauthenticity. . . ."[69] An indication of this shift in favor of non-Pauline authorship is Edgar Krentz's presentation in the final session of the SBL Seminar on the Thessalonian Correspondence in 1983.[70] He provides a comprehensive review of earlier studies, laying particular stress on stylistic and rhetorical differences between 1 and 2 Thessalonians. Some of the arguments are less compelling than others. The second letter has long sentences such as 1:3–12,[71] but there are similar sentences in 2 Cor 6:3–10 and 11:24–31. There is a lack of diatribe

---

[61] Laub, *Eschatologische Verkündigung*, 96–119, 146–57.
[62] Friedrich, *Der zweite Brief*, 252–57.
[63] Vielhauer, *Geschichte*, 89–102.
[64] Koester, *Introduction to the New Testament* 2:241–46; Koester's earlier study, coauthored with Robinson, *Trajectories through Early Christianity*, 153f., took a similar line.
[65] Lindemann, "Zum Abfassungszweck," 35–47.
[66] "Zum Abfassungszweck," 40.
[67] Marxsen, *Die zweite Thessalonicherbrief*.
[68] Bailey, "Who Wrote II Thessalonians?" 131–45, esp. 142.
[69] Marshall, *1 and 2 Thessalonians*, 29.
[70] Krentz, "A Stone That Will Not Fit." The recent dissertations by Hughes, *Second Thessalonians*, and by Glenn Holland also presuppose inauthenticity. Holland's dissertation, *The Tradition that You Received*, was not completed in time to be incorporated into this study, but his conclusions are presented in "Let No One Deceive You."
[71] Krentz, "A Stone That Will Not Fit," 11.

style in the second letter,[72] but the same could be said for other authentic
Pauline letters such as Philemon. That the parallelisms in 2 Thessalonians are "primarily synonymous . . . more rarely synthetic, almost
never antithetic"[73] is clearly different from the other Pauline letters,
however. Krentz concludes that the linguistic and stylistic details raise
questions about authenticity, but allow one to choose either the peculiar
historical situation Paul faced or the option of forgery.[74] This is a surpris-
ingly evenhanded, preliminary conclusion about the bearing of the crucial
philological evidence, given the thrust of Krentz's earlier argument, but I
believe it is forthright and apt. If a compelling case for forgery cannot be
made on the basis of this relatively objective evidence, it certainly cannot
stand on the subjective foundations of argumentative parallels and theological differences, the subjects to which Krentz turns in the decisive
sections of his article. He rehearses the arguments of Wrede and Trilling
about the parallels between 1 and 2 Thessalonians, but these could all be
explained by an adequate analysis of the congregational situation as it
evolved between the two letters. His recital of the differences in theological emphasis fails to address the essential weaknesses of such arguments noted above: many of the arguments concerning differences would
eliminate 1 Thessalonians as well as 2 Thessalonians and comparable
differences surface when one compares other authentic Pauline letters.
While many of the participants of the Thessalonian Seminar reportedly
felt otherwise, I am not convinced on such grounds that one ought to set
the ambiguity aside by concluding that 2 Thessalonians "is pseudonymous
and later than Paul's own life-time."[75]

4. CONCLUSIONS

The evidence concerning the authenticity of 2 Thessalonians is equivocal,
with the likelihood remaining fairly strongly on the side of Pauline

---

[72] "A Stone That Will Not Fit," 12.
[73] "A Stone That Will Not Fit," 15.
[74] "A Stone That Will Not Fit," 19.
[75] "A Stone That Will Not Fit," 37. If the arguments of Trilling, Krentz, et al. are accepted,
however, the task of finding a suitable setting for the forgery of 2 Thessalonians would be
the crucial desideratum. Hughes has presented the most compelling *Sitz im Leben* I have
seen for such a forgery, suggesting that the realized eschatology of Colossians and Ephesians
would have appeared to an advocate of right wing Paulinism toward the end of the first
century as a false claim that "the day of the Lord has come." 2 Thessalonians would thus be
a refutation of a perceived heresy advocated by a competitive branch of the Pauline
tradition. Hughes argues (*Second Thessalonians*, 214) that this theory explains ". . . the
paradox of the rather slavish use of I Thessalonians by II Thessalonians along with the
apparent eschatological incongruities between these two letters."

authorship. While 1 Thessalonians remains on the list of indisputable Pauline letters, 2 Thessalonians must be placed in a category of "probably Pauline." The argument of the first letter is condensed in the second with a very sure touch by someone who had complete command of Pauline idiom. The abbreviated sections are identical in style with the expanded sections, each utilizing typical Pauline vocabulary. Yet the tone of 2 Thessalonians is substantially different from that of 1 Thessalonians, implying a more irritable relation between writer and audience. Pauline authority is much more emphatically expressed in the second letter, the burden of whose argument is a refutation of false views concerning the parousia that had been imputed to Paul's earlier teaching and writing. Despite the fact that 2 Thessalonians is both an abbreviation and an expansion of 1 Thessalonians, its purpose is significantly different.

However one assesses these differences, the contrast between 2 Thessalonians and other pseudonymous writings in the New Testament remains striking. The marks of authentic use of Pauline vocabulary, style and argumentative form are sufficiently extensive that any forgery hypothesis is hard to sustain. I remain impressed by the conclusion of Martin Dibelius at this point: "Where it is a matter of the repeated use of established expressions with minor variations, one should not draw the inference of literary dependency."[76] If a forgery occurred, it was remarkably skillful, which presents a major barrier to the acceptance of any forgery hypothesis hitherto proposed. It is difficult to believe that such skill could be combined with the awkward claim in 2 Thess 3:17, which in light of 2 Thess 2:2 implies that all letters not bearing the mark of Paul's handwriting are inauthentic. This reference jeopardizes the acceptance of the forged second letter as Pauline because to accept it would be to eliminate the entire Pauline letter corpus as inauthentic. It is therefore obvious that the unparalleled skill in forging a letter with Pauline style and vocabulary is strangely dissonant with an effort to discredit the very letters being emulated. The dilemma is particularly acute when the author explicitly reaffirms a previous letter to the congregation in 2 Thess 2:15 as the appropriate basis for shared belief. On these points, the margin of probability in any of the available forgery hypotheses is extremely low. It seems unlikely that any new forgery hypothesis can succeed after so many brilliant specialists have failed to bend these details into some plausible shape.

Thus the dilemma of 2 Thessalonians could be summed up as follows: While the likelihood of definitively proving Pauline authorship of 2 Thessalonians remains at a modest level, the improbability of forgery is

---

[76] Dibelius, *An die Thessalonicher I, II*, 52.

extremely high. Given the options, the more probable alternative is to accept the the authenticity of both letters.

The difficulties that plague the forgery hypotheses would disappear if the same author wrote both 2 Thessalonians and 1 Thessalonians. But the crucial requirement to make such an approach plausible would be to provide an adequate audience hypothesis that explains the peculiar relation between writer and audience in each letter. A careful sifting of the evidence concerning the precise historical relation between the letters and an impartial rhetorical analysis of each letter are required, however, as the foundation for the construction of such an audience hypothesis. It is to these preliminary issues that we turn in the next three chapters.

Chapter Two

THE ISSUES OF
SEQUENCE AND RECIPIENTS

Even scholars who have been convinced of the Pauline authorship of both letters have often been so struck with the incongruity of their relationship that hypotheses other than the forgery type were developed. Various theories have been worked out regarding the intended recipients of 2 Thessalonians either to a special group within the congregation or to another congregation entirely. Others have suggested reversing the order of the letters or dividing the correspondence into smaller letters. An examination of these hypotheses will serve to bring important exegetical observations to light and may help clarify the dimensions of the problem of the Thessalonian correspondence.

1. THEORIES OF SEPARATE RECIPIENTS

One of the most frequently discussed theories was worked out by Adolf von Harnack, that 2 Thessalonians was written by Paul to a Jewish-Christian faction in Thessalonica.[1] His goal was to account for the anomaly brought to light by Wrede, namely the juxtaposition between the peculiar similarity of 2 Thessalonians to 1 Thessalonians on the one hand and the marked change of tone in the two letters on the other. Since Harnack was unconvinced by Wrede's forgery argument, he sought to explain how Paul could have written such similar letters at virtually the same time to the same city. Having written 1 Thessalonians mainly to the Gentile portion of the congregation and insisting that it be read to the other portion as well (1 Thess 5:27), Paul decided to write a special letter to the Jewish Christians to avoid any possibility of offense. The original address of this second letter, 'to the church of the circumcised Thessalonians,'[2] was changed for some reason when the letters were edited in the Pauline corpus. The difference of tone was accountable, according to Harnack, by Paul's lack of friendliness to this Jewish-Christian group. Paul felt himself thrust into a synagogue atmosphere with its liturgical tradition.[3]

---

[1] Harnack, "Das Problem," 560–78.
[2] "Das Problem," 574.
[3] "Das Problem," 566.

Unfortunately, Harnack's contentions were not documented in any detail. The apocalyptic interest of 2 Thessalonians was explained in terms of the Jewish background of its recipients, but in this connection Harnack failed to account for either the libertinistic, disorderly tendencies or the apocalyptic presumption that the day of the Lord had already arrived, both of which appear quite unlikely in a traditional Jewish-Christian congregation. Aside from claiming that 1 Thessalonians does not utilize Jewish tradition at all—which is belied by the use of Rabbinic marriage traditions[4] in 1 Thessalonians 4—Harnack's only other proof was 2 Thess 2:13, taken with the variant reading "God chose you as the first to be saved. . . ." But Acts 17:4, to which Harnack referred, does not necessarily imply that the Jews were converted "first"; and ἀπαρχήν, the less well attested variant,[5] carries not so much the connotation of strict chronological priority as of honor and certainty of salvation within the eschatological plan of God.[6] The most improbable aspects of this theory, however, are that Paul would have encouraged the existence of factions in Thessalonica by writing separate letters, or that he would have been so obtuse not to have sensed the rage this cold and impersonal second letter would have aroused in a faction which was explicitly being read the warmer, more friendly letter directed to its rivals. Thus, except for Kirsopp Lake[7] and F. C. Burkitt[8] this theory gained very little adherence.

Maurice Goguel accepted some of the observations in the Harnack article and suggested a variation, that 2 Thessalonians was addressed to the Beroean church at the same time that Paul wrote 1 Thessalonians to the Thessalonian congregation.[9] This might explain the similarity in subject matter and organization in the two letters, while accounting for the difference in tone on grounds of the synagogal origins of Christianity in Beroea (Acts 17:10–13). But most of the rest of the evidence remains unaccounted in this hypothesis. The references in 2 Thess 2:2, 15 and 3:17 to another letter that has been misunderstood or forged are unexplainable without some reference to 1 Thessalonians. The stiff references to the necessity for thanksgiving (2 Thess 1:3 and 2:13) are likewise incomprehensible without the prior letter with its extensive thanksgiving. Finally, as Best points out,[10] the supposition that the address of the Beroean letter was somehow missing at the time of the collection of the Pauline corpus

---

[4] Cf. Baltensweiler, "Erwägungen zu 1. Thess. 4, 3–8."
[5] Cf. Rigaux, Thessaloniciens, 682.
[6] Neil, Thessalonians, 181; Delling, "ἀπαρχή," TWNT 1:483f.
[7] Lake, The Earlier Epistles.
[8] Burkitt, Christian Beginnings, 133.
[9] Goguel, Introduction au nouveau Testament 4:327–37.
[10] Best, Thessalonians, 40.

and was mistakenly entered as "to the Thessalonians" seems highly implausible. It is certainly not susceptible to proof with any of the evidence at hand.

A similar hypothesis, though quite independent from the work of Goguel, was developed in 1945 by Eduard Schweizer. He suggested that 2 Thessalonians might be the second Philippian letter to which Polycarp referred.[11] This would account for the similarities in content and the difference in tone between the two letters. But Wilhelm Michaelis pointed to the decisive weakness in this suggestion, namely the incongruity of sending the strangely impersonal 2 Thessalonians as the first letter to the Philippians with whom Paul appears to have had the warmest relationship.[12] Michaelis also showed that there are no significant similarities between the situations reflected in 2 Thessalonians and Philippians.

A variation of the special recipient theory was suggested in brief remarks at the end of Martin Dibelius' commentary. The first letter may have been written to leaders of the congregation while the second was dispatched a short time later for use in the worship setting.[13] Some of the evidence that Dibelius adduced for this suggestion, however, speaks more strongly against it than for it. He cited 1 Thess 5:27 where Paul urged his letter should be read "to all the brethren," which hardly sounds limited to leaders alone. It also would have been inappropriate for Paul to appeal to the congregation to respect its leaders (1 Thess 5:12f.) in a letter addressed only to such leaders.

A reversed version of the special recipient theory has been advanced by E. Earle Ellis, that 2 Thessalonians was addressed to leaders of the Thessalonian congregation at the same time as 1 Thessalonians was sent to the congregation as a whole.[14] While Ellis refers to Harnack's study as "a brilliant piece of detection"[15] whose basic observations are "well taken," his reconstruction in fact overlooks the stiff and unfriendly relations that Harnack found in 2 Thessalonians. Not only is the rhetoric of 2 Thessalonians unsuitable for Paul's trusted coworkers, but also the striking disparity in his approach to the "disorderly ones" would have brought Paul under the accusation of speaking out of both sides of his mouth. The gentle advice to "admonish the idle" in 1 Thess 5:14 would appear flatly contradictory to the command of strict separation in 2 Thess 3:6, if the two letters were sent simultaneously. Any effort on the part of Paul's coworkers to enforce the ban would be undercut by the public reading of 1

[11] Schweizer, "Der zweite Thessalonicherbrief."
[12] Michaelis, "Der zweite Thessalonicherbrief."
[13] Dibelius, *An die Thessalonicher I, II*, 58.
[14] Ellis, "Paul and His Co-Workers."
[15] "Paul and His Co-Workers," 19.

Thessalonians with its much more lenient attitude. Finally, that "brothers" in 2 Thessalonians refers only to church leaders is unsupportable[16] and "first fruits" as a potential reference to leaders in 2 Thess 2:13 is a problematic variant reading.[17]

2. THEORIES OF REVERSED SEQUENCE

An alternative approach to the Thessalonian dilemma has been to reverse the sequence of the letters. This kind of hypothesis was first worked out by Hugo Grotius primarily as a way to explain the strange reference to Paul's signature in 2 Thess 3:17.[18] Since this reference is related to the suspicion of forgery, stated in 2 Thess 2:2, Grotius' argument was not very convincing. He combined it with an identification of the "man of lawlessness" in 2 Thess 2:3–12 with Caligula and a suggestion that 2 Thessalonians was addressed to Jews and 1 Thessalonians was sent later to address the Gentile wing of the church.

The reversal hypothesis was further developed by J. C. West[19] and Johannes Weiss.[20] It was set forth in definitive form by T. W. Manson, namely that 2 Thessalonians was written in 49 C.E. from Athens and that 1 Thessalonians was sent the following year from Corinth.[21] By reworking previously advanced arguments and joining them with new considerations, Manson made the following case. First, he felt that the changing persecution situation demands reversal of the order, since 2 Thessalonians refers to the persecution as a present experience and 1 Thessalonians views it as a past event. This argument would be valid except for a situation where persecution was intermittent, and in fact Paul speaks of the persecution as a past event as well as a continuing threat in 1 Thess 3:3: ἐν ταῖς θλίψεσιν ταύταις. Manson argued next that the internal

---

[16] Cf. Marshall's citing of Ollrog's study, *Paulus und seine Mitarbeiter*, 78 n. 93, in *1 and 2 Thessalonians*, 27. That "brother" ordinarily carries an egalitarian implication in Pauline usage has been confirmed by Funk, *Status und Rollen*, 124; cf. also Meeks, *The First Urban Christians*, 86f.

[17] Cf. Rigaux, *Thessaloniciens*, 682, who shows that the reading ἀπαρχήν has been influenced by James 1:18; Rom 16:5 and 1 Cor 16:15.

[18] Cf. the translation of key sections of Grotius's various writings on this question in Hughes, *Second Thessalonians*, chap. 1.

[19] West, "The Order of 1 and 2 Thessalonians," 66–74.

[20] Weiss, *The History of Primitive Christianity* 1:213–23. For a brief critique of this theory written a few years after Weiss' study was translated into English, cf. Thompson, "The Sequence of the Two Epistles," 306f.

[21] Manson, "St. Paul in Greece"; essentially the same solution is favored by Rigaux, *Thessaloniciens*, 69. Hurd states his agreement with the reversal scheme in "The Sequence of Paul's Letters," 198. Cf. also the less technical advocacy of the reversal hypothesis by Thurston, "Relationship between the Thessalonian Epistles," 52–56.

difficulties are dealt with in more detail in 2 Thessalonians whereas in 1 Thessalonians "they are referred to as completely familiar to all concerned."[22] This is an inconclusive argument for the priority of 2 Thessalonians because in a rapidly developing situation it would be natural to deal in detail in the second letter with those matters that had become further inflamed. The same objection stands against Manson's further argument that Paul's statement in 1 Thess 5:1 refers to the instructions in 2 Thessalonians regarding the seasons and the times.

Manson's final argument is that the "now concerning . . ." sections in 1 Thess 4:9–5:11 are related to problems arising out of a previous letter. The difficulty with this assertion is that 1 Thess 4:9–12 does not really deal with congregational hesitancy at applying the harsh discipline commanded by 2 Thess 3:6–15 as Manson supposed. Nor does 1 Thess 5:1–11 necessarily presuppose a previous discussion of the parousia identical with that set forth in 2 Thessalonians 2. Much the same could be said about Manson's argument that 1 Thess 4:13–18 answers the question of the fate of the dead which arose out of his argument for the postponed parousia in 2 Thessalonians 2. It might be so, but need not necessarily be so, because the death of Christians would be a shock to any congregation believing it would live to see the Lord's return. Since the problem resulted from apocalyptic structure of early Christian proclamation and expectation, it need not have arisen out of Paul's discussion in 2 Thessalonians 2. In fact, as shall be argued below, the character of 2 Thessalonians would be much more adequately accounted for on the assumption that it attempts to deal with a fever of eschatological expectation that had heightened since the writing of 1 Thessalonians.

R. Gregson also suggested a reversal of 1 and 2 Thessalonians, although his article does not reflect any dependence on previous hypotheses.[23] His major aims were to eliminate the conflict between Acts 17:14–15, Acts 18:5, and 1 Thess 3:1f. concerning the movements of Timothy and to answer the question of the purpose of 2 Thessalonians. Gregson was convinced that 1 Thessalonians reflected a more mature form of Pauline thought. But that Paul's reference to the punishment of the lawless in 2 Thessalonians is any less mature than his reference to the blessedness of the redeemed in 1 Thess 4:16–17 depends on the unlikely assumption that the lawless and the redeemed had a parallel situation in face of the parousia. Gregson's inference requires a rather modern standard of measuring maturity.[24] And whether a letter of joy (1 Thessa-

---

22 Manson, "Saint Paul in Greece," 441.
23 Gregson, "A Solution to the Problem."
24 Gregson, "A Solution to the Problem, 77.

lonians) is more likely to follow a letter of anxiety (2 Thessalonians) as Gregson argues, is surely beyond the reach of any known historical laws of probability. Gregson does solve the conflict between 1 Thess 3:1f. and Acts by suggesting the second letter was sent with Timothy from Athens while the first was sent later from Corinth. This, of course, assumes a journey from Beroea to Athens about which Acts is silent, and in this connection, reversing the sequence of the letters is not a necessary component to the solution Gregson offers, since the journey Acts deletes could just as well have been the second as the first.

A prominent recent presentation of the reversal hypothesis is that of Charles Buck and Greer Taylor.[25] Without reference to the work of Manson or Gregson or addressing any of the weaknesses noted above, they adopt the reversal scheme of Grotius and West. The major argument they advance has to do with the evolution of Pauline theology. 1 Thessalonians is seen to modify the view found in 2 Thessalonians, that Christians will not experience death prior to the parousia. This hardly seems plausible, because 2 Thessalonians does not really address the question of the death of believers in a manner parallel with 1 Thess 4:13–18. In addition to this alleged development in Pauline eschatology, Buck and Taylor contend that 2 Thessalonians contains a more "primitive" Christology.[26] While 1 Thess 1:10 and 4:14 refer to the resurrection, there are no such references in the second letter. This argument from silence is buttressed by the reference to Christ returning as an avenger in 2 Thess 1:7–8; while it may indeed be true that such violence is "unworthy of the mature Paul,"[27] it is no proof that the resurrection of Christ is not being presupposed. It is hard to imagine that an early Christian writer could have conceived of the return of Christ without also holding to the resurrection. The final argument they advance is that 2 Thessalonians lacks a legal theory such as one finds in later letters like Galatians, but since the same could be said for 1 Thessalonians, the argument bears little weight.

3. Reasons for the Canonical Sequence

If none of the theories of separate recipients or reversed sequence has proven plausible, it would appear that the best alternative is to allow the traditional sequence of 1 and 2 Thessalonians to stand. I would not wish to assume, however, that there is an intrinsic historical logic in the

---

[25] Buck and Taylor, *Saint Paul,* 140–45.
[26] Buck and Taylor, *Saint Paul,* 143.
[27] Buck and Taylor, *Saint Paul,* 144.

traditional sequence. I agree with Bruce in this regard, that "There is nothing antecedently improbable in dating 2 Thessalonians before 1 Thessalonians. The traditional sequence of Pauline letters to churches is based on length, not on date."[28] It is therefore necessary to show that the rhetorical and historical details in 1 and 2 Thessalonians can best be taken into account with the traditional sequence. I believe that the details brought to light by past researchers make it plain that only the traditional sequence is plausible. There are three major reasons why this is so.

(a) References to a Previous Letter

While there are no references to previous correspondence in 1 Thessalonians, there are three such references in the second letter. 2 Thess 2:2 refers to a letter "as from us" which purportedly proved that "the day of the Lord has come." After sifting the various efforts to explain the implications of this verse, it appears there are only two viable approaches. Either the letter in view here was actually a forgery or this is a reference to an earlier Pauline letter that was being cited in a way that Paul disapproved. If there was in fact a forgery, we do not have access to it now; but if an authentic Pauline letter was being misinterpreted, we have only one candidate: 1 Thessalonians. The only viable way to explain the evidence with the data that we have in hand is to conclude that 2 Thess 2:2 is a reference to 1 Thessalonians as misunderstood or misinterpreted by the Thessalonians.

2 Thess 2:15 urges the Thessalonians to "hold to the traditions which you were taught by us, either by word of mouth or by letter," and the past tense of the verb makes it difficult to avoid the conclusion that this is a reference to an earlier letter.[29] Both expressions, "by word" and "by letter" are combined in the same $\epsilon\check{\iota}\tau\epsilon \ldots \epsilon\check{\iota}\tau\epsilon$ construction, dominated by the aorist passive verb $\grave{\epsilon}\delta\iota\delta\acute{\alpha}\chi\theta\eta\tau\epsilon$, so they must both be antecedent to the point of the current communication in 2 Thessalonians. If 2 Thessalonians were an earlier epistolary communication with the congregation than 1 Thessalonians, one would have to hypothesize that another letter had preceded it. Again, the best way to account for the evidence we actually have is that 1 Thessalonians preceded the reference in 2 Thess 2:15.

The third reference to another letter is 2 Thess 3:17 where Paul refers to the "sign" of his peculiar handwriting. When combined with the earlier reference to a possible forgery, this must be interpreted as a means of

---

[28] Bruce, *Thessalonians*, xli.
[29] Cf. Bruce, *Thessalonians*, 194; Dobschütz, *Die Thessalonicher-Briefe*, 301; Masson, *Thessaloniciens*, 109.

authentication. The verse insists that such authentication is on "every letter of mine," which implies that the congregation has access to at least one of Paul's previous letters. Since there is an indication of such a closing greeting in Paul's own hand in 1 Thess 5:27,[30] that letter would fit the requirement of 2 Thess 3:17. Again, if we did not have 1 Thessalonians, we would have to hypothesize a letter like it containing such a closing greeting.

In sum, the fact that there are three references to a previous letter in 2 Thessalonians but none in 1 Thessalonians thus makes a *prima facie* case that 2 Thessalonians must have been written later, a case that is strengthened since 1 Thessalonians contains the details to which 2 Thessalonians refers. If we had no other evidence, these details alone would force one to place 2 Thessalonians after 1 Thessalonians.

(b) References to Persecution

Both 1 and 2 Thessalonians have references to persecution, and nothing is to be gained by attempting to assess the probability of such events increasing or decreasing between the writing of the two letters. What can be assessed are the rhetorical implications of the references. In 2 Thess 1:4–7 Paul refers to their experience of persecution as a sign of the eschatological judgment of God and thus as an indication of the authenticity of their faith. He promises vengeance on their persecutors in 2 Thess 1:8–10. Nowhere in 2 Thessalonians is concern expressed about how the congregation is responding to persecution; Paul simply reinforces their sectarian, apocalyptic outlook that understands persecution as a sign of belonging to the new age rather than the old. In contrast, Paul provides in 1 Thessalonians an elaborate explanation of the apocalyptic significance of persecution.[31] Their imitation of Paul's and the Judean churches' experience of persecution (1 Thess 1:6; 2:14) is construed in such a way as to place their experience within the context of a new age buffetted by the evil forces of the old. Paul reminds the congregation that he and his colleagues had been persecuted prior to the Thessalonian mission and had faced severe opposition in Thessalonica itself (1 Thess 2:2), with the apparent intent of allaying the impression that persecution was somehow inappropriate to the faith. He reminds them in 1 Thess 3:3–4 that persecution should have been anticipated, a reminder that would have hardly been necessary if its eschatological significance had been understood. The mission of Timothy is explicitly linked to Paul's concern that the congre-

---

[30] Cf. Bruce, *Thessalonians,* 135.
[31] Cf. Meeks, "Social Functions of Apocalyptic Language."

gation might be "shaken by these afflictions" (1 Thess 3:2–3), and Paul's joy at his positive report is related to their continued firmness in face of persecution (1 Thess 3:8).

A chronological inference can be drawn from the differing rhetoric of Paul's discussion of persecution in these two letters. If what was argued in 1 Thessalonians concerning the eschatological significance of persecution is treated as having been accepted in 2 Thessalonians, it seems likely that 1 Thessalonians was written earlier. Assuming that information cannot be unlearned, a letter revealing acceptance of a certain doctrine appears to be chronologically later than a letter that teaches such a doctrine in a style that reveals the congregation has not yet accepted it.

(c) References to the Founding Mission

In epistolary rhetoric, it is logical to refer back to the previous phases of a relationship.[32] Ordinarily, however, references to a past contact should be construed as relating to the last contact before writing unless there are clear indications to the contrary. It is perceived as unnatural in an epistolary situation to refer to distant phases of a relationship without taking into account the intervening phases that alter the relationship or add critical new information. It is striking in this connection to observe that the references to previous phases of Paul's direct relationship in 1 Thessalonians are exclusively in connection with the the founding mission. In 1 Thess 2:1–12, there are repeated references to Paul's behavior in Thessalonica and the events that immediately preceded his arrival there. It is clear from this discussion that Paul had only been in contact with the congregation once, which correlates to his reference in 2:17 of having been "orphaned" from them in an untimely manner. In 1 Thess 1:5, 9–10 there are additional references to Paul's relations with the congregation, again exclusively in connection with the founding mission. In 1 Thess 3:1–10, Paul reviews the most recent phase of his relations with the congregation by means of the intermediary, Timothy, whose report had stimulated the writing of the letter.

The contrast with 2 Thessalonians is rather substantial at this point, because the only reference to the founding mission is in a sentence that explicitly mentions a more recent phase of the relationship, namely through a previous letter. 2 Thess 2:15, as we noted above, refers both to a past letter and Paul's oral teaching on the founding mission. This is perfectly consistent with epistolary rhetoric, because it does not refer to an early phase of communication without indicating the most recent phase as

---

[32] Cf. Koskenniemi, *Studien zur Idee,* 35–37, 88–97.

well. But it highlights the implausibility of the suggestion that 1 Thessalonians may have been preceded by another letter, whether 2 Thessalonians or some other.[33]

These reflections are strengthened by the content of Paul's so-called "apology" in 1 Thess 2:1–12. Paul's intent in this section is to differentiate his behavior from that of others who act from "uncleanness . . . guile . . . flattery . . . greed. . . ." There are references here to the manner of Paul's interaction with the congregation, "gentle . . . as a nurse," and "like a father with his children." It would be highly incongruous in this context not to mention the manner of his most recent interaction with the congregation in the form of a letter, if such had been written prior to the dictation of 1 Thess 2:1–12. But all of the references in this section are to Paul's behavior during the founding mission. Both in 1 and in 2 Thessalonians, therefore, the evidence concerning Paul's previous communications with the recipients demand the canonical sequence.

4. Conclusion

After examining the evidence and the related historical hypotheses, one would have to say that none of the reversal or special recipient theories provides a really satisfactory solution to the Thessalonian dilemma. The evidence of the relation between the two letters is much better accommodated by the traditional sequence of 2 Thessalonians being written after 1 Thessalonians. On the basis of examining these hypotheses and reflecting on the implications of the evidence they bring to light, it appears likely that 1 and 2 Thessalonians were written to the same recipients in the canonical sequence.

---

[33] Cf. Best, *Thessalonians*, 45.

Chapter Three

THE QUESTION OF
LITERARY INTEGRITY

The peculiar structure of 1 and 2 Thessalonians, particularly the prominently extended thanksgiving that dominates the opening sections of each letter, has given rise to redactional theories of various sorts. The content of 1 Thess 2:13–16 and 5:1–11 has provoked the emergence of interpolational theories. A fairly comprehensive survey of such theories has recently been provided by Raymond F. Collins.[1] Given the extensive work that Walter Schmithals has done on the Thessalonian correspondence, it seems appropriate to begin with an evaluation of his contribution.

1. SCHMITHALS' REDACTIONAL HYPOTHESIS

Compared with the somewhat primitive redactional theory by Robert Scott,[2] the work of Walter Schmithals[3] impresses the reader with its imaginative qualities and its thorough research. Schmithals suggested a solution to the peculiar literary structure as well as the relationship between 1 and 2 Thessalonians by dividing them into four separate letters. His contention was that these four letters reflect a more rational picture of the development of the Thessalonian situation than can be drawn on the basis of the canonical letters. The resultant letters are as follows:

Letter a = 2 Thess 1:1–12 + 2 Thess 3:6–16
Letter b = 1 Thess 1:1–2:12 + 1 Thess 4:3–5:28
Letter c = 2 Thess 2:13–14 + 2 Thess 2:1–12 + 2 Thess 2:15–3:5
         + 2 Thess 3:17–18
Letter d = 1 Thess 2:13–4:2

This division hypothesis rested on two rather questionable observations. First, the thanksgiving which begins in 1 Thess 1:2 appeared to Schmithals to end at 1:10 and begin again in 2:13. He felt this would be

---

[1] Collins, "A propos the Integrity of I Thes."
[2] Scott, *The Pauline Epistles*, 215–33, posits the construction of two letters from fragments of 1 and 2 Thessalonians, written by Silas and Timothy respectively at approximately the same time.
[3] Schmithals, "Die Thessalonicherbriefe." A slightly revised version of this article appeared in *Paulus und die Gnostiker*. A preliminary version of Schmithals' analysis was presented in "Zur Abfassung." For a discussion of the evolution of Schmithals' view between these three articles, see Collins, "A propos the Integrity of I Thes.," 89–95.

best explained if 1 Thess 2:13 formed the beginning of a separate letter. This suggestion has been made before, notably by Eckart, and as noted above, Paul Schubert has demonstrated that 1 Thess 2:13 is not a new and separate thanksgiving. It in an integral portion of the lengthy but formally normal thanksgiving that extends from 1 Thess 1:2 to 3:13.

Second, in 1 Thess 3:11 and 4:1 Schmithals contended that Paul is reciting typical closing phrases, just as he does in 2 Thess 2:16. This parallel feature of the two letters was viewed as the editorial work of the compiler of the Pauline collection of letters. Bjerkelund's discovery of exhortative sentences containing λοιπόν rendered implausible the idea that 4:1 was a closing formula.[4] It is also clear that a blessing such as 3:11–13 serves to summarize and conclude the arguments of the preceding section.[5] The reference to augmenting love in 1 Thess 3:12 is related to the argument concerning the Thessalonians' labor of love in 1:3, just as the reference to strengthening the heart for the eschatological struggle in 1 Thess 3:13 is related to the argument about the parousia in 1 Thess 3:3ff. Likewise in the case of the second letter, 2 Thess 2:16–17 serves to summarize the entire preceding argument regarding the importance of the Thessalonians' own good works and faith as eschatological fruits providing their adherence to the kingdom and assuring their safety in the parousia. To divide up the materials leading to these epistolary benedictions would be to sever them from a major portion of the arguments they are intended to recapitulate. These observations are related to the pervasive weakness in Schmithal's understanding of the peculiar, eschatologically oriented argument in the long thanksgiving sections.[6] He felt the "apology" in 1 Thess 1:5–2:12 would be inappropriate in the same letter as the reference to the Thessalonians' love and devotion to Paul in 1 Thess 3:6ff., whereas actually both sections fit into the basic argument that in the apostolic behavior and the believers' response, the Thessalonians had experienced the presence of the new aeon. This is not an "apology" that answers objections raised by the Thessalonians but rather an argument that Paul's behavior had been a visible sign of the kingdom.[7] Thus the basic observations upon which Schmithals' hypothesis rests cannot be accepted as valid.

When one examines the resultant portions of the Thessalonian correspondence as Schmithals has rearranged it, they seem to make little sense rhetorically or historically. The transitions between the various sections are barbarous and illogical. For example in letter b the first section would

---

[4] Bjerkelund, *Parakalô*, 128–34.
[5] Cf. Jewett, "Form and Function," 18–34.
[6] Cf. Thieme, "Die Struktur."
[7] Cf. Denis, "L'Apôtre Paul."

end with 1 Thess 2:12 where Paul reminds the congregation that his apostolic activity had included exhortations to the new believers. The focus suddenly shifts in 1 Thess 4:3 when Paul turns away from the discussion of his own activity and begins to talk about fornication. To what then would τοῦτο γάρ refer? The transitions in letter c would be even rougher. The letter is supposed to begin with 2 Thess 2:13 where the δέ obviously sets the description of the holy calling of the eschatological congregation in contrast with something that went before. The most natural contrast would be with 2 Thess 2:10–12 where the adherents of the realm of darkness are described. But Schmithals has placed this section in a later portion of the letter. Likewise the transition from 2 Thess 2:14 to 2 Thess 2:1 is illogical and rough; after the reminder in verse 14 that they had already gained the glory of the new aeon, one would logically expect the indicative to shift to the imperative. That is what one finds in the canonical letter with 2 Thess 2:15. But if 2 Thess 2:1 followed hard on 2 Thess 2:14 as Schmithals suggests, then the force of the eschatological argument in 2 Thess 2:13–14 would be broken by the confusing insistence in 2 Thess 2:1ff. that the parousia had not yet taken place. The natural order of the argument is just as it appears in the canonical epistle, with the issue of the parousia being settled first and then the insistence on the inruption of the new aeon following afterwards. The transition from 2 Thess 2:12 to 2 Thess 2:15 is likewise all too abrupt. If the ἄρα οὖν in verse 15 referred back to the behavior of the adherents of the old aeon in verse 12, the result would be an absurdity.

A serious rhetorical problem in the Schmithals hypothesis is that in the last three letters Paul would be constantly referring back to things he said during his founding mission without making any reference to the discussion of those same topics in the immediately preceding letters. For example, in letter b Paul refers back to his relationship with the Thessalonians during his founding visit (1 Thess 1:5ff. and 2:1ff.) without mentioning his latest communication with them via letter a. This would have struck the readers of letter b as rhetorically incongruous. Then in letter d, presumably written months after the first letter and a long time after his missionary visit, Paul speaks as if the only encounter they had had with him was in responding to the "word of hearing" in his missionary proclamation (1 Thess 2:13ff.). Paul confides that he had tried several times to visit Thessalonica (1 Thess 2:18) because being out of touch with them pained him so greatly (1 Thess 2:17). But he does not mention the three communications that had supposedly passed between them in the meantime. Would it be natural to say, as Paul allegedly did in letter d, that "when we were with you we warned that tribulations would be your lot" (1 Thess 3:4), thus referring back to the missionary preaching rather than to the fact that these matters had recently been impressed upon them in the immediately preceding letter c (2 Thess 2:5–12)? In each of these instances, it would be more consistent with ancient epistolary practice to refer to one's latest discussion of the issue rather than reaching back to the original missionary preaching as if nothing had been added to it in the meantime.

The Schmithals hypothesis also contains some serious historical and rhetorical discrepancies. The "disorderly ones" are treated gently in letter b (1 Thess 5:14) as members in good standing although they were supposedly placed under disciplinary isolation by Paul in letter a (2 Thess 3:6, 14, 15).[8] Another example of incongruity may be seen in letter a which supposedly opens with εὐχαριστεῖν ὀφείλομεν. The expression "we are bound . . ." presupposes that an earlier thanksgiving had been misunderstood as gratuitous flattery. 'No,' answers Paul, 'we must give thanks because of the eschatological gift of your faith and love.' Such a heavy emphasis appears to be rhetorically inappropriate in the opening letter of a correspondence.

Finally, there are difficult redactional barriers against accepting the Schmithals hypothesis. The editorial process by which these supposed letters were cut into the present canonical epistles is too complicated to be credible. In contrast Günther Bornkamm has demonstrated a relatively simple editorial process in the creation of 2 Corinthians.[9] Even in the case of the more complicated redaction of 1 Corinthians, the process is straightforward and comprehensible as compared with the much shorter Thessalonian correspondence.[10] No redactional theory was worked out by Schmithals to account for these complications.

When one adds up all these shortcomings, it appears clear that the Schmithals hypothesis fails to provide a resolution to the Thessalonian dilemma. The evaluation of this extensive and cogent literary-critical analysis results in rendering the original integrity of the canonical Thessalonian letters even more plausible than before.

2. THE QUESTION OF THE INTERPOLATION
OF 1 THESS 2:13–16 AND 5:1–11

In comparison with Schmithals' elaborate redactional theory, which seems to have limited persuasive power, a number of recent researchers

---

[8] Cf. Schmithals, *Paul and the Gnostics*, 212.
[9] Cf. Bornkamm, "Die Vorgeschichte."
[10] Cf. Jewett, "The Redaction of I Corinthians," 411–20.

have indicated a deep interest in the suggestions that 1 Thess 2:13–16 and perhaps also 1 Thess 5:1–11 were inserted into the text by later editors. The modern history of this kind of theory begins in 1905 with Rudolf Knopf's suggestion that 1 Thess 2:16c was a marginal gloss, inserted into the text after the fall of Jerusalem in C.E. 70.[11] Knopf's argument was that no historical event prior to the writing of 1 Thessalonians fits the description of final wrath as well as the fall of Jerusalem. Although this was essentially an argument from silence, it was accepted by James Moffatt,[12] Alfred Loisy,[13] Maurice Goguel,[14] and a number of more recent exegetes.[15] A mediating position, that Paul simply made extensive use of synoptic tradition in 2:13–16 was suggested by Orchard, Schippers and others.[16]

The hypothesis of an interpolation in 1 Thess 2:13–16 has its most persuasive development in the work of Birger A. Pearson.[17] He insists quite correctly that the aorist verb ἔφθασεν in 1 Thess 2:16c "must be taken as referring to an event that is now past, and the phrase εἰς τέλος underscores the finality of the 'wrath' that has occurred."[18] Dismissing suggestions that this catastrophy could be the death of Agrippa in C.E. 44, the insurrection of Theudas in 44–46, the famine in Judea in 46–47 the Jerusalem riot between 48–51, or the expulsion of Jews from Rome under Claudius in 49, Pearson contends it could only refer to the destruction of Jerusalem in 70. That Christian writers interpreted the destruction as a sign of divine wrath is clear,[19] but there is an unmistakable quality of retrospection in Pearson's argument. From the perspective of those who know about the Jewish-Roman War, it is surely the most appropriate choice. But to someone who lived before that catastrophe, several of the other events could easily have appeared to be a final form of divine wrath. In particular, the suggestion made by Sherman Johnson concerning Josephus' account of the riot and massacre in Jerusalem after C.E. 48 needs to be taken into account.[20] I developed this suggestion in "The Agitators and

---

[11] Knopf, *Das nachapostolische Zeitalter,* 139. For an account of nineteenth-century interpolation theories, cf. Clemen, *Die Einheitlichkeit der paulinischen Briefe,* 13–18.

[12] Moffatt, *Introduction to the Literature,* 73, accepts Knopf's argument that the expression ἡ ὀργὴ εἰς τέλος is suitable only for the catastrophy of the fall of Jerusalem, but he does not acknowledge that this verse is an interpolation.

[13] Loisy, *Les Livres du Nouveau Testament,* 135–37.

[14] Goguel, *Introduction au Nouveau Testament* 3:305–7.

[15] Cf. Collins, "A propos the Integrity of I Thes.," 71–74.

[16] Orchard, "Thessalonians and the Synoptic Gospels," 23ff.; for an account of other exegetes who subscribed to this approach, cf. Schippers, "The Pre-Synoptic Tradition."

[17] Pearson, "1 Thessalonians 2:13–16."

[18] "1 Thessalonians 2:13–16," 82f.

[19] Cf. Gaston, *No Stone on Another,* 340–65. Lampe has recently provided a sober sifting of this evidence in "A.D. 70 in Christian Reflection," 166–71.

[20] Johnson, "Notes and Comments," 173ff.

the Galatian Congregation," arguing that Paul was in fact referring to the twenty to thirty thousand Jews that Josephus reported were massacred in this riot.[21] One could also consider the possibilities of the Theudas insurrection and the famine in this connection; the important fact is that there were large-scale disasters that someone might have described in terms of wrath upon the Jews at the time of writing 1 Thessalonians. Contrary to Pearson's assertion, the wording of 1 Thess 2:16c does not require a date after C.E. 70.

The impact of Birger Pearson's study was enhanced by combining the argument for a post 70 date of 1 Thess 2:16c with other details in 1 Thess 2:13–16. He argued on structural grounds against the resumption of the thanksgiving in 1 Thess 2:13, contending that it interrupts the transition from 2:12 to 2:17, the beginning of what Robert Funk called "the apostolic *parousia*."[22] From a more recent rhetorical perspective, however, the transition from the description of the apostolic action in 2:10–12 to the impact of that action on the Thessalonians is smooth and logical, as the analysis in chapter 5 will demonstrate. More impressive are the historical and theological issues that Pearson discusses. That "the Jews" killed Jesus as 1 Thess 2:15 maintains is indeed singular, as Pearson points out, but hardly less sweeping than the reference to the "rulers of this present age" in 1 Cor 2:8, which could include leaders of every nationality. And in light of recent studies of the crucifixion, it is inappropriate to deny complicity on the part of Jewish authorities;[23] there is no glaring historical inaccuracy at this point that would have to be explained by resorting to an interpolation theory. The presence of vicious *ad hominem* details in verse 15b and c is undeniable, however, and the efforts of commentators to tone down the rhetoric to answer Pearson's charge seem to me misguided.[24] That Paul was capable of such viciousness is clear from Gal 5:12, and the mere fact that Paul expresses himself more mildly in Romans 9–11 on the question of his fellow Jews is no proof that he did not write 1 Thess 2:13–16. There are many instances in which Romans differs from earlier letters, but arguments for inauthenticity based on such details have not succeeded in proving to current scholarship that Paul did not write Galatians or the Corinthian letters. While one could wish that Paul had expressed himself more mildly, particularly on the sensitive issue of anti-

---

[21] Jewett, "The Agitators and the Galatian Congregation," 205 n. 5. The references are to Josephesus, *Ant.* 20.112 and *Bell.* 2.224–27.

[22] Funk, *Language, Hermeneutic, and Word of God,* 163ff.

[23] Cf. Bammel, "The Trial before Pilate," 415–51, esp. 436.

[24] Cf. Marxsen, *Der erste Brief,* 49. The frank admission of Bruce is appreciated at this point: "Such sentiments are incongruous on the lips of Paul. . . ." *1 and 2 Thessalonians,* 47.

Judaism, only those desiring a sanitized picture of Paul and the early church are likely to find Pearson convincing on this point.

There has been considerable discussion since Pearson's article on the question of whether 1 Thess 2:14 is the only indication of persection of Christians in Judea prior to the opening of the Jewish-Roman War. He relied on the assessment of Douglas Hare,[25] S. G. F. Brandon,[26] and Leonhard Goppelt[27] in contending "there was no significant persecution of Christians in Judaea before the war."[28] But the evidence in Gal 6:12 clearly indicates the presence of such persecution,[29] and Bo Reicke has recently concluded primarily on the basis of evidence within the gospels that "Christians were repeatedly the victims of Jewish patriotism and zealotism during this period."[30] This is a crucial point also for an understanding of the imitation ethic in 1 Thess 2:14 which Pearson rightly observes is structured differently than other Pauline letters where Paul typically exhorts congregations to model themselves after his own behavior.[31] The point of comparison that the author wishes to lift up is that "you suffered the same things from your own compatriots as they (i.e., the Jewish Christians in Judea) did from the Jews. . . ." Since a major issue in the congregation was the relation between persecution and faith, it is understandable that Paul should have selected the earliest Christian communities as having experienced the same thing as the Thessalonians. Since this is not the only example of Paul's exhorting congregations to model their behavior after that of other churches (cf. 2 Cor 8:1–9:4), it seems inappropriate to contrast 1 Thess 2:14 with "the otherwise coherent picture of the *mimesis* terminology in the Pauline letters. . . ."[32]

Pearson concludes his influential article with a discussion of the method and motivation of the redactor, suggesting that he used phrases and words from the earlier portion of the letter, especially the opening thanksgiving, "in order to provide a putative 'Pauline' framework for a new message."[33] The motivation for the insertion of verses 13–16 in 1 Thessalonians 2 was to create a "'united front' of all Christians against the Jews who have at last suffered in the destruction of their city and temple the ultimate rejection and judgment from God."[34] The interpolation is then brought

---

[25] Hare, *The Theme of Jewish Persecution*, 30ff.
[26] Brandon, *Jesus and the Zealots.*
[27] Goppelt, *Jesus, Paul and Judaism*, 105ff.
[28] Pearson, "1 Thessalonians 2:13–16," 87.
[29] Cf. Jewett, "The Agitators and the Galatian Congregation," 206–8.
[30] Reicke, "Judaeo-Christianity," 149. Okeke argues for the same conclusion on general grounds in "The Fate of the Unbelieving Jews," 129.
[31] Pearson, "1 Thessalonians 2:13–16," 87f.
[32] "1 Thessalonians 2:13–16," 88.
[33] "1 Thessalonians 2:13–16," 91.
[34] "1 Thessalonians 2:13–16."

into correlation with the polemic against Judaism in later strands of the gospels, responding to the expulsion of Christians from the synagogues of Palestine. If the argument for an interpolation had been more compelling, this is surely the historical context in which it was most likely to have occurred. Given the current need to disentangle the interpretation of New Testament texts from the tradition of anti-semitism,[35] I can only say that I wish Pearson were right. It would relieve Pauline theology of a major embarrassment if he were.

A number of articles have taken up key issues raised by Pearson's article. Hendrikus Boers made a plausible case that the form critical analysis of 1 Thessalonians would be aided by the elimination of 2:13–16, making it into a more "normal" Pauline letter.[36] J. Coppens offered a more critical response, listing a series of national disasters that might be referred to in the expression "wrath to the end," and pointing out a similarly hostile Pauline polemic in Phil 3:2. He does concede, however, that these verses appear to be somewhat of a disgression in the flow of the argument in 1 Thessalonians 2.[37] G. E. Okeke addressed the question of whether 1 Thess 2:13–16 is inconsistent with Pauline thought. He showed that the attitude toward unbelieving Jews is different from Romans 9–11 but contended that "the difference does not make the Thessalonian passage non-Pauline."[38] In contrast, Raymond F. Collins minimized the differences between 1 Thessalonians and Romans but argued that the occasional nature of Paul's letters and the development of his thought undermine Pearson's arguments concerning inconsistency.[39] Ingo Broer provided an extensive defense of the authenticity of 1 Thess 2:14–16 and placed the passage in the tradition of the persecution of the prophets.[40] He prefers a dehistoricized interpretation of the wrath in 2:16c, placing the passage in the context of Rom 1:18ff., but he does not hesitate to speak of Paul's conscious use of inner Jewish polemic in response to persecution.[41]

Daryl Schmidt develops an innovative, positive support for Pearson's position by an analysis of the syntactical pattern of 1 Thessalonians.[42] There are similar patterns in 1:2–2:12 and 2:17–3:10 which differ slightly from 2:13–16, but this hardly constitutes support for an interpolation. Paul's syntactical and stylistic range is remarkably broad and varied in

---

[35] Cf. the provocative study by Gager, *The Origins of Antisemitism*. Earlier discussions include Michel, "Frägen zu 1 Thessalonicher 2:14–16"; Hyldahl, "Jesus og joderne ifolge 1 Tess 2:14–16."

[36] Boers, "The Form Critical Study," 152.

[37] Coppens, "Miscellanées bibliques."

[38] Okeke, "The Fate of the Unbelieving Jews," 136.

[39] Collins, "A propos the Integrity of I Thes.," 75–76, 97–99.

[40] Broer, "'Antisemitismus' und Judenpolemik."

[41] "'Antisemitismus' und Judenpolemik," 86–89.

[42] Schmidt, "1 Thess 1:13–16."

every letter. That 2:14–16 has more imbeds, or subordinate clauses, than adjoining sentences is clear, but it is still less than in the long opening sentence of the thanksgiving (1:2–7), which Schmidt believes is authentically Pauline. The few other unique linguistic details that he finds in this section could be paralleled by a similar analysis of key sections in other letters; part of the freshness of Paul as a stylist is his capacity for unique formulation. Hence Schmidt's arguments are compelling only for someone who has already accepted the Pearson viewpoint.

The most recent defense of the authenticity of 1 Thess 2:13–16 is by Karl Paul Donfried.[43] By taking the apocalyptic pattern of Pauline theology seriously, Donfried shows "that neither all nor part of the text in 1 Thessalonians 2:13–16 is a later interpolation."[44] He shows how the themes of imitation and affliction announced in 1:6–9a are taken up in 2:13–16 and argues that Paul refers to "wrath" as the apocalyptic judgment of God manifest in the cross event. While this latter contention fails to explain the specific focus of the polemic in 2:16, that wrath had fallen upon the "Jews" rather than on the human race in general, the presence of a typically Pauline style of apocalyptic in this passage seems clear to me. But given the serious problems in the theological and ethical content of these verses, it is unlikely that agreement can be reached. The recent restatement of the form-critical and theological arguments in favor of interpolation by Norman Beck proposes to excise these four verses from the Christian canon as "an embarrassment."[45] Agreeing with him about the theological and ethical implications of 1 Thess 2:13–16, I only regret that the evidence for an interpolation is so weak. The language, rhetoric and apocalyptic theology of these verses remain thoroughly Pauline.

On a much smaller scale than for 1 Thess 2:13–16, questions have been raised concerning interpolations in other passages.[46] In particular 1 Thess 5:1–11 has been suggested as an interpolation by Gerhard Friedrich because it appears to disparage a false sense of security concerning the return of Christ.[47] Friedrich understands 1 Thess 4:13–18 as addressing anxieties that deceased Christians will not experience the parousia, recommending the very sense of security that the following verses oppose. Since he finds the two-sided audience theory of Dobschütz implausible,

---

[43] Donfried, "I Thessalonians 2:13–16."
[44] "I Thessalonians 2:13–16," 245.
[45] Beck, *Mature Christianity*, 46.
[46] The effort by Ernst Fuchs, in "Meditationen über 1 Thess 1,2–10," 299f., to question the authenticity of 1 Thess 1:2–10 on grounds of the lack of typical elements of later Pauline theology is briefly discussed by Gerhard Friedrich in "1 Thessalonicher 5,1–11," 290. Although the Fuchs article was unavailable to me at the time of completing this monograph, it does not sound very plausible.
[47] Friedrich, "1 Thessalonicher 5, 1–11," 288–315.

with 5:1–11 addressed to enthusiasts and 4:13–18 addressed to non-apocalyptic Christians, Friedrich suggests that an interpolator from the Lukan circle sought to correct the impression that Paul expected to experience the parousia. The interpolator ". . . was concerned to show that Paul had not even spoken about an imminent expectation. He had expected the times and seasons and even his own death [before the parousia]. 1 Thess 5:10 would therefore be a direct correction of 4:15."[48] This article clearly indicates the necessity of a more adequate audience theory for the Thessalonian correspondence, because in the absence of such a theory the thematic transition between chapters 4 and 5 is problematic. But Friedrich's efforts to shore up his hypothesis by discovering non-Pauline elements in 5:1–11 were unsuccessful, as the critiques by Rigaux[49] and others[50] have demonstrated.

3. Elaborate Theories that Involve Redaction and Multiple Interpolation

We come now to a series of studies whose plausibility is on a rather problematic level. The debate over combining redactional with inter-polational theories begins with the work of Karl-Gottfried Eckart.[51] In a study that received devastating critical reviews,[52] Eckart suggested that two separate letters as well as a series of interpolations are combined in 1 Thessalonians. His first observation was that the thanksgiving theme in 1 Thess 1:2ff. is repeated in 2:13ff. He called this a doublet and rejected 2:13ff. as a later interpolation, which has the disadvantage of miscon-struing the form and function of the Pauline thanksgiving. Paul Schubert has shown that the seemingly separate thanksgivings in 1:2ff., 2:13ff., and 3:9ff. are in fact one long thanksgiving, consistent in structure with those in other letters.[53] The leading clause that begins with "we give thanks" (1 Thess 1:2) is followed by three participial constructions and other typical features while the true final clause typical for the thanksgiving form does not come until 3:11. The thanksgiving in 1 Thessalonians, while extend-

---

[48] "1 Thessalonicher 5,1–11," 314.

[49] Rigaux, "Tradition et redaction," shows that while traditional apocalyptic motifs are employed in these verses, the redactional transitions and theological outlook are typically Pauline.

[50] Cf. Marshall, 1 and 2 Thessalonians, 12f.; Collins, "A propos the Integrity of I Thes.," 100f.; Plevnik, "1 Thess. 5,1–11," 72–74.

[51] Eckart, "Der zweite Brief."

[52] Kümmel, "Das literarische und geschichtliche und geschichtliche Problem"; and Thieme, "Die Struktur."

[53] Schubert, Form and Function.

ing for the extraordinary length of forty-three verses, is a "highly complex though formally orthodox thanksgiving."[54] Schubert showed that the thanksgiving was used to introduce and deal with the vital themes of a Pauline letter. He further noted that in the more intimate letters, the thanksgiving tends to be longer than otherwise. In short, a grasp of the form and function of the Pauline thanksgiving would indicate that Paul does not start over again with a doublet in 1 Thess 2:13 as Eckart believes.

As a further indication that two letters are conflated in 1 Thessalonians, Eckart notes that in 1 Thess 3:1–2 Paul says he sent Timothy to Thessalonica, while in 3:6 he says Timothy returned. But Eckart fails to find evidence why Paul could not have explained his reasons for sending Timothy in a letter written after Timothy's return with good news. Such a review of his relations with a congregation is actually not at all unusual for Paul (Cf. 2 Cor 1:1–2:13 and 7:5–8:24). In actuality Eckart's reasons for seeing two reports in this section speak against his hypothesis rather than for it: the parallel between $\Delta\iota\grave{o}$ $\mu\eta\kappa\acute{\epsilon}\tau\iota$ $\sigma\tau\acute{\epsilon}\gamma o\nu\tau\epsilon s$ (3:1) and $\kappa\grave{a}\gamma\grave{\omega}$ $\mu\eta\kappa\acute{\epsilon}\tau\iota$ $\sigma\tau\acute{\epsilon}\gamma\omega\nu$ (3:5) is perfectly understandable as Paul's recapitulation of his motivation and feelings after Timothy returned, whereas 3:5 has no features characteristic of transitional interpolation. Its vocabulary and style are thoroughly Pauline and it extends and explains Paul's motivations rather than drawing a line between two alien sections.

The letters that Eckart derives from 1 Thessalonians are as follows:

Letter a = 1:1–2:12 + 2:17–3:4 + 3:11–13
Letter b = 3:6–10 + 4:13–5:11 + 4:9–10a + 5:23–26 + 5:28

Since neither of these letters meets minimal standards of rhetorical or epistolary coherence, the major significance of this hypothesis has been to stimulate the next phase of research.

The weaknesses of the Eckart hypothesis are compounded, it seems to me, in the work of Ebba Refshauge.[55] He contends that both 1 and 2 Thessalonians were created by combining extensive interpolations with fragments of original Pauline letters. In an elaborate and quite incredible extension of the nineteenth-century "flying fragments" hypotheses, Refshauge posits that the original letters were as follows:

1 Thess = 2:13 + 2:1–2 + 1:6 + 2:17–20 + 3:5–10 + 4:13–14 + 5:1–
              5a + 5:9–11 + 5:16–21(22) + 3:11–13 + 5:25–28
2 Thess = 2:13–14 + 2:1–2 + 3:11–15 + 2:16–17 + 3:17–18

Since the arguments for some of the extensive interpolations have been dealt with above, it suffices at this point to make brief comments about the

---

[54] Schubert, *Form and Function.* 23.
[55] Refshauge, "Literaerkritiske overvejelser."

resultant letters. Both letters commence with the reiteration of the thanks-giving motifs in the canonical letters, thus dropping the portions of the thanksgivings that provide the agenda for the letters. One would not surmise in a letter that opened with 1 Thess 2:13 that the contents were going to deal with the steadfastness required by adversity or the specific issues related to Christian hope, dealt with in 1 Thess 4:13–14 and 5:1–5a, 9–11. Similarly there is no indication in the thanksgiving in 2 Thess 2:13–14 that the second letter contains material about the second coming or the "idlers," both of which Refshauge includes in the truncated 2 Thes-salonians. One could make a similar point about the benedictions that Refshauge selects for the shortened versions of the two letters. 1 Thess 3:11–13 does not include a potential reference to the problem of "spirit" as required by the inclusion of Paul's discussion in 1 Thess 5:19–22. In this regard, the benediction that concludes the present letter, 1 Thess 5:23, would be preferable. 2 Thess 2:16–17 provides no recapitulation of Paul's discussion about the conflict in the congregation concerning the "idlers." From the point of view of epistolography, therefore, the letters do not function nearly as well as the canonical ones. In other respects the hypothesis works somewhat more smoothly than Schmithals', because the letters are retained in their canonical sequence, which eliminates many of the inappropriate references to earlier communications. Nevertheless, in the absence of a viable redactional theory, this hypothesis remains im-plausible.

An independent though similar effort to combine redactional with interpolational methods was worked out by Christoph Demke.[56] Five sections of 1 Thessalonians are attributed to Paul's hand: 2:17–3:2a + 3:5b–11 + 4:9–10 + 4:13–17 + 5:1–22. The other sections were added by a redactor in an effort to make Paul conform to the image of the Pastoral Epistles. This means that despite their thoroughly Pauline vocabulary and style, the sections presenting Paul as a model for the behavior of the Thessalonians as well as those dealing with ethical holiness are attributed to the redactor. There is an acknowledged ideological factor in Demke's redaction-critical method, in that disparities with the later, more clas-sically "evangelical Protestant" letters are taken as proof of inauthen-ticity.[57] Since the original components that presumably derive from Paul make no sense rhetorically or epistolographically, and since Demke's approach requires one to subscribe to a static view of Pauline theology, the results are far from convincing.

Winsome Munro's study offers a reconstruction of the Thessalonian

---

[56] Demke, "Theologie und Literarkritik."
[57] Demke, "Theologie und Literarkritik," 65.

correspondence that is reminiscent in its ideological rationale to Demke's hypothesis, but neither Demke or Refshauge are mentioned.[58] She identifies as interpolations those sections that embody concerns typical of the Pastoral Epistles. Thus the injunctions concerning the disciplining of the ἄτακτοι in 2 Thess 3:6–15 as well as the references to Paul's authoritative tradition in 2:15 and 3:4 are ascribed to an ecclesiastical redactor working in Rome or Asia Minor between c.e. 90–140. Stylistic factors such as the high incidence of antithetic parallelism and distinctive vocabulary are adduced to support the assignment of the ethical admonitions in 2 Thessalonians 3 to the redactor, but this is hardly convincing. If anything, the presence of antithetic parallelism should point to authentic Pauline style, as Weiss and Trilling have shown.[59]

The difficulty in agreeing upon objective criteria for the identification of the interpolations suggested by Munro is illustrated by a comparison with Eckart and Refshauge. Eckart identifies 2 Thess 3:6–10 and Refshauge identifies 2 Thess 3:11–15 as Pauline, each assuming that the other half of the pericope is an interpolation, while Munro eliminates both halves. The lack of sufficiently objective criteria for determining the presence of inauthentic material is also visible in the treatment of 1 Thessalonians, where Munro discerns the "pastoral stratum" in 1:5b, 6a, 7; 2:1–16; 4:1–12; 5:12–15, 21b and 22. Overlooking the careful study of 1 Thess 5:1–11 by Friedrich[60] and making only marginal use of Pearson's study of 1 Thess 2:13–16,[61] she eliminates every reference to the Pauline ethical example, sexual conformity and congregational order. Antithetic parallelism is consistently adduced as evidence of non-Pauline authorship, which would be absurd when applied to indisputably authentic letters. Similarity in vocabulary and content with other Pauline passages that had earlier been eliminated by Munro is asserted without recognition of the circular quality of such an argument. Finally, the remaining fragments that constitute the original Pauline letter in Munro's reconstruction do not reflect a requisite level of rhetorical coherence.[62] Munro's reconstructed letter fails to include some of the most important themes announced in the opening verses of the thanksgiving that are recapitulated in the closing benediction. Although I am far from adverse to accepting redactional and interpolational hypotheses, I find Munro's elaborate reconstruction no more plausible than that of her three predecessors.

---

58 Munro, *Authority in Peter and Paul,* 82–93.
59 Weiss, "Beiträge zur Paulinischen Rhetorik," 168–82; Trilling, *Untersuchungen,* 52–54.
60 Friedrich, "1 Thessalonicher 5,1–11," 288–315.
61 Pearson, "1 Thessalonians 2:13–16."
62 Munro, *Authority in Peter and Paul,* 93.

4. CONCLUSIONS

Finishing this chapter with an examination of Eckart, Refshauge, Demke and Munro does not leave the impression of solid scholarly progress. In a very real sense, each of these elaborate theories cancels the other out by identifying contradictory components of the Thessalonian correspondence as interpolations. One gets the sense that things have not really advanced beyond the level of Schmithals' work, with which the chapter began. While compelling cases have been made concerning limited interpolations and redactional activity in several other Pauline letters, the matter stands very differently with the Thessalonian correspondence. With the exception of 1 Thess 2:13–16 for which more substantial stylistic and material reasons have been advanced, scholarly support for redactional and interpolational theories has not extended very far beyond the persons originally proposing such theories. Even in the case of 2:13–16, as argued above, Pauline authorship is likely.

The major positive contribution of this discussion has been to make it clear that a well designed audience hypothesis is required to explain the peculiar content of the Thessalonian letters. The problems addressed in most of these hypotheses are real, but they are simply compounded by additional, irresolvable contradictions posed by the untenable redactional and interpolational theories themselves. Plausible resolutions are more likely to be found in the peculiar historical and cultural circumstances related to each letter. As we advance toward the analysis of these circumstances, we can proceed with considerable confidence on the premise that both letters are integral Pauline creations.

Chapter Four

THE QUESTION OF CHRONOLOGY

A series of closely related chronological issues must be dealt with in order to provide a firm foundation for dating the Thessalonian correspondence. Despite the fact that the traditional way of putting the question presupposes a correlation between evidence in the Pauline letters with the chronological framework in the Book of Acts, the most serious underlying question is precisely that correlation. Current Pauline chronologists are divided on this question between the traditionalists who work out compromises between the letters and Acts and the followers of John Knox who give priority to the letters.[1] Both positions offer a range of options in the assessment of the Thessalonian evidence. Since most of the Thessalonian commentators in the past have been indebted to the compromise method, a grasp of the evolution of this debate requires that we begin with the traditional discussion.

1. The Problem of Correlation with Acts

From the point of view of those whose chronologies are based primarily on the Book of Acts, the main question concerning the dating of the Thessalonian letters was whether they were written from Corinth during the so-called "second missionary journey" or from Ephesus during the "third journey." Since this would make a difference of some three to five years in the development of the Thessalonian congregation, it was a rather crucial issue.

The later, third journey hypothesis, has been advocated by W. Hadorn, Wilhelm Michaelis, and Walter Schmithals. Hadorn felt that Paul's apologetic self-defense in 1 Thessalonians 2 as well as the many difficulties in the Thessalonian congregation were explainable only if Paul had been absent from the church for a longer period than the traditional, second journey, view would allow.[2] In reality, however 1 Thessalonians 2 is not so much a personal defense as a clarification of the apostolic

---

[1] Cf. the account of the 1980 colloquy on this issue in Corley, ed., *Colloquy on New Testament Studies*, 263f.

[2] Hadorn, "Die Abfassung der Thessalonicherbriefe in der Zeit der dritten Missionsreise," 213–35; Hadorn, "Die Abfassung der Thessalonicherbriefe auf der dritten Missionsreise."

behavior in terms of a sign of the presence of the new age.[3] And there is no reason why questions about the character and timing of the new age would not have arisen very quickly in the new congregation in Thessalonica. Hadorn's theory appears to presuppose a slow, regular, evolutionary development in the early church, and it hardly requires emphasis today that patterns of evolution found in the natural world cannot be applied in any simple fashion to historical phenomena.

In a somewhat similar vein, Wilhelm Michaelis argued that the reference to the Thessalonians becoming "an example to all the believers in Macedonia and in Achaia" (1 Thess 1:8) would be an exaggeration if the churches in Asia and Macedonia had not been in existence for a long time.[4] Again, this presupposes some regular and ascertainable pattern of development in the early church. Furthermore, as can be observed from 2 Thess 3:1 and elsewhere, such statements by Paul are uttered with eschatological perspective and do not result from statistical observations or opinion polls. Michaelis' second argument was that the reference to the dead in the congregation (1 Thess 4:13ff.) indicates a substantial span of time between the founding of the congregation and the writing of the letter. Paul's reference, however, relates to the persecution situation in Thessalonica and cannot be subjected to the laws of probable life expectancy. We have no evidence to prove that one or more persons might not have died within a short time after Paul's departure from Thessalonica. In explaining the eschatological significance of persecution, Paul argued that the Thessalonians suffered the same as the Judean Christians (1 Thess 2:13ff.). Michaelis mistakes the intention of these remarks when he asserts that Paul in 1 Thess 2:14 is giving expression to his "fresh impressions" of the situation in Judea. For Michaelis, this provides a basis for moving the date of writing past the visit recorded in Acts 18:22 when Paul presumably would have received such impressions.[5]

It appears, however, that the fundamental reason Michaelis wanted to postpone the date of 1 and 2 Thessalonians was to confirm the reliability of Luke's account of the movement of Paul's associates. He notes that Timothy and Silas were left in Beroea (Acts 17:14) and rejoined Paul only after he was well established in Corinth (Acts 18:5). This appears to contradict 2 Thess 3:1–2 which states that Timothy met Paul in Athens and was sent back to Thessalonica on an errand. Michaelis' attempt to protect the credibility of Acts failed, however, because he could not set the correspondence in any later time which Luke's account would support. In

---

[3] Cf. Denis, "L'Apôtre Paul."
[4] Michaelis, *Einleitung in das Neue Testament*, 223–25.
[5] Michaelis, *Einleitung in das Neue Testament*, 224.

placing the date in the first year of the Ephesian ministry (ca. C.E. 52), he rightly rejected linking Timothy's travels with those referred to in Acts 19:22 because there is no reference to the Jerusalem Offering in the Thessalonian letters. Michaelis admitted that Acts does not provide any positive confirmation relating to Timothy's travels in the first year at Ephesus, but committed a logical error in using this as proof that the letters must have been written from Ephesus before the travels reported in Acts 19:22. All that could rightly be concluded is that they were written sometime before the travels of Acts 19:22 and this could point equally well to an even earlier provenance in Corinth. In fact, if one were to lay weight on the lack of a reference to the offering in 1 and 2 Thessalonians, then the earlier dating is preferable since the agreement to take up the offering in the Gentile churches was made after the first Corinthian visit, i.e., after the time both letters were composed.[6] Finally, while Michaelis admitted that Acts provides no confirmation for the writing of the Thessalonian letters from Ephesus, he overlooked the decisive evidence in 2 Thess 3:1–2 that Paul's travels involved Athens at the very time Michaelis assumed he was in Ephesus. The result is that in seeking to defend the Lukan chronology, Michaelis succeeded only in casting graver doubts upon it by bringing it into direct contradiction with the primary evidence in the letters themselves.

The "third missionary journey" hypothesis of Walter Schmithals rested on the arguments developed by Hadorn and Michaelis, but its motivation was entirely different.[7] In order to sustain an elaborate audience theory involving invading gnostic missionaries from Paul's Corinthian congregation, Schmithals needed to place the Thessalonian correspondence after the Corinthian letters.[8] Since there is no evidence of such missionaries in the Thessalonian correspondence, this motivation is hardly compelling. None of the weaknesses of the Hadorn-Michaelis approach was resolved by Schmithals, and one gains the impression from recent discussions that this rang the death knell for the third journey option.[9]

At the level of historical details, it is relatively simple to deal with the dating of the Thessalonian correspondence on the premise of the compromise chronologies. Most commentators have used this method to argue that the letters were written during the so called "second missionary

---

[6] This presupposes the three Jerusalem journey chronology suggested by John Knox in which the Apostolic Conference takes place at the time of Acts 18:22; cf. Knox, *Chapters in a Life of Paul*, 61–73; Jewett, *A Chronology of Paul's Life*, 78–104.

[7] Schmithals, *Paul and the Gnostics*, 181–91.

[8] Cf. the discussion of this motivation by Luedemann, *Paul, Apostle to the Gentiles*, 208f.

[9] Cf. Marshall, *1 and 2 Thessalonians*, 21f.; Reese, *1 and 2 Thessalonians*, xii; Best, *Thessalonians*, xxxiv–xxxv.

journey." A major consideration is that the letters bear the impression of having been written a relatively short time after Paul's enforced departure from Thessalonica. In 1 Thess 2:17 Paul refers to having been cut off from them for a short time. The unusual combination of the synonyms πρὸς καιρόν and πρὸς ὥρας into one expression has the intention of producing an impression of the "greatest heightening of the concept of brevity."[10] This expression is appropriate after an enforced absence of several months whereas it is problematic after an absence of three or four years. Throughout the letters one observes that Paul had only visited Thessalonica once (1 Thess 2:1, 18; 2 Thess 2:5; 3:10) and that soon after his departure he grew anxious about the Thessalonians, going so far as to be left alone in Athens in order to send Timothy back to inquire about their welfare (1 Thess 3:1). The first letter was written immediately upon Timothy's return from this mission (1 Thess 3:6). Dobschütz notes that Ἄρτι δὲ ἐλθόντος Τιμοθέου πρὸς ἡμᾶς ἀφ᾽ ὑμῶν implies the first letter was written "under the fresh impression of arrival"[11] since ἄρτι means "now, just . . . at the present time."[12] It may also be that the use of ταχέως in 2 Thess 2:2 suggests a short span of time between Paul's founding of the church and the emergence of the Thessalonian difficulties.[13] Thus the internal evidence indicates that 2 Thessalonians was written soon after Paul's departure from his founding mission.

The question that those indebted to the compromise chronolological method must confront is whether Acts can be reconciled with the sending of the Thessalonian letters from Corinth on the second journey. Whatever one's reasons for preferring this approach, it is essential to recognize that the author of Acts had no intention of providing an account of Paul's missionary partners. If anything, the tendency of Acts is to limit the scope of their activities in order to make Paul the central actor.[14] All that is reported in Acts is that Timothy and Silas had been left in Beroea with orders to come as quickly as possible to Paul in Athens (Acts 17:15). Acts probably would not have reported Timothy's arrival and departure from

---

[10] Dobschütz, *Die Thessalonicher-Briefe*, 120; cf. also Bruce, *Thessalonians*, 55 and Best, *Thessalonians*, 124.

[11] Dobschütz, *Die Thessalonicher-Briefe*, 139.

[12] Bauer, Arndt, Gingrich, Danker, *A Greek-English Lexicon*, 101; cf. Best, *Thessalonians*, 139: "Timothy came back only a short time before this letter. . . ." Bruce concurs in this assessment: "the letter was evidently written as soon as possible after Timothy's recent (ἄρτι) return." *Thessalonians*, 66.

[13] Dobschütz, *Die Thessalonicher-Briefe*, 265, disagrees with this suggestion. Best, *Thessalonians*, 275, concurs with Dobschütz by insisting that ταχέως "is used modally and not temporarally and there is no allusion to the shortness of time since their conversion or since I Th." Marshall, *1 and 2 Thessalonians*, 186, retains the temporal sense but relates it "to the swift effect that the news could have on an excitable people."

[14] Cf. Haenchen, *The Acts of the Apostles*, 513.

Athens even if the author had known about it, for it would have necessitated an explanation of Timothy's mission which would have countered
the basic purpose in Acts. That purpose, after all, included depicting the
triumph of the gospel, not the troubles of early churches. The omission of
these travel details actually causes no real problem if one simply assumes
that Timothy returned to Athens in accordance with Paul's wish while
leaving Silas in Beroea to supervise activities there. Timothy then returned to Thessalonica immediately and only later did he and Silas travel
together to Corinth where Paul was then working.[15] The likelihood is that
2 Thessalonians was written immediately after this rendezvous in Corinth,[16] as indicated by the references to Achaia in 1 Thess 1:7–8. Since the
reference to Athens in 1 Thess 3:2 indicates a recent departure, the evidence in the letters can be smoothly correlated with Acts 18:1.

Making chronological use of these details according to the compromise
method requires a correlation with one of the most widely accepted data in
early Christian history, the Gallio Inscription, which provides the parameters for the Corinthian ministry. This makes it clear that Paul arrived in
Corinth in the winter of C.E. 49–50,[17] making it possible to set the
Thessalonian letters shortly thereafter. With a unanimity that is rare in
New Testament scholarship, all of the recent commentators appear to
follow this method and place the writing of 2 Thessalonians circa C.E.
50.[18] The standard introductions to the New Testament agree.[19]

2. THE CHALLENGE OF THE KNOX CHRONOLOGY

The difficulty with the compromise approach is that this dating of the
Thessalonian correspondence causes insuperable conflicts with other
Pauline letters and the evolution of Pauline theology. The problem is not
with the dating of the Thessalonian letters as such but with their relation
to other Pauline activities. If the so called "second missionary journey"

---

[15] Neil, *Thessalonians*, 62.

[16] 1 Thess 3:6 mentions Timothy alone because Silas had not visited Thessalonica again and his arrival in Corinth with Timothy was irrelevant for the Thessalonian congregation.

[17] Cf. the standard reckoning of this date in Finegan, *Handbook of Biblical Chronology*, 319; for an account of the debate on this issue, cf. Jewett, *A Chronology of Paul's Life*, 36–40.

[18] Cf. Bruce, *Thessalonians*, xxxiv: "It is commonly agreed that 1 Thessalonians, together with 2 Thessalonians, if its authenticity is accepted, should be dated . . . about A.D. 50." In agreement are Friedrich, *Der zweite Brief*, 206; Marxsen, *Der erste Brief*, 14; Marshall, *1 and 2 Thessalonians*, 21; and Best, *Thessalonians*, 11.

[19] For example, cf. Kee, *Understanding the New Testament*, 400; Spivey and Smith, *Anatomy of the New Testament*, 302; Martin, *New Testament Foundations* 2:161; Gundry, *A Survey of the New Testament*, 364; Koester, *Introduction to the New Testament* 2:112; Guthrie, *New Testament Introduction*, 181f.

took place after the rise of the Judaizer crisis, involving the Jerusalem Conference and the subsequent conflict between Paul, Peter, and Barnabas in Antioch, it is impossible to explain why no marks of these conflicts are visible in the Thessalonian letters. In Galatians Paul describes the theological arguments he developed in response to these challenges, involving justification by faith and repudiation of Gentile circumcision as a form of justification by works (Gal 2:14–16). There is not a hint of such a theology in either 1 or 2 Thessalonians. Furthermore Paul refers in a highly negative manner to the "mystery of lawlessness" and the "lawless one" in 2 Thess 2:7–9, categories that are flatly contradicted by the extensive critique of the law in Gal 3:1–4:31. The problem is not limited to 2 Thessalonians, because in 1 Thess 4:1–8, Paul insists on the continued validity of a highly legalistic marital ethic, derived almost verbatim from Rabbinic regulations. Yet it is clear from Paul's description of his stance both in the Jerusalem Conference and the conflict at Antioch that he had juxtaposed faith with law, a critical viewpoint visible in all of the later Pauline letters. But if the traditional chronologies are correct, he abandoned this entire theology in the first letters written after the conference. Then to make the zigzag more complete, he presumably wrote Galatians in approximately the same period as he wrote 1 Thessalonians!

These contradictions are heightened when one takes Paul's statements about his political relations with the Judean churches into account. In 1 Thess 2:14–16, he identifies very strongly and positively with the Judean Christians who are suffering persecution from their Jewish opposition. The Thessalonians are described as "imitators" of these Judean churches, an expression so unlike the attitude revealed in Galatians that it has provided a major argument against the authenticity of this passage.[20] In Galatians there are numerous indications of a highly strained relationship with the Judean churches. Paul argues for both his independence and his relative isolation from these churches (Gal 1:17–22). In his account of the Jerusalem Conference, Paul expresses bitter feelings about the radical Judaizers from the Judean churches (Gal 2:4) and sarcasm about the leadership claims of the "pillars" (Gal 2:2,6). He denounces Peter's hypocrisy in the later encounter at Antioch when he submitted to the political pressures from Jerusalem (Gal 2:11–15). These striking reversals in attitude between Thessalonians and Galatians remain impossible to explain if these letters were written at the same time.

The contradictions caused by the traditional placement of the Thessalonian correspondence in the period after the Apostolic Conference exert

---

[20] For the literature concerning the authenticity of 1 Thess 2:14–16, see sec. 2 of chap. 3 above.

pressure on the evidence both in Thessalonians and in Galatians. Scholars who wish to avoid these contradictions sometimes resort to exegetically desperate measures such as paring back the hostility of Paul's attitude toward the Judean churches as revealed in Galatians.[21] These contradictions would be eliminated if 1 Thessalonians were placed in the period prior to the emergence of the conflicts surrounding the Judaizer crisis.

These observations are sustained by Thessalonian commentators who express in one way or another the impression that 1 Thessalonians is the earliest Pauline letter. James M. Reese refers to 1 Thessalonians as "Paul's first apostolic letter,"[22] a judgment that Willi Marxsen[23] and other commentators share. Without acknowledging the questions it raises for the compromise chronology he uses, Marshall states that "the general character of the teaching suggests an early date in relation to Paul's other letters. This is particularly so with regard to Paul's teaching about the parousia. . . . The teaching about church order also appears to be very primitive. A good deal of Paul's characteristic doctrine is also absent from this letter. . . ."[24]

All of these contradictions would be eliminated if the John Knox type of chronology were adopted. Knox's breakthrough lay in recognizing the insertion of extra Jerusalem journeys in the book of Acts, which has five as compared with the three reflected in the Pauline letters. Accepting the historical canon of favoring primary over secondary evidence, Knox argued for the elimination of the two extraneous Jerusalem journeys in Acts. He identified the first Jerusalem journey of Gal 1:18f. with Acts 9:26-29 and the third journey of 1 Cor 16:4 and Rom 15:25-32 with the account in Acts 21-23. The crucial point in relation to the Thessalonian problem was that Knox identified the second Jerusalem journey at the time of the Apostolic Conference (Gal 2:1-10) with the fourth of Acts' Jerusalem trips (Acts 18:22). This meant that the conference took place at the end of the second missionary journey rather than the first. In other words, the Judaizer crisis and the conflict over the law did not arise until *after* the formation of the European churches and therefore, *after* the writing of the Thessalonian letters. Aside from the superior methodological clarity and the many other chronological advantages of the Knox hypothesis, I consider the resolution of the tangle of the Thessalonian

---

[21] Cf. Best, *Thessalonians*, 113: "Paul . . . cannot have been at such odds with the Judean churches as the Tübingen hypothesis proposes if he chose them as examples" in 1 Thess 2:14-16.

[22] Reese, *1 and 2 Thessalonians*, xii.

[23] Marxsen, *Der erste Brief*, 15.

[24] Marshall, *1 and 2 Thessalonians*, 21; cf. Best, *Thessalonians*, 9. On the other hand, Bruce, *Thessalonians*, xlvii, resists drawing conclusions about the evolution of Pauline doctrine on the basis of important categories missing in 1 and 2 Thessalonians.

correspondence in relation to the Apostolic Conference, the foundation of the European churches, and the writing of Galatians one of the major contributions of his chronology.[25]

There are some serious chronological disagreements, however, between those who attempt to carry through with the Knox method. John Knox himself places the Thessalonian correspondence "perhaps not long after A.D. 40,"[26] suggesting they may have been written from Athens or perhaps from Corinth. His most recent statement on Pauline chronology gives the impression that he would still place this correspondence in the early 40's. Denying the chronological relevance of the Gallio inscription, the Edict of Claudius and the Escape from Aretas for the calculation of the early period of Paul's ministry, Knox uses the timespans in Acts and general estimates to place Paul's arrival in Macedonia in C.E. 40 and the arrival in Corinth in C.E. 43.[27] The rather vague quality of these estimates is visible in the following argument that Paul's travels southward from Macedonia in the period before reaching Corinth can be reconstructed entirely from details in the letters:

> This movement southward 1 Thessalonians and Philippians make altogether clear and certain, and the fact that the Acts story agrees in this respect adds nothing to our assurance. But as to how long he stayed in these cities we have no definite indication. One would gather that he may have remained in Philippi and Thessalonica a year at least— perhaps several years in both of the Macedonian cities—and, from silences, that he spent a shorter time in Athens. These, again, are hardly more than guesses, as anyone's estimates must be.[28]

Knox makes no attempt to correlate these estimates with evidence concerning road conditions, distances traveled, seasonal exigencies, or the length of founding visits based on a detailed reconstruction of Paul's relations with the Philippians or Thessalonians as visible in these letters. About all one can say is that the sum total of the estimates adds up to three years from arrival in Philippi to arrival in Corinth. But there is no basis in Knox's argument to eliminate the possibility that it could just as easily have been two years or five years. In its details the Knox chronology requires one to trust the person rather than his calculations; there appears

---

[25] Cf. Jewett, *A Chronology of Paul's Life*, 103.

[26] Knox, *Chapters in a Life of Paul*, 86.

[27] Knox, "Chapters in a Life of Paul." In his *Chapters in a Life of Paul*, 81, Knox wrote that "Paul must have first reached Corinth hardly later than A.D. 45, perhaps several years earlier."

[28] Knox, "Chapters in a Life of Paul," 350.

to be no way precisely to replicate his results or disconfirm his conclusions.[29]

A book length effort to provide a more reliable basis for the Knox hypothesis was written by Charles Buck and Greer Taylor.[30] Accepting his critical principle of eliminating the conflicts with Acts by relying exclusively on the Pauline letters, they suggest a developmental scheme as the "method of establishing at the outset the order in which the letters were written."[31] 1 Thessalonians had to have been written at about the same time as 1 Corinthians in their view because it counters "the older and simpler teaching . . . that all Christians would live until the parousia,"[32] a doctrine that Paul presumably had reiterated in the "previous letter" to the Corinthians. This lacks the kind of plausibility that might convince other scholars,[33] because the reconstruction of the lost Corinthian letter is so hypothetical and there is no way to eliminate the possibility that the Thessalonians simply drew their own inference concerning the abolition of death until the parousia. In order to move from this inference concerning the sequence of letters to an historical anchor point, Buck and Taylor argue that the "wrath" of 1 Thess 2:16 refers to the Judean famine. But in view of the various possibilities that have been suggested by researchers,[34] it hardly seems appropriate to conclude "There is really only one event in this period that completely satisfies the requirements of the case . . . the famine that occurred in Judea in the year 46."[35] Despite the fact that commentators and historians need to make educated guesses about the likely reference in this verse, I would continue to feel that a reference as open ended as this "lacks the kind of specificity required for chronological usefulness."[36]

Buck and Taylor use some unfortunately vague references from 2 Thessalonains 2 to argue for the placement of 2 Thessalonians in C.E. 44. The "man of lawlessness" is identified with Caligula and the "restrainer"

---

[29] It is rather ironic in this connection that Knox's advocate, John C. Hurd, Jr., refers to my effort to achieve experimental testability in Pauline chronology as "a throwback to the dawn of science when experimenters regularly selected those of their experimental readings that most nearly fit the theory that they were proposing." "Introduction," 269. I would continue to insist that whatever differences of opinion there may be as to which pieces of evidence one includes in the historical data base, the mark of a scientific method is testability. If a chronological hypothesis cannot be disproven by an objective test against the evidence, it is not in this sense scientific.

[30] Buck and Taylor, Saint Paul.

[31] Saint Paul, 9.

[32] Saint Paul, 46.

[33] Cf. Best, Thessalonians, 12f.

[34] Cf. chap. 3, sec. 2 above where the riot and massacre in Jerusalem, the Theudas insurrection, and the Jewish-Roman War are discussed as possible identifications of the "wrath" of 1 Thess 2:16.

[35] Buck and Taylor, Saint Paul, 148.

[36] Jewett, A Chronology of Paul's Life, 35.

with Claudius, with the result that a presumed three and a half year period after the death of the former is brought into relation to the day of the Lord prophecy in 2 Thess 2:2.[37] But since neither of these identifications is convincing, and since there is no way to prove that the Thessalonians were using the Danielic three and a half year scheme, the entire series of inferences appears groundless.[38]

Of the several other scholars who have attempted to develop the Knox hypothesis,[39] Gerd Luedemann has provided the most extensive argument in favor of the writing of 2 Thessalonians around C.E. 41.[40] On several grounds, he builds a compelling case that the Pauline mission in Macedonia, Thessalonica and Corinth antedated the Jerusalem Conference. It is far more difficult, however, to make a case for precisely how many years before the conference these missionary activities required. Luedemann's selection of the year 41 rests on his acceptance of the reference in Acts 18:2 to the Edict of Claudius, which he places in C.E. 41.[41] Roman historians and New Testament scholars are split on the complicated question of the placement of this datum, most of them assigning it to C.E. 49.[42] Luedemann argues that two reports of Corinthian ministries are conflated in Acts 18, and that the opening verses refer to the founding mission in the 40's. This aspect of his chronology is sustained by a literary-critical analysis of Acts 18 that I have critically evaluated in another study.[43] Rather than repeating myself at this point, I shall cite the sharply formulated critique by Jerome Murphy-O'Connor: "It is difficult to evaluate Lüdemann's discussion of Acts XVIII because it cannot be considered a serious literary analysis. All we are offered is an incomplete series of observations developed by means of one-sided dogmatic assertions. Mere possibility is regularly confused with probability. What he says may be correct, but he certainly has not proved it."[44]

Having laid out this chronological argument for the early placement of the Corinthian ministry on literary-critical and historical grounds, Luedemann develops an extensive case that the eschatology of 1 Thessa-

---

[37] Buck and Taylor, *Saint Paul*, 146–62. For the more plausible argument that "the restrainer" in 2 Thess 2:6–7 is God, see Aus, "God's Plan and God's Power."

[38] For a more detailed discussion of the Buck and Taylor hypothesis, with particular reference to its correlation with other data in Pauline chronology, cf. Jewett, *A Chronology of Paul's Life*, 34–36, 76–78.

[39] Cf. Suggs, "Concerning the Date"; Hurd, "Pauline Chronology and Pauline Theology"; Hurd, "The Sequence of Paul's Letters"; Hurd, "Chronology, Pauline," 167.

[40] Luedemann, *Paul, Apostle to the Gentiles*, 201–38, 262.

[41] *Paul, Apostled to the Gentiles*, 164–70.

[42] Cf. Smallwood, *The Jews Under Roman Rule*, 211–15; Scramuzza, *The Emperor Claudius*, 287; Momigliano, *Claudius*, 37.

[43] Jewett, *A Chronology of Paul's Life*, 82f.

[44] Murphy-O'Connor, "Pauline Missions," 87.

lonians 4–5 antedates that found in 1 Corinthians 15.[45] But he runs into serious difficulty in making plausible that this development would have required eight to eleven years. That span of time is obviously required by his chronological calculations of the time available between the writing of 2 Thessalonians in C.E. 41 and the writing of 1 Corinthians in 49; it certainly does not follow any known laws of mental development. The most problematic aspect of Luedemann's chronology, however, is that it requires him to deny the validity of the Aretas datum (2 Cor 11:32f.) and to pare back the size of the seventeen year period that Paul states lay between his conversion and the Jerusalem Conference (Gal 1:18–2:1). Since Luedemann places the Conference in C.E. 47, this requires him to violate these details from the Pauline letters, which, according to the Knox principle he is following, should have absolute priority over any detail in the Book of Acts, such as the reconstruction of the Corinthian ministry. Despite its superior testability as compared with the Knox chronology, the negative assessment of reviewers indicates the lack of plausibility.[46] Thus at this point, the argument for an extremely early placement of the Thessalonian correspondence has not stood up to critical examination.

3. The Calculation of the Dates

I worked out an alternative approach to the problem of dating the Thessalonian correspondence in *A Chronology of Paul's Life,* combining the John Knox hypothesis with an extensive series of chronological details both from the letters and from Acts. The critical principle employed in this chronology is derived from Knox, that no detail in Acts should be allowed to enter the data base if it conflicts with a detail in the primary evidence, the Pauline letters. This principle is connected with a thoroughly experimental approach to the problem of Pauline chronology, which reasons on the basis of interlocking chronological periods, and then calculates the implications as precisely as possible by use of maps, travel schedules, and climatic contingencies. This chronology places the founding mission in Thessalonica in the latter part of C.E. 49 and the mission in Corinth starting at the beginning of C.E. 50, more than a year and a half before the Jerusalem Conference in October, C.E. 51. With this frame-

---

[45] Luedemann, *Paul, Apostle to the Gentiles,* 239–44.

[46] Murphy-O'Connor's conclusion in "Pauline Missions," 88, is quite devastating: "Lüdemann's chronology is nothing more than a lofty edifice of speculation floating in mid-air; he has committed himself to a chimera." For a more nuanced appraisal, cf. Hübner, "Review of Gerd Lüdemann," cols. 741–44. Luedemann's chronology has been accepted, on the other hand, by Schade, *Apokalyptische Christologie bei Paulus,* 173–90. For a discussion of other evaluations, cf. Luedemann, *Paul, Apostle to the Gentiles,* 289–93.

work, the dating scheme that Thessalonian commentators have adopted can be accepted without difficulty and the contradictions in the evolution of Pauline theology and his relations with the Judean church are eliminated. The Thessalonian letters can be placed during the founding mission to Corinth and still reflect the circumstances prior to the emergence of the Judaizer crisis.

On the basis of this form of the Knox chronology, the more precise dating of the Thessalonian letters depends on inferences drawn from the references to Timothy and Silas with Paul at the time of writing (1 Thess 1:1; 2 Thess 1:1). The letters must have been written sometime after these colleagues rejoined Paul in Corinth. Since Paul arrived in Corinth in the winter of C.E. 49–50, it seems probable that the rendezvous did not take place until early spring. Paul shared the widespread dislike of winter traveling and Acts indicates that Paul was already "occupied with preaching" in Corinth before their arrival (Acts 18:5). A further consideration is that shipping did not usually open on the Aegean Sea until February or March and the extremely short lapse between 1 and 2 Thessalonians suggests the presence of rapid transportation. If Timothy arrived in Athens during October or November, C.E. 49, and had been sent back by land to Thessalonica (a ten day journey covering approximately 350 kilometers), he would have had ample time to spend several months "strengthening and exhorting" the congregation (1 Thess 3:2) before returning in early spring to Corinth with his report. 1 Thessalonians was sent to answer the particular questions that Timothy brought and to cope with the congregational dilemmas that he reported. Reckoning several weeks to a month for the results of Paul's first letter to be evident, it appears that some word came to Paul about the reactions of the congregation. The second letter could very well have followed the first within a period of five to seven weeks.[47] The extraordinary similarity in argument and vocabulary, the continuance of the persecution in Thessalonica (2 Thess 1:4), and the fact that Timothy and Silas were still with Paul in Corinth—all of these factors demand as short a lapse of time as possible between the two letters. The result of these considerations is a placement of both of the Thessalonian letters in the spring of C.E. 50, the first being written six to eight months after Paul's departure from Thessalonica.

---

[47] Cf. Dobschütz, *Die Thessalonicher-Briefe,* 22 and Frame, *Thessalonians,* 19.

Chapter Five

THE RHETORIC OF
THE THESSALONIAN LETTERS

Previous studies of the integrity, sequence and audience of the Thessalonians letters have thrown considerable light on the question of its rhetoric. Many of the crucial exegetical observations on which such reconstructions rested had to do with the peculiar organization of each letter. We have had occasion to remark several times, for example, that both letters contain very prominent thanksgiving sections that are unparalleled in other Pauline writings. Yet up to the present moment, no commentary has been written that takes full account of the rhetoric of these letters. Two recent dissertations have been written about the rhetoric of 2 Thessalonians and one study was published in 1979 on the genre of 1 Thessalonians.[1] The first monograph that includes a short discussion of the rhetoric of the two letters was written by George A. Kennedy in 1984.[2] The relevance of this work for our effort to grasp the communicative situation reflected in the Thessalonian correspondence is captured in Kennedy's statement that the "ultimate goal of rhetorical analysis, briefly put, is the discovery of the author's intent and of how that is transmitted through a text to an audience."[3]

1. AN APPROACH TO EPISTOLARY RHETORIC

Classical rhetoric aimed at training speakers and writers to persuade their audiences to make some kind of change in their situation.[4] While some advice was offered to tailor rhetoric to the psychology of specific audiences,[5] the main concentration was on the activity of the communicator.[6] It was therefore natural that earlier studies of the rhetoric of Pauline

---

[1] Hughes, *Second Thessalonians*; Holland, *The Tradition that You Received*; Koester, "I Thessalonians."
[2] Kennedy, *New Testament Interpretation.*
[3] *New Testament Interpretation.* 12.
[4] Cf. Lausberg, *Elemente der literarischen Rhetorik*, 15f.; Martin, *Antike Rhetorik*, 2–12. Cf. also Mainberger, "Rhetorik oder die Technologie des Scheins," 7–10; Mainberger's second article, "Der Leib der Rhetorik," deals with the widely assumed task of classical rhetoric as a means of persuading audiences rather than dealing with truth in any final sense.
[5] Cf. Wuellner, "Paul's Rhetoric of Argumentation," 156; Perelman and Olbrechts-Tyteca, *The New Rhetoric*, 23–26.
[6] Cf. Brock and Scott (eds.), *Methods of Rhetorical Criticism*, 33–37.

material concentrated on the literary style, structure and argumentative devices employed by the author.[7] The tendency to construe rhetoric largely in terms of the invention and arrangement of the argument, using the sophisticated categories developed by Greek and Latin rhetoricians, is characteristic of the important recent work of Hans Dieter Betz.[8] He has identified the rhetorical genre of the letters and letter fragments he has analyzed, and has provided well-grounded analyses of the literary structure of the arguments. But his orientation to classical rhetoric and traditional form and literary criticism predisposes him to overlook the potential of rhetoric to aid in the reconstruction of the audience situation and the external circumstances related to the writing. Significant efforts by recent scholars to grasp the wider ramifications of rhetoric are available in studies by Edwin A. Judge,[9] Wilhelm Wuellner,[10] Michael Bünker,[11] Folker Siegert[12] and others.[13] None of these studies, however, presents the total communication process implicit in a Pauline letter, including detailed reconstructions not only of the author's message but also of the audience to which it was directed and the circumstances surrounding the communication.[14]

While I wish to make extensive use of the resources of classical rhetoric, since it offers the clearest access to the way material was formed in the Greco-Roman world, I believe that the New Rhetoric and closely associated linguistic theories offer a more comprehensive grasp of epistolary communication. The various theorists associated with the New Rhetoric ". . . share a rejection of the speaker orientation of the traditional perspective."[15] They draw attention to the social context of human communication, thereby placing the insights and tools of classical rhetoric within a larger framework accessible to modern social sciences. A definitive

---

[7] Cf. Wilke, *Die neutestamentliche Rhetorik,* 469–75; Weiss, "Beiträge zur Paulinischen Rhetorik"; Koenig, *Stilistik, Rhetorik, Poetik*; Norden, *Die antike Kunstprosa* 1:492–510; Bultmann, *Der Stil der paulinischen Predigt,* 96–103; Allo, "Le défaut d'éloquence," 36–39.

[8] Betz, *Der Apostle Paulus*; *Galatians*; "The Literary Composition"; *2 Corinthians 8 and 9.*

[9] Judge draws inferences not only from the social setting of Paul's proclamation but also from a rhetorical appraisal that ranks him "as an orator and writer of rare distinction" in "The Early Christians," 137; cf. also his "St. Paul and Classical Society."

[10] Wuellner, "Paul's Rhetoric of Argumentation"; Wuellner, "Greek Rhetoric and Pauline Argumentation."

[11] Bünker, *Briefformular and rhetorische Disposition.*

[12] Siegert, *Argumentation bei Paulus gezeigt an Römer 9–11.*

[13] Wilder's *Early Christian Rhetoric,* deals primarily with literary genres and gospel material but there is a brief discussion of epistolary materials on 31–34. Edmund Arens offers a sophisticated application of modern speech-act theory and other linguistic resources in *Kommunikative Handlungen.*

[14] Petersen's recent investigation of the "story" implicit in a Pauline letter relies on the theory of literary criticism rather than rhetoric, but his aim is similar to that in the present investigation; cf. *Rediscovering Paul.*

[15] Brock and Scott, *Methods of Rhetorical Criticism,* 267.

statement of this position is provided by Perelman and Olbrechts-Tyteca whose orientation provides prominent space for the discussion of "The Speaker and His Audience," "The Audience as a Construction of the Speaker," and the "Adaption of the Speaker to the Audience."[16] They contend that "since argumentation aims at securing the adherence of those to whom it is addressed, it is, in its entirety, relative to the audience to be influenced."[17] It follows that "knowledge of those one wishes to win over is a condition preliminary to all effectual argumentation,"[18] and that the social functions of writer and audience have a decisive effect on the rhetorical genre that is selected.[19] These observations are relevant for historical research, offering the possibility of inferences drawn from the structure and genre of a writing to the identity and social roles of audience and speaker alike.

An impressive body of linguistic research could be correlated with the concerns of the New Rhetoric in ways that are productive for historical exegesis. David Hellholm has provided the most extensive synthesis of a wide range of hermeneutical, linguistic, and semiotic theories that I have found, stressing the decisive significance of the "communication situation."[20] He employs the comprehensive model of the communication process developed by Elisabeth Gülich and Wolfgang Raible, taking into account the language and intention of the speaker or writer, the form and language employed in the communication, the predisposition and reaction of the hearers or readers, and the situation both inside and outside of the specific communication exchange.[21] This elaboration of Karl Bühler's use of the classical Greek conception of communication involving a speaker, a text, an audience and a subject matter[22] allows us to confirm the link between ancient and modern communication theory. It is also related to the oft-cited triad of the means of persuasion in classical rhetoric: the *ethos* of the speaker, the *pathos* that can be evoked in the audience and the *logos* of the spoken or written message.[23]

The field of sociolinguistics confirms the effort to place the interpretation of written discourse such as a Pauline letter within the broader

---

[16] Perelmann and Olbrechts-Tyteca, *The New Rhetoric*, 17–26.

[17] *The New Rhetoric*, 10.

[18] *The New Rhetoric*, 20.

[19] *The New Rhetoric*, 21.

[20] Hellholm, *Das Visionenbuch*, 42; for a much more simplistic approach to the social setting of discourse, using common sense and some categories from classical rhetoric, cf. Bitzer, "The Rhetorical Situation," and Brandt, *The Rhetoric of Argumentation*.

[21] Gühlich and Raible, *Linguistische Textmodelle*, 25.

[22] Bühler, *Die Axiomatik der Sprachwissenschaften*; Bühler, *Sprachtheorie*, 24ff; cf. Innis, *Karl Bühler*.

[23] Aristotle *Rhetoric* 2.1355–56; Cicero *De Oratore* 2.115, 183–85; Cf. Kennedy, *Classical Rhetoric*, 67–70.

social context. The fundamental conviction of sociolinguistics, in John B. Pride's words, is that "the setting (or context, context of situation, etc.) in which verbal behavior takes place is also part of its meaning. . . ."[24] Siegfried J. Schmidt has worked to clarify the concept of "context," showing that it contains (1) available semantic codes, (2) economic factors, (3) social situation and roles, (4) political situation, (5) cultural situation, (6) the communication situation, including the identity and reactions of the communication partners, and (7) the intentions of speakers and hearers.[25] Along with others[26] influenced by Charles W. Morris,[27] Charles J. Fillmore uses the term "pragmatics" to refer to the social context of discourse, showing that particular uses of syntactic and semantic codes are "largely explainable by an appeal to pragmatic conditions."[28] Fillmore's reasoning is similar to that employed in this historical investigation, inferring from the content of discourse what its pragmatic circumstances must have been. An interest in the total scope of the communication process and its setting in the social world shared by speaker and audience is also manifest in the work of Teun A. van Dijk,[29] Erwin Morgenthaler[30] and Ernest W. B. Hess-Lüttich.[31]

It must be kept in mind that the use of classical rhetoric, the New Rhetoric, and associated linguistic theories in an investigation like this is somewhat different from their traditional intent. Unlike modern communication situations where the viewpoints of audiences as well as writers or speakers are susceptible to social-scientific research, in the case of the Pauline letters we are forced to resort to historical reconstructions. Our major access to the mind-set of the audience and to the social issues addressed in the Pauline letters is in the letters themselves, which means that we employ rhetorical resources to reason backwards from *logos* to *pathos*. In a very real sense, we are forced to trust what Perelman and Olbrechts-Tyteca referred to as the speaker's "construction" of the au-

---

[24] Pride, "Sociololinguistics," 12.1608.
[25] Schmidt, "Some Problems of Communication Text Theories," 51f.; for an amplification of this scheme cf. his *Foundations for the Empirical Study of Literature*, 29–37.
[26] Cf. Stalnaker, "Pragmatics," 272–89; Wunderlich, *Foundations of Linguistics*, 256–93; Wunderlich, *Studien zur Sprechakttheorie*, 51–118; Plett, *Textwissenschaft und Textanalyse*, 79–92; Plett, *Einführung in die rhetorische Textanalyse*.
[27] Morris, *Signs, Language and Behavior*; Morris, *Writings on the Social Theory of Signs*.
[28] Fillmore, "Pragmatics and the Description of Discourse," 2:103.
[29] van Dijk understands language as "an integral part of social interaction" (p. 167), interpreting "context" as the dynamic, historical aspect of communication situations (pp. 191—95); *Text and Context*. But his primary focus is on the theoretical relations between texts and contexts, which provides only general support for the Thessalonian project.
[30] Morgenthaler has a particular interest in institutional factors that influence communication, *Kommunikationsorientierte Textgrammatik*, 37–41, 93–100.
[31] Hess-Lüttich deals primarily with the social contexts and implications of literary texts in *Soziale Interaktion*.

dience. We must infer from the genre, rhetorical structure, and content of Paul's epistolary discourse what was going on in the Thessalonian congregation. It is therefore somewhat misleading to entitle this chapter the "rhetoric of the Thessalonian letters," because it concentrates largely on the rhetorical structure, the *logos*, of the letters to provide a basis for inferring the larger rhetorical framework of the audience and the circumstances. The subsequent chapters of this investigation that deal with the audience and the external circumstances are equally a part of the rhetoric of the Thessalonian correspondence.

There are preliminary questions that must be dealt with before rhetorical analyses of particular letters can be developed. What type of letters are 1 and 2 Thessalonians, from the perspective of ancient epistolary theory? What is the rhetorical genre of the two letters? There has been a certain amount of confusion on these questions in the debate thus far, because epistolary type has sometimes been referred to with terms that imply rhetorical genres. William G. Doty outlined the types of letters that were characteristic of the ancient world: the "typical common letter," the "business letter," the "official letter," the "public letter," the "non-real" or pseudonymous letter, and the "discursive letter" or "letter-essay."[32] Cicero had a threefold classification of letters as literary, public and private,[33] while the later epistolary handbooks provided 20–40 different types. Helmut Koester discusses the alternative identifications of "the genre" of 1 Thessalonians, concluding that it is a "private letter" that performs something of an official function.[34] But this should be kept separate from the question of the rhetorical genre in the strict sense of that term. The study of ancient epistolary theorists by Abraham J. Malherbe shows why these questions must be dealt with somewhat separately.[35] "Epistolary theory in antiquity belonged to the domain of the rhetoricians, but it was not originally part of their theoretical systems," he observes.[36] The extant epistolary handbooks by Pseudo-Demetrius and Pseudo-Libanius do not contain rhetorical theory. While it is possible to find rough models for 1 and 2 Thessalonians in these handbooks, these do not provide immediate clues about the rhetorical genres. Yet it is clear that epistolary materials were included in the curriculum of ancient schools,[37] and the letters of

---

[32] Doty, *Letters,* 4–8.
[33] Cicero *pro Flacco* 37.
[34] Koester, "I Thessalonians," 34f.
[35] Malherbe, "Ancient Epistolary Theorists."
[36] "Ancient Epistolary Theorists," 4.
[37] "Ancient Epistolary Theorists," 12–15; Clark, *Rhetoric in Greco-Roman Education,* 64, 105f.; Marrou, *A History of Education,* 240; Schubart, *Einführung in die Papyruskunde,* 397; Kroll, "Rhetorik," cols. 1117–19.

well-educated writers[38] reveal an integration of rhetorical skills. It was a kind of integration, however, that was not prescribed in the epistolary handbooks or the rhetorical theories.

2. Non-rhetorical Approaches to 1 Thessalonians

Prior to the appearance of the rhetorical studies by Koester, Kennedy, Hughes and Holland, the research that has been done on the structure of the Thessalonians letters fell in two general categories: analyses of the logical or thematic development, and analyses of the epistolary form. While the positive contributions of each of these approaches will be evaluated below, the methodical shortcomings should be pointed out in advance. Outlines of Pauline letters that seek to reveal logical or thematic developments suffer from theological biases that are difficult to control. Scholars tend to have favorite doctrinal interests that come to the fore in the thematic analyses they create. In the case of the Thessalonians letters, there is very little discussion in the commentaries as to why one outline is preferred over another, which indicates the unmethodical quality of the research up to this point. The difficulty with studies of epistolary form is that the component parts are difficult to relate to each other, and in the case of 1 Thessalonians in particular, the extraordinary length of the thanksgiving section seems to postpone the introduction of the body of the letter until the beginning of chapter 4, which leads to a misconstrual of the main argument of the letter, as we shall see. A final problem is that neither of the methods employed heretofore has sufficient grounding in the conceptual framework of ancient letter writing, which was provided by rhetoric.

In the sections that follow, I illustrate this dilemma by an overview of various kinds of outlines of 1 and 2 Thessalonians. The charts below (see charts 1· and 2, pp. 216–20) indicate the internal divisions of the outlines devised by the commentators. The eighty-nine verses of 1 Thessalonians are divided proportionally in the horizontal sections of the charts.

The outlines on charts 1 and 2 are agreed on several points in the analysis of 1 Thessalonians. They all place a major division at the end of chapter 3. With the exception of Frame, all of the other outlines also place a major division at the end of chapter 1. In addition there is a point of agreement that was not possible to exhibit in the small scale of these charts: each commentator places an internal division in chapter 1 after

---

[38] Forbes has recently made a case that the sophistication of Pauline rhetoric indicates formal education in a rhetorical school. "Paul's Boasting and Hellenistic Rhetoric," 22–24.

verse 1, calling verses 2–10 a thanksgiving or the like. Yet it is clear that the extended length of the thanksgiving causes considerable confusion. Schürmann limits the thanksgiving to 1:2–3 while Morris suggests it extends through to verse 4.[39] Following the path of Milligan,[40] Best, Bruce and Hurd[41] speak of 2:13–16 as a kind of renewal of the thanksgiving theme while Boers[42] leaves the material unassigned. Donfried follows Marshall in vaguely identifying these verses as "reception of the gospel."[43] Bailey refers to 2:13 with the awkward description "thanksgiving in the middle."[44] Frame extends the thanksgiving section to 3:10, but severs it from its natural conclusion in 3:11–13. Rigaux and Friedrich properly hold the material from 1:2–3:13 together,[45] but fail to make a clear identification as an extended thanksgiving. Doty's[46] analysis reveals the difficulty most clearly, because he identifies the material from 1:2–2:16 as the thanksgiving, but suggests that the body of the letter begins at 2:1. The identification of the actual conclusion of the long thanksgiving period, which according to Schubert and O'Brien extended to 3:13,[47] is also a matter of confusion. Spivey and Smith identify 3:11–13 as a prayer that ends the first major section of the letter,[48] while Roetzel leaves these verses unassigned.[49] Boers identifies 2:17–3:13 with the technical epistolographic category, "apostolic parousia,"[50] while Hurd uses the more general category, "apostolic visitation." Doty identifies 3:11–13 as an eschatological conclusion. Very substantial differences are also apparent in the identification of 2:1–12, which Bruce, Marxsen and Boers identify as an apostolic apology, with most of the other outlines using vague descriptive terms such as the "initial behavior of the apostles." Frame identifies the entire first half of the letter as "The Apologia" (1:2–3:13).

The identifications of the components of the hortatory part of the letter differ mainly on the terminological level, with Adeney going the furthest in the separation of thematic sections.[51] More significant for our purposes

---

[39] Schürmann, *Thessalonians,* xxi; Morris, *Thessalonians,* 43.
[40] Milligan, *Thessalonians,* 2.
[41] Hurd, "Thessalonians, First Letter," 900.
[42] Boers, "The Form Critical Study."
[43] Donfried, "Thessalonians, the First Letter," 1064.
[44] Bailey, "Who Wrote II Thessalonians?" 133.
[45] An outline identical to Rigaux's and very close to Friedrich's is provided by Heinrich Schlier, *Der Apostel und seine Gemeinde,* 7f.
[46] Doty, *Letters,* 43.
[47] Schubert, *Form and Function,* 17–27; O'Brien, *Introductory Thanksgivings,* 141–64.
[48] Spivey and Smith, *Anatomy of the New Testament,* 302; their outline closely resembles that of Milligan, *Thessalonians,* and Plummer, *First Epistle to the Thessalonians,* xix–xx.
[49] Roetzel, *The Letters of Paul,* 28.
[50] Cf. Palmer, "Thanksgiving, Self-Defence, and Exhortation," for an outline of 1 Thessalonians that is virtually identical with the one created by Boers.
[51] Adeney, *The Epistles of Paul,* 34f.

are the disagreements concerning the end of the letter. Bornemann does not identify the closing verses as separate from the admonitions, while Milligan, Marshall, Rigaux, Schürmann and Friedrich allow the admonitions to extend through verse 24 and Spivey/Smith through verse 27. This reveals uncertainty about the function of the unit I have identified as the homiletic benediction in 5:23–24, with some scholars placing it with the foregoing material which it summarizes. Hurd separates what he calls the "blessing" of 5:23–24 from the "autograph coda" of 5:25–28. Most of the outlines, in one way or another, hold 5:23–28 together as the conclusion of the letter.

There is a significant evolution of analytic method visible in these outlines. Adeney[52] and Guthrie provide little more than a listing of topics in the letter, eschewing either an identification of formal elements or logical development. Bornemann and Milligan[53] are also typical of the period before the rise of form criticism in showing little consciousness of the technical components of a Pauline letter. Frame provided a more accurate identification of these components, although the grasp of the function of the thanksgiving was not available at the time he wrote in 1912. Most of the more current outlines reveal a methodical confusion between epistolary and topical categories.[54] There is usually a proper identification of the epistolary prescript and postscript as well as a portion of the thanksgiving. But such categories are interspersed with topical titles, whose variations from scholar to scholar reveal substantial differences in the construal of the argument and rhetoric of 1 Thessalonians.[55] It would appear that a methodical improvement is available with the emergence of the epistolary outlines of Bailey, Boers, Doty, Hurd, Peterson and Roetzel. Yet these six analyses tend to present 1 Thessalonians as a series of isolated epistolary components, sometimes leaving unidentified those portions that do not fit. None of the six provides a satisfactory resolution of the extended thanksgiving in 1:2–3:13, which leads one to

---

[52] Adeney, *The Epistles of Paul,* 33–35. The outlines by Findlay, *Thessalonians,* lxx–lxxi and Whiteley, *Thessalonians,* 29f. are virtually identical to Adeney's.

[53] Milligan's two main divisions: 1:2–3:13, "Historical and Personal" and 4:1–5:24, "Hortatory and Doctrinal," were adapted by Plummer, *First Epistle to the Thessalonians,* xix and Bailey, *Thessalonians,* 251. The same basic outline is found in Lueken, *Der erste Brief,* 6.

[54] For example, in the case of Donfried, "Thessalonians, the First Letter," 1064, the Marshall outline is adopted with minor changes in the thematic titles so that it is unclear whether an epistolary analysis is intended.

[55] An example is Schürmann, *Thessalonians,* xxi–xxiii who provides three overlapping levels of analysis, not all of which could be illustrated in the chart. He calls 1:1 the "Opening of the Letter," 1:2–5:14 the "Body of the Letter," and 5:25–28 the "Close of the Letter," which sound like epistolary categories, but he places on a different level the "Introductory Thanksgiving" of 1:2–3 and avoids the use of other epistolary terms. He divides the letter into "Affectionate Memories," 1:2–313, and "Instructions in the Christian Life," 4:1–5:24, in addition to providing the more typical divisions listed in the chart.

conclude that the peculiar integration of argument, apology, and apostolic parousia in this extraordinary thanksgiving cannot be solved by epistolary analysis alone. While Peterson discusses this lengthy thanksgiving, for example, he reverts to a traditional division of the material reminiscent of the older study by Milligan.[56] There is a need for a more comprehensive analytical method that can incorporate valid exegetical insights from these earlier analyses into a a more convincing view of the letter as a whole. In short, there is a need for a rhetorical theory.

3. The Rhetoric of 1 Thessalonians

There are preliminary questions that must be dealt with before a rhetorical analysis can be suggested. What type of letter is 1 Thessalonians, from the perspective of ancient epistolary theory? What is its rhetorical genre?

(a) The Question of Rhetorical Genre

As suggested earlier in this chapter, the first step in determining the rhetorical genre of epistolary materials is to identify the epistolary type. Both Pseudo-Demetrius and Pseudo-Libanius provide epistolary types that seem to fit 1 Thessalonians quite closely. The former, which may well have been available in Paul's time, describes the "praising letter" and the "thankful letter" in which approval is expressed, encouragement is given, and gratitude is shown.[57] Pseudo-Libanius, stemming approximately from the fourth to sixth centuries C.E., refers to the "thankful style" of letter, εὐχαριστικη, which seems to match 1 Thessalonians. But if we are to grasp the relation between writer and recipients and follow the development of a specific letter, it is essential to move beyond mere identification of the epistolary type to a discussion of the rhetorical genre of the letter. The first explicit discussion of this question that I know about is in Kennedy's recent study, which identifies 1 Thessalonians as a deliberative letter.[58] It seems more likely, however, that the rhetorical genre most closely associated with 1 Thessalonians is demonstrative/epideictic because it concentrates on praise and blame with a prominent traditional subject being thanksgiving to the gods.[59] Another way of describing this genre of rhetoric is that it reveals a writer seeking "to persuade them to hold or reaffirm some point of view in the present, as when he celebrates

---

[56] Peterson, *Second Thessalonians*," 42.
[57] Malherbe, "Ancient Epistolary Theorists," 34–35, 38–39.
[58] Kennedy, *New Testament Interpretation,* 142.
[59] Lausberg, *Handbuch,* 131f.

or denounces some person or some quality. Praise or blame is taken by
Aristotle to be the characteristic feature of epideictic."[60]

The classification of 1 Thessalonians as demonstrative matches quite
closely the view of the purpose and character of 1 Thessalonians as found
in standard commentaries and introductions. For instance James Moffatt
inferred from the content of 1 Thessalonians that Paul felt the Christians
in Thessalonica "were on the right path; what they chiefly needed was
stimulus and direction."[61] Willi Marxsen comments on the contrast with
Galatians or Romans where doctrinal instruction and ethical advice
appear much more crucial in the argument than in 1 Thessalonians: "The
congregation, though facing adversity, is on the right path . . . [which]
leads Paul to appeal to the congregation concerning experiences they
themselves have had."[62] I. Howard Marshall concurs in this widely held
judgment: "The whole letter is a masterly piece of pastoral encouragement
based on the existing progress made by the readers."[63] Helmut Koester
shows how the letter stresses the elements of commonality in the experiences of suffering between Paul and the congregation.[64]

The following analysis attempts to convey the epideictic nature of the
argument, which opens with the thanksgiving prayer of 1:2–5 and concludes with the homiletical benediction of 5:23–24, followed by closing
greetings. The main argument of the letter is an extended narration of the
grounds for giving thanks to God in 1:6–3:13. Praise of God for having
granted the Thessalonians a place in the new age is used to clarify the
shape of that age in a way that deals with the confusions in the congregation.[65] On the basis of construing this main argument as a thanksgiving
to God, the concrete issues in the congregation are expressed as reminders
of the pattern of praiseworthy and blameworthy behavior suitable to the
new age in which they have become participants.

(b) A Rhetorical Analysis of 1 Thessalonians

1:1–5   I.   Exordium
1:1   A. Epistolary prescript
                     1. Superscript: senders—Paul et al.
                     2. Address: the Thessalonians
                     3. Salutation: grace and peace

---

[60] Kennedy, *New Testament Interpretation,* 19.
[61] Moffatt, *Introduction to the Literature,* 69; cited with favor by Best, *Thessalonians,* 15.
[62] Marxsen, *Der erste Brief,* 28.
[63] Marshall, *1 and 2 Thessalonians,* 10.
[64] Koester, "Apostel und Gemeinde," 287–92.
[65] Cf. O'Brien, *Introductory Thanksgivings,* 165.

1:2–5		B. Thanksgiving
1:2		1. Introductory thanks for "all of you"
1:3		2. Immediate reasons for thanks: "work of faith, of love, and steadfastness of hope"
1:4		3. Foundational reasons for thanks: "beloved by election"
1:5		4. Causative reasons for thanks: power of word and apostolic transmission
1:6–3:13	II.	Narratio of grounds for thanksgiving
1:6–10		A. Congregational imitation
1:6–7		1. Imitation of Paul and Christ
1:6a		a. Declaration of imitation
1:6b		b. Reception of word in affliction
1:6c		c. Joy in the Holy Spirit
1:7		d. Becoming an example for others
1:8–10		2. Proof of Thessalonian imitation
1:8a		a. "From you the word sounds forth"
1:8b		b. "Your faith . . . has gone everywhere"
1:8c		c. Statement of self-evidence
1:9–10		d. The report of imitation
1:9a		i) Apostolic reception
1:9b–10		ii) Congregational conversion
2:1–12		B. Clarification of apostolic example
2:1		1. Basic contention: Paul's visit "not in vain"
2:2		2. Apostolic courage in adversity
2:3–8		3. Apostolic ethos
2:3		a. Antithesis to "error, uncleanness . . . guile"
2:4a		b. "Approved by God to be entrusted with the gospel"
2:4b		c. Pleasing God rather than humans
2:5–6		d. Refusal of missional manipulation or exploitation
2:7		e. Apostolic gentleness . . . "like a nurse"
2:8		f. Summary: genuine affection and readiness to share the gospel
2:9–12		4. Apostolic behavior
2:9		a. Paul's "labor and toil" in Thessalonica
2:10		b. Paul's "holy and righteous and blameless" behavior
2:11–12		c. Paul's "fatherly" exhortation
2:13–16		C. Clarification of Judean example
2:13		1. Reiteration of thanksgiving

2:13a		a. Statement of thanks
2:13b–c		b. Reason: Thessalonian reception of apostolic word as "the word of God"
2:13d		c. Consequence: "God's word is working in you believers"
2:14–16		2. Thessalonian imitation of Judean Christians
2:14a		a. Statement of imitation
2:14b–16b		b. Clarification of type of imitation: suffering from fellow citizens
2:14b		i) Parallel persecution
2:15–16a		ii) Judean persecution described
2:16b		iii) Wrathful consequences
2:17–3:10	D.	Paul's desire for apostolic visit
2:17–20		1. Repeated efforts to revisit Thessalonica
2:17–18a		a. Affectionate reasons to revisit
2:18b		b. The hindrance of Satan
2:19–20		c. Eschatological significance of Thessalonians to Paul: "hope, joy, crown, boast, glory"
3:1–5		2. Substitute visit of Timothy
3:1a		a. Paul's anguished response to the separation
3:1b		b. The willingness to be "alone" in Athens
3:2–3a		c. The status and mission of Timothy
3:2a		i) "our brother and God's coworker"
3:2b		ii) Positive mission: "establish faith and exhort"
3:3a		iii) Negative mission: to keep the congregation from being "moved by afflictions"
3:3b–4		d. Reiteration of Timothy's message
3:5		e. Recapitulation of Paul's motives and concerns in sending Timothy
3:6–10		3. The result of Timothy's visit
3:6		a. The positive report: "faith . . . love" and and loyalty to apostle
3:7		b. Paul's response: comfort in affliction
3:8		c. Eschatological dimension of Paul's response: "we live . . ."
3:9–10		d. Pauline thanksgiving and intercession
3:11–13	E.	Transitus in benedictory style
3:11		1. The requested divine intervention to "direct our way to you"
3:12		2. The requested increase of love
3:13		3. The requested status at the parousia

4:1–5:22 III. Probatio
4:1–8   A. The first proof concerning the marriage ethic
4:1–2   1. Reiteration of previous grounding of ethics
4:3–6   2. The admonition concerning holiness in marriage
4:7–8   3. The divine grounding of the admonition
4:9–12   B. The second proof concerning the communal ethic
4:9–10a   1. Reiteration of previous grounding and accomplish-
                     ment of the love ethic
4:10b–12   2. The admonitions
4:10b   a. Continue in the ethic
4:11a   b. Live quietly
4:11b   c. Be self-supporting
4:12a   d. Gain public respect
4:12b   e. Be independent
4:13–18   C. The third proof concerning the dead in Christ
4:13   1. The issue: hopeless grief
4:14   2. The premise: resurrection of Christ implies resur-
                     rection of believers at parousia
4:15–17   3. The inference: "Dead in Christ will rise first" and
                     will be reunited at the parousia
4:18   4. The conclusion: a call to mutual comfort
5:1–11   D. The fourth proof concerning the eschaton
5:1   1. The issue with a reminder of previous teaching
5:2   2. The premise from previous teaching: parousia
                     comes unexpectedly
5:3   3. The first inference: no escape for the complacent
5:4–5   4. The second inference that Thessalonian Christians
                     are "children of light"
5:6–8   5. The argument to respond appropriately
5:6   a. The first admonition to sober wakefulnes
5:7   b. The ground of the admonition in the asso-
                        ciation of darkness and complacency
5:8   c. The second admonition to sobriety and the
                        defensive armor of faith, love and hope
5:9–10   6. The inference concerning the assurance of election
                     to salvation
5:11   7. The conclusion: a call to mutual encouragement
5:12–22   E. The fifth proof concerning congregational life
5:12–13   1. The first exhortation to respect and love congrega-
                     tional leaders
5:14   2. The second exhortation to deal with congrega-
                     tional disorders

5:15		3. The third exhortation to respond to evil with good
5:16–18		4. The fourth exhortation to retain joyous devotion
5:19–22		5. The fifth exhortation to balance charismatic with theological control
5:23–28	IV.	Peroratio
5:23		A. The homiletic benediction
5:24		B. The formula of assurance
5:25		C. The prayer request
5:26		D. The admonition on holy greetings
5:27		E. The adjuration in Paul's own hand
5:28		F. The final blessing in Paul's own hand
5:23–24		G. The concluding benediction
5:25–27		H. The closing greetings and requests
5:28		I. The final greeting

(c) Comparison with Other Rhetorical Analysis

There are several important differences in the assessment of the rhetorical structure of 1 Thessalonians, as chart 3 indicates (see p. 221). The first is the identification of the exordium or proem. That this section could continue through the end of chapter 3 as Koester suggests would be to exceed the generally accepted guidelines in ancient rhetoric.[66] A more serious question is whether it ends with verse 5 as I suggest or continues on through verse 10 of chapter 1. Since the rhetorical function of the exordium is to introduce the subject in such a way as to gain the sympathy of the audience, the question is whether this function is completed at the end of verse 5 or whether it continues through 10. I would argue for the former, because all of the themes of the letter are announced in the thanksgiving sentence beginning with verse 2 and ending with verse 5. The emphasis on the "work of faith" (1:3) relates to the active example of the apostles' labor (2:9–12) and to the problem of work in the congregation (5:12–18). The parallel expression "the labor of love" announces the themes of the marriage and communal ethic (4:1–8; 4:9–12; 5:12–22). The reference to the "steadfastness of hope"(1:3) alludes to the eschatological issues to be dealt with later in the letter (4:13–5:11). The theme of the congregation's election by the love of God (1:4) relates to the question of the authenticity of their conversion and membership in the new age (1:6–10), which had been shaken by the experience of persecution and death (2:1–16; 3:1–6; 4:13–18). The power of the gospel alluded to in 1:5

---

[66] Cf. Lausberg, *Handbuch*, 162.

is described in detail in 1:6–10 and 2:13–17, while the issue of the Holy Spirit (1:5) is developed in later sections dealing with ethical implications (4:8) and congregational order (5:19–22). The reference to Paul's example in 1:5 is developed in 2:1–12 while his motivation to act "for your sake" (1:5) is elaborated in 2:9–12 and 2:17–3:10. In sum, the proper task of an exordium is completed by the end of 1:5.

A skilled rhetor was taught to create a smooth transition at the end of an exordium so that the flow of thought into the narratio was uninterrupted.[67] This is precisely what Paul has achieved with 1 Thess 1:6 which begins the narration of his relations with the congregation and their experience of conversion as a result of his preaching. The references to past experience in verses 6–10 are clear signs of a narratio section, which continues on without interruption at 2:1ff., the location where Hughes and Kennedy believe the narratio starts. Commentators have observed the continuity of thought between 1:6–10 and 2:1–12,[68] noting that while Paul shifts to a description of his own behavior, the narrative of their relation to him continues from 1:9. It appears appropriate, therefore, to assign the material from 1:6 through chapter 3 to the narratio section.

The question of precisely where the narratio ends is also in dispute, with Hughes suggesting a partitio section in the final three verses of chapter 3. He is correct in perceiving 3:11 as a reference to the narratio section, with its description of the frustrated plans to return to Thessalonica. But this would seem to link it more closely with the prior discussion than with the sections yet to come. That the reference in 3:12 to an "increase in love" relates nicely to the forthcoming section 4:9–12 is well taken, but it also picks up the theme of the "faith and love" of the Thessalonians toward Paul that was discussed in 3:6–10. The reference to the parousia in 3:13 serves to introduce themes that are developed in 4:13ff., but again, it picks up the earlier topic of the apocalyptic orientation of the Thessalonians' conversion (1:9–10) as well as the apocalyptic horizon of Paul's mission to Thessalonica (cf. the use of παρουσία in 2:19). The reference to "holiness" in 3:13 connects tightly with the forthcoming discussion in 4:1–8, but it also recapitulates a crucial component in the apostolic example discussed in 2:10. The function of 3:11–13 therefore is more likely that of a transitus, which is the typical ending of a narratio section. The affective qualities of the benediction match the requirements for such a transitus[69] much more closely than the usual

---

[67] Lausberg, *Handbuch*, 163, citing Quintilian 4.1.76 and 79.
[68] Frame, *Thessalonians*, 92; Marshall, *1 and 2 Thessalonians*, 62; Best, *Thessalonians*, 88; Dobschütz, *Die Thessalonicher-Briefe*, 82f.; Morris, *Thessalonians*, 42.
[69] Lausberg, *Handbuch*, 188f.

listing of propositions in a partitio.[70] But the function of a transitus is very close to that of a partitio: in the case of 1 Thess 3:11–13, the preceding argument is recapitulated and the themes of the forthcoming argument are introduced.

The final points of dispute are whether the second half of the letter should be divided at 5:12 as Hughes and Koester suggest, and whether 5:4–11 constitutes a peroration. In light of the exhortations in 4:3–8; 4:10–12; 4:18; 5:6 and 5:11, it seems strange to speak of the exhortative section starting only with 5:12. That a shift of exhortative topic occurs at this spot is clear, but the material both before and after this juncture must be classified as parenetic. Given the interlacing of exhortation and topical argument in 4:1–5:22, I would prefer the general classification of this material as probatio,[71] which I take to be a technical term for what Kennedy designates as "headings" in this section. Whether the material in 5:4–11 should be designated a peroratio depends on one's assessment of preceding verses. Hughes allows the third proof in his analysis to extend from 4:13 through 5:3, which seems to obscure the change of subject indicated by περὶ δὲ in 5:1. This was used in 4:9 and 13 to indicate earlier topics about which the Thessalonians had expressed concerns. I am inclined to follow current commentators who see a section beginning in 5:1 and ending in 5:11, with the theme of sleeping and waking in 5:4–10 designed to emphasize the argument against apocalyptic complacency in 5:1–3.[72]

4. NON-RHETORICAL APPROACHES TO 2 THESSALONIANS

We turn now to the question of the rhetorical structure and genre of 2 Thessalonians, beginning with an account of those scholars using thematic analysis as illustrated on charts 4–6 below (pp. 222–25). There is a somewhat higher measure of agreement in these outlines of 2 Thessalonians than was the case for 1 Thessalonians. Donfried[73] follows Marshall exactly while only the assignment of the final verses separate Marshall from Bailey, Friedrich from Best[74] and Findlay from Egenolf.[75]

---

[70] *Handbuch*, 190.

[71] This identification expresses Bjerkelund's contention that 4:1ff. constitutes the main point or corpus of 1 Thessalonians; *Parakalô*, 134.

[72] Cf. Best, *Thessalonians*, 203; Reese, *1 and 2 Thessalonians*, 55–60.

[73] Donfried, "Thessalonians, the Second Letter," 1064.

[74] Others adopting an identical outline to that of Best, using different titles, are Morris, *Thessalonians*, 191; Whiteley, *Thessalonians*, 30; Adeney, *The Epistles of Paul*, 56f.

[75] Egenolf, *The Second Epistle*, 91f.

Hurd's outline[76] is very close to Guthrie's. Every outline provides some sort of division at 2:1 and all but five place a division at 3:1. Major disagreements in the assessment of the thanksgiving are apparent, with Holland[77] confining it to 1:3, Findlay and Guthrie assigning it to 1:3–4, Bailey extending it from 1:3–12 and Hughes from 1:3–10.[78] Peterson sees the thanksgiving recurring in 1:11–12 and 2:13–14, but is unable to incorporate this into his outline in a coherent manner.[79] Similarly, Hurd identifies 2:13–17 as a renewal of the thanksgiving in 1:3–12 and Holland calls 2:13–14 a "description of an act of thanksgiving."[80] It is also apparent from the variety of headings provided for the material in 1:1–12 that this section may contain more than the thanksgiving which provides the usual exordium for a Pauline letter. Best and Bruce refer to "Encouragement, Prayer" and Rigaux to "Exhortations and Encouragements" as contained in this section, while Marxsen describes its content as "Teaching on Judgement at the Parousia." Holland assigns 1:5–12 to the narratio that provides the basis for the subsequent proofs. Krodel refers to 1:11 as "the transition," presumably to the next section of the letter.[81] This can be accounted for in part by acknowledging that the formal thanksgiving is followed by an intercessory prayer in 1:11–12.[82] If one is inclined to allow the thanksgiving to extend beyond 1:4, it remains clear that the material in 1:3–10 includes a substantial portion of the argument of this letter, just as in the case of the long thanksgiving in 1 Thessalonians.

Some of these dilemmas can be resolved by a rhetorical analysis of the opening sections of 2 Thessalonians, designating the material in 1:1–12 as the exordium which consists of the prescript, the thanksgiving and the prayer. The exordium introduces the letter and establishes the apocalyptic premises of the subsequent discussion. Paul's confidence in the status of the congregation is confirmed by their experience of persecution (1:5–10) but the question of their being "worthy of God's call" (1:11) is related to

---

[76] Hurd, "Thessalonians, Second Letter," 901. In his brief discussion, no identification is made of the opening and closing, and one must infer from the discussion that he would identify 2:1–12 as the "body," using the category he employed in the outline of 1 Thessalonians.
[77] Holland, "Let No One Deceive You," 327f.
[78] Hughes, Second Thessalonians, 165–67.
[79] Peterson, Second Thessalonians, 44f.
[80] Holland, "Let No One Deceive You," 328.
[81] Krodel, 2 Thessalonians, 79.
[82] Schubert, Form and Function, 28, contends that the thanksgiving consists only of 1:3–4, followed by an eschatological proof and then by the intercessory prayer in 1:11–12. It should be observed, however, that 1:4 does not fit his paradigm of the thanksgiving much better than 5–10. O'Brien cites Schubert on this disposition as if he agreed in Introductory Thanksgivings, 169, but states on the preceding page that the "opening thanksgiving period . . . extends from vv. 3–12." Bruce, Thessalonians, 155, prefers to designate 1:1–12 a "prayer report."

the confusion about the apocalyptic plan and the disciplining of the "disorderly," which are taken up in the rest of the letter.

The question of how to dispose of the opening verses of chapter 3 is considerably more complicated. The expression τὸ λοιπόν, "finally," leads most of the commentators to begin a new section with 3:1, but the content of 3:1–5 is very closely associated with the preceding section dealing with the status of the Thessalonians in the apocalyptic drama. Krodel designates these verses as the second of two cycles, each concluding with a benediction, that constitute a major section of the letter running from 2:13–3:5. Similar assessments are implicit in the analyses of Findlay, Egenolf and Marxsen. Rigaux appears to be on solid ground in arguing that the emphatic style of 3:6 designates a new section, while 3:1–5 is transitional, picking up the themes of 2:13–17.[83] But Rigaux does not provide an entirely satisfactory explanation for the term "finally," which in other Pauline letters designates either the end of the letter as a whole (2 Cor 13:11; Phil 4:8) or a change of topic (1 Thess 4:1; Phil 3:1; 1 Cor 4:2). If it does not designate a new section, it would appear to have an inferential sense in this verse, meaning "therefore."[84]

The content of 3:1–5 has appeared somewhat ambiguous to commentators, with Best, Bruce and Friedrich identifying it properly as prayer or request for prayer, but not finding a way to integrate it into the argument. Holland achieves a more integral solution by identifying these verses as a request for prayer that opens the exhortatio section of 3:1–13, but this does not do full justice to 3:3–4, which contain a confession of confidence and an epistolary benediction. Frame provides the odd title of "Finally" for these verses. Despite the suggestions of Milligan, Guthrie, Marshall, Donfried, Hughes and Holland, it does not seem appropriate to designate 3:1–5 as the beginning of the exhortative section of 2 Thessalonians. While προσεύχεσθε is in the imperative in 3:1, the succeeding verses are not exhortative. There are also imperatives in 2:15, but they also do not indicate the beginning of an exhortative section despite the suggestion of Trilling.[85] By following Rigaux, the solemn command in 3:6 can be taken with full seriousness as the opening of the final topic of the letter, which is exhortative in content though not stylistically consistent with the exhortative material of 1 Thess 5:12–22. This may indicate that 2 Thessalonians belongs to a different rhetorical genre than 1 Thessalonians.

---

[83] Rigaux, *Thessalonians*, 692f.

[84] Cf. Bauer, Arndt, Gingrich, and Danker, *A Greek-English Lexicon*, 480.

[85] Trilling, *Der zweite Brief*, 124–27, suggests that four similarly structured exhortative "packages" beginning with 2:15, 3:1; 3:6 and 3:13 make up the parenetic section of 2 Thessalonians, but he admits that 3:1–5 does not conform to the pattern very well. His suggestion does not account for the prominence of the benediction formulas in 2:16–17 and 3:5, nor for the argumentative rather than exhortative content of 3:1–5.

A final point of disagreement in the outlines of 2 Thessalonians is whether the closing section starts with 3:16 or 3:17. When one takes into account the function of such benedictions to summarize and bring to conclusion sections of the preceding letter, then the content should provide a clue as to whether it is only the immediate section or the entire letter that is being summarized.[86] If it is the former, the benediction logically belongs at the end of the exhortative section; if the latter, it is more natural to think of it as the beginning of the peroratio. The reference to the "Lord of peace" granting you "peace" relates closely with the immediately preceding discussion (3:6–15), but the expression "at all times in all ways" refers more naturally to the discussion of the times and seasons that dominated earlier sections of the letter (1:5–10; 2:1–12; 2:13–3:5).[87] I would therefore prefer to place 3:16 in the peroratio of 2 Thessalonians.

5. THE RHETORIC OF 2 THESSALONIANS

(a) The Question of Genre

On the basis of the preliminary judgments made above concerning the appropriate outline for 2 Thessalonians, we are now in a position to take up the question of its epistolary type. 2 Thessalonians seems to be marked by a combination of what Pseudo-Libanius called "the denying style" and "the reproving style."[88] The rebuttal of the claim that the "Day of the Lord has come" in 2:1–12 plays a prominent role in the letter, with Paul denying that his previous letter had implied such a doctrine. The unusual emphasis on being "bound" to give thanks (1:3; 2:13) conveys a mild and indirect reproof to the Thessalonian congregation, a sense that "Paul is not entirely satisfied with the congregation."[89] In contrast to 1 Thessalonians, the relation between Paul and his audience is marked by authority and the demand of obedience.[90] The combination of denial and reproval would place 2 Thessalonians in the category of the "mixed letter."[91] Despite the similarity in content between 1 and 2 Thessalonians, there is no possibility of fitting the latter into the category of a "thankful letter" that seemed so natural a classification for the former.[92]

---

[86] Cf. Jewett, "Form and Function," 24.

[87] Jewett, "Form and Function," 25.

[88] Malherbe, "Ancient Epistolary Theorists," 65–67.

[89] Dobschütz, Die Thessalonicher-Briefe, 236. Frame suggests an even milder form of reproof as conveyed in the expression "we are bound to give thanks" in Thessalonians, 221: ". . . Paul is replying to the utterances of the faint-hearted . . . to the effect that they did not consider themselves worthy of the kingdom or entitled to the praise accorded them in the first epistle."

[90] Cf. Koester, "Apostel und Gemeinde," 287f., 293–96.

[91] Pseudo-Libanius, par. 92; tr. by Malherbe, "Ancient Epistolary Theorists," 77.

[92] Findlay, Thessalonians, lxxi, offers a related formulation of the different genres of the two

A similar conclusion needs to be drawn concerning the probable rhetorical genre of 2 Thessalonians, which is deliberative rather than demonstrative.[93] In deliberative rhetoric the speaker or writer "seeks to persuade them to take some action in the future,"[94] which in the case of 2 Thessalonians involves a reassessment of the eschatological expectation and a stiffened policy toward the "disorderly." The typical emphasis in the deliberative genre is on "the question of self-interest and future benefits,"[95] which matches the extensive discussion of the status of the Thessalonians in relation to the apocalyptic events already experienced (1:3–12) as well as those yet to come (2:13–3:5). The repeated expression, "we are bound to give thanks," (1:3; 2:13) conforms to this genre by using the idea of obligatory worship for the sake of gaining the future blessings of God that had been widely popularized in Judaism.[96] Each of the three benedictions that convey the burden of Paul's message (2:16–17; 3:5; 3:16) concentrates on the granting of personal stability and peace in view of the Day of the Lord which is yet to come. The traditionally political context of deliberative rhetoric comes to expression in Paul's direct commands about how to deal with the ἄτακτοι in 3:6–15,[97] using a style and approach that is considerably different from the exhortative section of 1 Thessalonians.

The following outline attempts to incorporate these rhetorical and epistolary assessments.

(b) A Rhetorical Analysis of 2 Thessalonians

1:1–12	I.	Exordium
1:1–2		A. Epistolary prescript
1:1a		1. Senders: Paul, Silvanus, Timothy
1:1b		2. Address: the Thessalonians
1:2		3. Salutation: grace and peace
1:3–10		B. Thanksgiving
1:3		1. Introductory thanks for "you, brethren"
		a. Claim of suitability: "bound . . . as is fitting
		b. Content of thanks: growing faith and increasing love

---

letters: ". . . 1 Thessalonians is an unconstrained, discursive *letter*; 2 Thessalonians is more of a calculated *homily*."

[93] Cf. Holland, "Let No One Deceive You," 327.

[94] Kennedy, *New Testament Interpretation*, 19.

[95] *New Testament Interpretation*, 20.

[96] Aus has explored this background in "The Liturgical Background," building on the research of Günther Harder in *Paulus und das Gebet*.

[97] Cf. Lausberg, *Handbuch*, 54.

1:4		2. Missional consequence of thanksgiving: Paul's boast
		a. Arena: "in the churches of God"
		b. Achievement: "steadfastness and faith"
		c. Context of achievement: "persecution and afflictions"
1:5-10		3. Apocalyptic implications of thanksgiving
1:5		a. Suffering as evidence of apocalyptic "judgment"
1:6-9		b. Apocalyptic "rest" for the elect and "vengeance" for persecutors when Christ returns
1:10		c. Apocalyptic context: the parousia when Christ is Glorified, confirming "our testimony to you"
1:11-12		C. Intercessory prayer
1:11a		1. Reason: "because of this" apocalyptic confirmation
1:11b		2. Orant and subject: "we always pray for you"
1:11c-d		3. Content of prayer
		a. "make you worthy of God's call"
		b. "fulfill every good resolve and work of faith"
		c. Means: "by power"
1:12		4. Apocalyptic purpose of prayer
1:12a		a. Glorification of Christ "in you"
1:12b		b. Glorification of "you in him"
1:12c		c. Means of glory: "grace"
2:1-2	II.	Partitio
2:1		A. Topics for discussion
		1. Parousia of Christ (=first proof 2:3-12)
		2. Eschatological involvement of believers (=second proof 2:13-3:5)
2:2		B. False doctrine to be disputed
		1. Warning about being "shaken" by false doctrine
		2. Possible sources of false doctrine: "spirit, letter as from us"
		3. Citation of false doctrine: "that the Day of the Lord has come"
2:3-3:5	III.	Probatio
2:3-12		A. The first proof: parousia has not yet come
2:3a		1. Warning about being deceived
2:3b-12		2. Signs that must preceed the parousia
2:3b		a. First sign: the "rebellion"
2:3c-4		b. Second sign: the "Man of Lawlessness"
2:5		c. Digression: reminder of consistency with previous doctrine

2:6-7   d. Third sign: the "Restrainer" and his removal
2:8   e. Fourth sign: destruction of "Lawless One" by
               Jesus at the parousia
2:9-10   f. Digression: explanation of deception of the
               "Lawless One"
2:11-12   g. Fifth sign: delusion sent upon unbelievers
2:13-3:5 B. The second proof: believers have assurance that they
               will prevail until the parousia
2:13a   1. Paul's thanksgiving
               a. Claim of suitability: "bound to give thanks"
               b. Object of thanksgiving: "you, brethren, beloved
                  by the Lord"
2:13b   c. Reason of thanksgiving: election of the Thessa-
                  lonians to be saved
2:13c   d. Means of salvation: "santification by the spirit
                  and belief in truth"
2:14   2. The apocalyptic effect of the gospel
               a. Calling by God to join the elect
               b. Purpose of sharing apocalyptic "glory"
2:15   3. The exhortation to "stand firm and hold to" the
               Pauline teachings
2:16-17   4. The assuring benediction
2:16   a. The subject
                  i) The Lord Jesus
                  ii) God our Father
                  iii) Assuring actions in the past: "love," "eternal
                      comfort," "good hope through grace"
2:17   b. The requested action of God
                  i) "Comfort your hearts"
                  ii) "Establish . . . good work and word"
3:1-2   5. The exhortation to prayerful intercession
3:1a   a. The request
3:1b-2   b. The content of intercession
3:1b   i) That gospel may triumph
3:2a   ii) That Paul may be delivered
3:2b   iii) Explanation: "for not all have faith"
3:3-4   6. The expression of confidence
3:3   a. The faithfulness of the Lord
3:4   b. The obedience of the Thessalonians
3:5   7. The benediction
               a. The subject: "the Lord"
               b. The requested action: "direct your heart to"

God and Christ, whose "love" and "steadfastness" provide apocalyptic assurance

3:6–15   IV.   Exhortatio
3:6   A. The first exhortation to discipline the "disorderly"
                     1. The source of the command: Paul and colleagues
                     2. The address: "you, brethren"
                     3. The action: exclusion of brothers
                     4. Illicit actions of brothers
                         a. Being disorderly
                         b. Refusing Pauline tradition
3:7–10   B. The ethical grounding of the first exhortation
3:7–9   1. The Pauline example of labor
3:7a   a. The obligation of imitation
3:7b–8   b. Pauline behavior as the model
                             i)   Not "disorderly"
                             ii) No eating without paying
                             iii) Rigorous labor
                             iv) Purpose: no burden for others
3:9   c. Explanation: right to support renounced to
                          provide example
3:10   2. The apostolic teaching about work
3:11–13   C. The second exhortation to the "disorderly"
3:11   1. The report about the "disorderly"
3:12   2. The exhortation
                       a. The authority of the exhortation: apostle
                          speaking "in the Lord Jesus Christ"
                       b. The content of the specific exhortation
                           i) "Work in quietness"
                           ii) "Earn their own living"
3:13   c. The general exhortation: "well-doing"
3:14–15   D. The third exhortation about exclusion
3:14a   1. The designation: those refusing to obey this letter
3:14b   2. The command of exclusion
3:14c   3. The purpose of exclusion: "that he may be
                      ashamed"
3:15   4. The proper attitude in exclusion: "not as an enemy
                      . . . but as a brother"

3:16–18   V.   Peroratio
3:16   A. The homiletic benediction
3:17   B. The postscript in Paul's hand
3:18   C. The final greeting

(c) Explanation and implications

A major contention in this analysis is that the partitio of 2 Thessalonians is found in 2:1-2, with the two main arguments being announced in verse 1 as ἡ παρουσία τοῦ κυρίου and ἡμῶν ἐπισυναγωγή ἐπ' αὐτόν.[98] The preliminary denial of the false teaching concerning the presence of the parousia and the status of believers is stated in verse 2. The two proofs that follow in 2:3-12 and 2:13-3:5 argue that a series of signs must preceed the coming of the parousia and that believers can have assurance that they will prevail until that time provided they stand firm in the Pauline teachings and example. Within this latter section, there is a request for prayerful intercession (3:1-2) that sustains the apostolic example of resolutely working for the gospel in the time between the ages, showing that Paul faces the same kind of opposition and ambiguity that the Thessalonians had hoped to transcend by accepting the idea that the parousia had already come. The prominent benedictions in this second proof (2:16-17; 3:5) express Paul's confidence that the Thessalonians will remain steadfast despite the adverse pressures of the old age.

The exhortatio section (3:6-15) follows immediately upon the benediction that concludes the probatio of 2 Thessalonians, providing an antithesis to "the steadfastness of Christ" (3:5). This indicates that the subject of the ἄτακτοι is directly related to the apocalyptic confusions rebutted in the two proofs. While a proper stance in relation to the parousia was shown in the proof to constitute a holding fast to τὰς παραδόσεις ἃς ἐδιδάχθετε (2:15), the behavior of the disorderly is described περιπατοῦντος καὶ μὴ κατὰ τὴν παράδοσιν ἣν παρελάβετε παρ' ἡμῶν (3:6). The apostolic example is then explicitly linked with working for one's own bread (3:7-10), which the ἄτακτοι are refusing to do.

On the basis of identifying 2 Thess 2:1-2 as the partitio, 2:3-3:5 as the probatio and 3:6-16 as the exhortatio, the function of the exordium and the peroratio can be more easily understood. The thanksgiving refers to the "steadfastness and faith" of the Thessalonians in face of persecution which, according to 1:5, is a confirmation that the apocalyptic scheme is proceeding according to the tradition of the suffering of the righteous.[99] This provides an apocalyptic grounding for the contention that those who fail "to obey the gospel of our Lord Jesus" will be punished in the forthcoming parousia (1:8-10). This introductory material effectively opens up the issue of the apocalyptic confusion and its relation to the ἄτακτοι who refuse to accept the message of the Pauline tradition. The

---

[98] Hughes, *Second Thessalonians,* 138-41.
[99] Cf. Bassler, "The Enigmatic Sign," 500-506.

peroratio of 3:16–18 provides the gift of eschatological peace "all the time and in every circumstance" draws together the issues of the futurity of the parousia, the continuation of apocalyptic woes, and the assurance available to the faithful in the time between the ages. Such peace includes not only the cessation of conflict between believers and the world that is anticipated in the parousia but also the successful resolution of the dilemma of the ἄτακτοι who are to be warned as brothers rather than as enemies (3:15). The redoubled reference to the blessing "with you all" (3:16, 18) conveys the hope that such congregational discipline will result in a united church of former ἄτακτοι and the rest. The reference to Paul's authenticating signature confirms the refutation of the doctrine ascribed to him in 2:2. Just as all of the themes of the body of 2 Thessalonians are announced and prepared for in the exordium, so also they are all drawn together in the brief peroratio.

Two observations may be drawn from this analysis that bear on the questions concerning the relation of 2 Thessalonians to its audience and to 1 Thessalonians, the themes of our next chapters. 2 Thessalonians is a tightly organized deliberative letter with a combination of reproof, denial and encouragement that reveals a complex situation of misunderstanding a previous piece of correspondence that had attempted to deal with apocalyptic confusions and congregational disorders. On the basis of the antithetical relation between the teachings of the ἄτακτοι and the teachings of Paul and also the remarkable integration of the proofs and the exhortation, it is clear that the activities of this group are directly related to the apocalyptic confusions. The rhetorical evidence concerning both letters may thus provide a basis for reconstructing the historical situation evoking the Thessalonian letters as well as the precise relation between the letters themselves.

Chapter Six

THE SITUATION IN THE
THESSALONIAN CONGREGATION

The Situation in the Thessalonian Congregation
Inferences from the Literary Evidence

The rhetorical analysis in the preceding chapter clears away one of the major impediments to assembling the clues to the audience situation that are available by a close reading of the literary evidence in the Thessalonian letters. The long narratio section in 1 Thessalonians that provides the grounds for giving thanks for the eschatological grounding of the congregation despite persecution from without and confusions within has a clearly argumentative purpose in demonstrative rhetoric. It sustains and clarifies the ethos the congregation requires to surmount its present difficulties, thus containing in a very real sense the primary argumentative burden of the letter. This means that the letter is misunderstood when taken to mean that there are no serious problems in the congregation, that the extended thanksgiving reveals a thoroughly positive, unproblematic situation.[1] Typical of the many commentators who fall into this trap was William Neil, who suggested that Timothy's report to Paul must have been almost wholly favorable and that 1 Thessalonians was motivated mainly by Paul's thankfulness at such positive prospects.[2] James M. Reese echoes these sentiments when he writes that "much of the letter is simply a recalling of the joyful experience of faith and hope they had received and shared generously with their fellow Macedonians. Paul writes this way to involve them more deeply in his personal desire to praise God as their savior. He knows that the best way to kindle their intense religious experience is to recall what God did for them."[3] The impression one gains from reading such comments is that the Thessalonians were analogous to a modern Christian congregation that simply needs a little more spiritual vitality to measure up. I contend that this is a fallacious inference drawn from a misunderstanding of the rhetoric of 1 Thessalonians.

It is interesting to observe that since Paul uses a different genre of rhetoric in 2 Thessalonians, employing a much stiffer and more directly argumentative tone, commentators are inclined to take that situation more

---

[1] For a more adequate approach to the problems in the congregation, cf. Lightfoot, "The Church of Thessalonica," 264–69.

[2] Neil, *Thessalonians*, xv.

[3] Reese, *1 and 2 Thessalonians*, xiii. For an extended statement of this benign assessment, cf. Dewailly, *La jeune Église de Thessalonique*, 63–109.

seriously. For example, Best concludes that the second letter was written "to meet a new situation in respect of eschatology and a deteriorating situation in respect of idleness. . . ."[4] The puzzle is that with the traditional chronology such commentators follow, the more serious difficulties of 2 Thessalonians appear to have arisen from a completely unproblematic congregational situation a few months earlier. Since both the issues of eschatology and "idleness" were addressed in 1 Thessalonians, it seems more logical to assume that the roots of the 2 Thessalonians situation were present at the time of writing 1 Thessalonians.

A more adequate starting point for the reconstruction of the audience situation at the time of writing the first letter is offered by Helmut Koester. Without allowing any of the details from the second letter to influence his image of the situation, Koester concludes that the congregation was facing "such questions as the credibility and integrity of the apostle, hostilities from the outside, consequences for Christian conduct, and the significance for life in the present of the newly acquired status of salvation. Paul discusses these questions in detail, which attests to his own insights into the real problems of a newly founded church. . . ."[5] This summary reflects a sound grasp of the rhetoric of 1 Thessalonians, and takes account of the justification of Paul's apostolic behavior in 1 Thessalonians 2 as well as the series of ethical clarifications and warnings in 1 Thessalonians 4–5. Paul's information about the situation was provided by Timothy's oral report based on a period of first hand observations. Also it is likely that Timothy brought a list of written or oral questions posed by the Thessalonian congregation, as evidenced by the sections in 1 Thessalonians beginning with "now concerning."[6] There are substantial reasons, therefore, for inferring a troubled situation in Thessalonica at the time of writing the first letter. It appears justifiable to assume that Paul's arguments were so closely related to this congregational situation that the latter can be inferred from the former.[7]

Given the problematic status of 2 Thessalonians at the present moment of research, it is prudent to build the picture of the congregational situation primarily on the basis of clues in 1 Thessalonians. In the para-

---

[4] Best, *Thessalonians,* 59; cf. also Guthrie, *New Testament Introduction,* 193.
[5] Koester and Robinson, *Trajectories through Early Christianity,* 112f.
[6] Cf. Faw, "On the Writing of First Thessalonians."
[7] Cf. Schmithals, *Paul and the Gnostics,* 123–218 for an exegetical justification for reconstructing the congregational situation from the argument of the letters; also Frank W. Beare, "The First Letter," 4–11, esp. p. 4: ". . . if we are to make anything of his letters at all, we must pick up his scattered allusions and references and put them together, and in one way and another piece out as clear a picture as we can of the place and the people and the particular circumstances that may have impelled him to write as he does." For a discussion of the method of drawing audience inferences, cf. Berger, "Die impliziten Gegner," 375–80.

graphs that follow, I draw inferences from the argument of the first letter, allowing subsidiary information from the second letter to enter the picture only on the two occasions when it appears to be completely consistent with the information available from the first. The close chronological proximity of the two letters makes this subsidiary use appear justified. But we shall postpone until the final chapter the detailed reconstruction of the situation as visible at the time of Paul's writing of 2 Thessalonians. By employing the information in this way, I hope that the reconstruction of the situation at the time of 1 Thessalonians can be made plausible even for those who reject the argument in chapter 1 concerning the authenticity of 2 Thessalonians.

1. THE PROBLEM OF PERSECUTION

From the opening lines of the narratio section in 1 Thessalonians we encounter references to the "affliction" and "suffering" that had marked the Thessalonian experience from the moment of the Thessalonians' conversion (1 Thess 1:6; 2:14). That persecution posed a real threat to the congregation is evident from the fact that Paul explains the sending of Timothy as his effort to sustain them in this crisis (3:1–5).[8] Paul uses a rare word meaning "shaken," "disturbed" or "perturbed" in 1 Thess 3:3 to convey his concern over their reactions.[9] His narration of what Timothy was commissioned to accomplish, however, does not involve the encouragement of courageous response to persecution as one might expect but deals rather with the question of whether persecution should have been anticipated. Paul reminds the congregation in 3:3 that "you yourselves know that this is to be our lot," which speaks to the question of appropriateness. The issue quite clearly is whether persecution should be expected as a normal concomitant of the faith.[10] Ernest Best captures Paul's point with his epigram, "normality is persecution."[11]

Paul goes on to reiterate the point of appropriate expectations in the

---

[8] Cf. Marxsen, *Der erste Brief*, 54.

[9] Cf. Chadwick, "I Thess. 3.3, "σαίνεσθαι," for the use of this term in a papyrus with the meaning "to perturb mentally"; Lang, "Σαίνω," *TDNT* 7:54–56 concurs that this is the appropriate translation here; cf. also Bauer, Arndt, Gingrich, and Danker, *A Greek-English Lexicon*, 747. Perdelwitz sought to eliminate the puzzles in the use of this term by a textual emendation, which proved implausible: "Zu σαίνεσθαι ἐν ταῖς θλίψεσιν ταύταις, I Thess. 3,3."

[10] Marshall comments, "If a person knows that something unpleasant is part of his destiny, something that is inevitable, then he will brace himself to meet it and will not think that it is a sign that he is on the wrong track or be taken by surprise by it." *1 and 2 Thessalonians*, 92.

[11] Best, *Thessalonians*, 135.

following sentence: "For when we were with you, we told you beforehand that we were to suffer affliction, and as you know, it has been so" (1 Thess 3:4). Not only does this reiteration sound superfluous in light of 1 Thess 1:6 which reveals that they had been converted during persecutions, but it is also hard to see how this kind of rhetoric could be designed to counter cowardice or despair in the face of adversity. It seems to imply instead that the Thessalonians were for some reason surprised or perturbed that persecution would be a part of their life in the new age, and that its presence cast doubt on the validity of their faith. William Neil infers similarly that Paul was countering some "arguments . . . that any religion that aroused such opposition must be unwholesome and perverse."[12] That the Thessalonians felt persecution was somehow inconsistent with their faith may be indicated also by 1 Thess 2:14 where Paul defines Christian ethical imitation primarily in terms of suffering persecution.[13]

2. THE RESPONSE TO THE DEATH OF CHURCH MEMBERS

The discussion in 1 Thess 4:13–18 indicates the congregation was in a state of shocked dismay at the death of some of the members. Paul spoke of their grief as if they had lost hope that they would ever see the deceased members again (4:13) and his emphasis was that while the dead would rise first at the parousia, those who remained alive would be "caught up with them at the same time that they shall be caught up."[14] Given the thrust of this argument, it appears that the congregation had not only discounted the possibility of mortal death for members of the new age, but also lacked the typical early Christian hope that death would be resolved by resurrection.[15] For some reason they were assuming the separation of death would be permanent.

Willi Marxsen has provided a ground clearing effort to understand the peculiar connection between the imminent parousia and the Thessalonian concern about the implications of the death of congregational members. Resisting the temptation to interpret these verses in a traditional dogmatic manner, isolating them from the situational context, he insists that the entire discussion was aimed at persons in Thessalonica whose hopeless-

---

[12] Neil, *Thessalonians*, 64.

[13] Bruce suggests that Paul's point in 1 Thess 2:14 is that "Persecution . . . is a natural concomitant of Christian faith. . . ." *1 and 2 Thessalonians*, 45.

[14] Frame, *Thessalonians*, 176, cites Ellicott at this point. Collins concludes in "Tradition, Redaction, and Exhortation," 333 that the argument in 1 Thess 4:13–18 is that ". . . the living have no precedence over the dead when it comes to being with the Lord."

[15] Cf. Laub, *Eschatologische Verkündigung*, 131 and Nepper-Christensen, "Das verborgene Herrenwort," 139f.

ness concerning the death of congregational members before the parousia was connected somehow with their spiritual enthusiasm.[16] Assuming that Paul's intense expectation of the parousia would have obviated the need for a traditional resurrection teaching during his founding mission in Thessalonica,[17] Marxsen contends that the problem for the congregation was not the death of members as such, but their death "before the parousia" which seemed to imply that they had "believed in vain."[18] The prospect of death prior to the parousia would logically also have threatened the faith of those still alive, a threat that Paul counters with his argument that the dead will not be disadvantaged because they will rejoin the living Christians at the sound of the last trumpet.

Several aspects of Marxsen's case require clarification. What is the precise connection between the despair of the Thessalonian congregation and the enthusiasm to which Marxsen refers? And how could the congregation have fallen into such despair unless they had literally believed that death had been abolished by the new faith? What could explain such an illusory belief? Wolfgang Harnisch refines the approach of Walter Schmithals in attempting to answer these questions, arguing that a gnostic doctrine of spiritual resurrection in the present was the logical foil of Paul's argument.[19] While the case for Gnosticism is not nearly as strong as in the Corinthian situation, Harnisch at least makes a case that a radical sense of realized eschatology is required by the evidence in 1 Thess 4:13–18. The wording of 4:15b indicates that the key issue for the Thessalonians was the relation of the living Christians to their deceased congregational members, while Paul's argument that the living shall not "precede" the dead in the parousia countered a tendency to consign the deceased to the realm beyond salvation.[20] Harnisch makes a less plausible case for paring back the implications of 1 Thess 4:13b to a Pauline warning about a possible level of grief rising as a consequence of Thessalonian beliefs.[21] His effort was designed to eliminate a major flaw in the Schmithals hypothesis, that the Thessalonian enthusiasts are mysteriously charged here with hopelessness,[22] but it is hardly convincing because persons in grief do not require logical instructions to grasp the level of their despair.[23]

---

[16] Marxsen, Der erste Brief, 63; for an earlier statement of his viewpoint, see "Auslegung von I Thess 4, 14–18."
[17] On this point, cf. also Becker, Auferstehung der Toten in Urchristentum, 46f.
[18] Marxsen, Der erste Brief, 65.
[19] Harnisch, Eschatologische Existenz, 19–51; Schmithals, Paul and the Gnostics, 160–67.
[20] Harnisch, Eschatologische Existenz, 27f.
[21] Eschatologische Existenz, 24f.
[22] Cf. Luz, Das Geschichtsverständnis, 321.
[23] Cf. also the critique of the Harnisch hypothesis in Luedemann, Paul, Apostle to the Gentiles, 206–8.

An alternate hypothesis is therefore required to explain the exegetical details that Marxsen and Harnisch uncovered. Joseph Plevnik has provided the basis for such an alternate view by showing that Paul's language concerning resurrection in 1 Thess 4:13–18 indicates he had taught a doctrine of assumption into paradise.[24] This apocalyptic doctrine involves the translation of the whole person from this world to the next, but it only functions for persons who have not experienced death. As Lohfink has shown in his definitive study of heavenly ascension and assumption narratives, "The one who is assumed does not have to taste death, and conversely, the one who is really dead cannot be assumed."[25] This could help explain the confusion of the Thessalonians, according to Plevnik: "If . . . Paul had already taught the Thessalonians that at the parousia of Christ they would all be assumed and gathered around the risen Lord forever, then the death of some of the faithful would obviously cause consternation in the community. They would naturally think that the dead could not participate in the assumption—one had to be *alive* to be assumed."[26] To draw out the implications of this doctrine in a manner congruent with the evidence in 1 Thessalonians 4, it appears that the Thesssalonians believed that the presence of the new age should have eliminated the possibility of death for true believers, so that when deaths occurred, they fell into despair about their eschatological faith, discounting the possibility of ever seeing their loved ones again. What remains unexplained in Plevnik's work is the peculiar resistance against a future eschatology in the Thessalonian piety, which leads us to the next clues.

3. THE QUESTION OF PREPAREDNESS FOR THE PAROUSIA

The use of the introductory formula "now concerning" in 1 Thess 5:1 indicates that the issue of the "times and the seasons" was one of the major concerns that Timothy reported on the part of the Thessalonians.[27] Our rhetorical analysis identified this as the opening sentence of the fourth proof in the letter, running from 5:1–11. Commentators have inferred from Paul's use of the adverb ἀκριβῶς, meaning "accurately, more

---

[24] Plevnik, "The Taking Up," an article that builds on the foundation of his earlier study, "The Parousia as Implication," 212–67. For a similar stress on rapture or assumption into paradise as the peculiar form of resurrection in this passage, cf. Hyldahl, "Auferstehung Christi." Klijn offers a less plausible explanation in "1 Thessalonians 4,13–18," namely that persons dying before the final act of history will miss the joy of Israel's triumph.

[25] Lohfink, *Die Himmelfahrt Jesu,* 74; translation by Plevnik, "The Taking Up," 280.

[26] Plevnik, "The Taking Up," 281.

[27] Despite its promising title, the essay by Blake, "The Apocalyptic Setting," does little more than confirm the significance of this theme.

exactly" in 5:2, that Paul may have been responding to a Thessalonian query, "Tell us *precisely* when the parousia is going to happen."[28] The outlook revealed in such a question apparently involved a refusal or inability to accept the traditional teaching of which Paul reminds them in 1 Thess 5:1–2 (cf. also 2 Thess 2:5). The warning about a false sense of security (1 Thess 5:3) would seem to indicate the congregation was discounting the possibility of future judgment.[29] They appear to have resisted maintaining the state of preparedness required for a life in the shadow of the parousia (1 Thess 5:6–8).[30] They apparently felt that given their election as members of the new age (1 Thess 1:4), they should have a secure status. But their experience of adversity seemed to contradict the premise of the presence of the new age. Hence they fit the description in 1 Thess 5:14 as "weak," in that they were "weary," "disheartened,"[31] and I would add, "impatient with ambiguity." Their intense experience of realized eschatology, so to speak, sustained an unwillingness to live with the uncertainty of a future eschatology.[32] In this context, the emphasis on sobriety in 1 Thess 5:6–8 involves primarily realism about the futurity and ineluctability of the parousia.[33] This would explain why Paul refuses in 1 Thess 5:1–11 to provide any softening of the unpredictability of the parousia.[34] The entire tenor of the argument, as Collins shows, is to maintain a proper sense of "urgency" in the expectation of the parousia.[35]

It seems to me that the reluctance of the Thessalonians to live with the ambiguity of an incalculable parousia is consistent with a readiness to accept the message reported in 2 Thess 2:2 that "The Day of the Lord has already come!"[36] The centrality of this issue for the argument of 2

---

[28] Cf. Marshall, *1 and 2 Thessalonians*, 132.

[29] Cf. Harnisch, *Eschatologische Existenz*, 77–84; also Schmithals, *Paul and the Gnostics*, 164–67; for a critical sifting of the Harnisch and Schmithals' contributions, see Plevnik, " 1 Thess. 5, 1–11." For a balanced statement of the Thessalonians' tendency to deny the ambiguity of life between the ages, without resorting to a gnostic hypothesis, cf. Laub, *Eschatologische Verkündigung*, 168–71.

[30] Cf. Mattern, *Das Verständnis*, 77–82.

[31] Black, "The Weak in Thessalonica," 318.

[32] Cf. Smalley, "The Delay of the Parousia."

[33] Cf. Lövestam, "Über die neutestamentliche Aufforderung," 90–94.

[34] Cf. Marshall, *1 and 2 Thessalonians*, 233f.: "he can only say that it will come at an unpredictable time. While Paul certainly envisaged that it could happen within the lifetime of his readers and perhaps indeed within a very short time, he did not delimit the time of its arrival within a definite period but left it quite open as to when it would appear, as A. L. Moore has rightly emphasized." The reference is to Moore's study, *The Parousia in the New Testament*, 73. Cf. also Laub, *Eschatologische Verkündigung*, 132f.

[35] Collins, "Tradition, Redaction, and Exhortation," 342.

[36] Despite the tendency of commentators to tone down the perfect verb used in this sentence, it is essential to take seriously the impartial conclusions of the grammarians. A verb in the perfect tense such as ἐνέστηκεν, "has come," carries the sense of an action completed in the past and continuing in its completed state into the present. Cf. Moulton, *A Grammar* 1:109. Kühner and Gerth write in *Ausführliche Grammatik* 2.1.146: "The perfect tense . . . conveys

Thessalonians is indicated by the rhetorical analysis that identifies this statement as the false doctrine to be disputed in the rest of the letter. Ernst von Dobschütz showed that the person uttering these words and the congregation accepting them could not have held orthodox Jewish-Christian assumptions about the futurity of the eschaton.[37] Although many commentators have been reluctant to confront the implications of a literal translation of 2 Thess 2:2,[38] it does no more than state in bald terms the tendency toward a radical kind of realized eschatology countered throughout 1 Thessalonians. At least since the time of Dobschütz, scholars have suggested that giving credence to a message about the parousia having already arrived would seem to presuppose a Hellenistic mentality that understood the apocalyptic scheme in a non-historical, spiritualized fashion. Willi Marxsen concludes that "the difficulty" in interpreting 2 Thess 2:2 "disappears if we recognize that here a Gnostic idea is being expressed apocalyptically. . . . The church has been confused by eschatological fanatics of Gnostic origin with the assertion that the fulfillment has

---

an action that from the perspective of the speaker appears to be completed, fully developed." Thus the clear sense of 2 Thess 2:2 is that the parousia has already come and that its presence is now being felt. The interpretation by Dobschütz, Neil, Bruce, Best and others in the sense that the parousia is "near at hand" is therefore unsupportable. Milligan properly insists that the expression is "denoting strictly *present* time" and should be translated "as if the day of the Lord is now present." *Thessalonians,* 97. Stephenson inadvertently supplies conclusive evidence in favor of this conclusion in his article promoting the translation "is just at hand." Cf. "On the Meaning of $\dot{\epsilon}\nu\dot{\epsilon}\sigma\tau\eta\kappa\epsilon\nu$ η $\dot{\eta}$ $\dot{\eta}\mu\dot{\epsilon}\rho\alpha$ $\tauο\hat{υ}$ $\kappa\nu\rho\dot{\iota}ο\nu$," He notes that since the middle of the last century, most exegetes and lexicographers have been driven to the sense of "presence" rather than "imminence" for $\dot{\epsilon}\nu\dot{\iota}\sigma\tau\eta\mu\iota$ because of LXX parallels, the use of the term in Hellenistic literature and papyri, and also the fact that the Greek expression for the present tense was $\dot{ο}$ $\dot{\epsilon}\nu\epsilon\sigma\tau\dot{ω}\varsigma$ $\kappa\rho\dot{ο}\nuος$. Stephenson discounts this evidence because he finds it impossible to believe that the Thessalonians could have thought the parousia had already come. The question is whether the degree of acceptability to the modern exegete's own common sense should have priority in determining what a Greco-Roman writer might have intended to say. For a straightforward discussion of the proper translation of this sentence as "the day of the Lord has come, is present," cf. Laub, *Eschatologische Verkündigung,* 138–40.

[37] Cf. Dobschütz, *Die Thessalonicher-Briefe,* 267: "That the day of the Lord in the proper sense as the day of judgment and salvation should already have arrived cannot possibly be the opinion of Christians suffering serious persecution; according to Old Testament and early Christian opinion the day of the Lord implied such a measure of externally observable, fundamental and world transforming, miraculous processes that no Christian could have spoken of that time as present in the sense that 'we live already in it'. . . ." The failure to recognize the unorthodox premises of the Thessalonian piety detracts from the value of Charles H. Giblin's hypothesis that the distortion of the eschatological teaching arose from the liturgical practices in Thessalonica; cf. *The Threat to Faith.* More recently John Gillman has rejected every effort to grasp these unorthodox premises, concluding that the problem in Thessalonica was the intellectual inability to integrate "the traditional teaching about the parousia and the resurrection of the dead." Cf. "Signals of Transformation," 270.

[38] Cf. Dobschütz, *Die Thessalonicher-Briefe,* 267–68; Dibelius, *An die Thessalonicher I, II,* 44; Bruce, *Thessalonians,* 165; Friedrich, *1 Thessalonicher 5, 1–11,* 262–63; Masson, *Thessaloniciens,* 93.

already come."[39] Although it would be inappropriate at this point in our investigation to accept Marxsen's thesis about the precise origin of the misconception implied in 2 Thess 2:2, it is at least clear that resistance against preparedness for a future parousia is evident in both letters.

An alternative construal of the prophetic announcement in 2 Thess 2:2 has recently been suggested by Glenn Holland.[40] He takes the expression, ἐνέστηκεν ἡ ἡμέρα τοῦ κυρίου, as referring to an event that had already occurred but denies that it implies the parousia. Since "the Day of the Lord" is frequently used in the Old Testament to refer to a day of wrath, Holland argues that some ἄτακτοι after 70 C.E. used the expression to refer to an historical crisis involving persecution that was perceived to be preliminary to the return of Christ.[41] In his effort to draw sharp lines between the views of the ἄτακτοι, the pseudonymous author of 2 Thessalonians, and the original apocalyptic theology of Paul, Holland makes decisive use of evidence in the other Pauline letters to buttress his case concerning 2 Thess 2:2. He argues that Paul's usage implies:

> . . . two "days," one the "day" of the Lord Jesus, the parousia, and the other "day" of wrath against the wicked, which the good, with proper spiritual armament, will survive, to find a blessing afterward. These two different "days" represent Paul's failure to integrate fully the idea of "the Day of YHWH" and of God as eschatological judge in the Old Testament with the Christian idea of the collective acceptance of the congregation on "the Day of Jesus Christ," when Christ appears as judge at the parousia.[42]

This strikes me as a rather strained distinction, given the proximity of the expressions, "parousia of the Lord" and "day of the Lord," in 1 Thess 4:15 and 5:2[43] and the resultant necessity to identify the "Lord" on the day of wrath as different from Christ. It may be theologically appealing to separate Christ from wrathful judgment, but it cannot be sustained by

---

[39] Cf. Marxsen, *Introduction to the New Testament*, 39; cf. also Schenke, "Auferstehungsglaube und Gnosis." Aus has explored a potential background of the belief reflected in 2 Thessalonians in "The Relevance of Isaiah 66:7." Although he confuses the outlook of the author with that of the audience and hedges on the precise implications of the ἐνέστηκεν ἡ ἡμέρα τοῦ κυρίου in 2 Thess 2:2, he infers the viewpoint of the Thessalonians in a manner somewhat congruent with my conclusion on 264f.: "Because the addressees believe their sufferings have reached their peak, they conceive of them as one of the elements in the messianic woes, themselves part of the coming of the Day of the Lord. They argue as follows: 'Our intense persecution shows that the End has come (that is, it has started to come).'"

[40] Holland, "Let No One Deceive You," 331–36.

[41] "Let No One Deceive You," 335f.

[42] "Let No One Deceive You," 332f.

[43] Cf. Marshall, *1 and 2 Thessalonians*, 127, 133; Friedrich, *Der erste Brief*, 243–45.

recent scholarship.[44] Even if Paul made such a distinction, this is hardly proof that the ἄτακτοι followed suit. If, as Holland argues by reference to Aune's study of Christian prophecy,[45] 2 Thess 2:2 is a typical "salvation-judgment oracle," there is every reason to expect that the κύριος in this oracle would have been Christ rather than YHWH.[46] Despite Holland's significant foray, which may become more plausible when buttressed by the availability of his dissertation, the most likely implication of 2 Thess 2:2 is that Christ has already returned, in one form or another, and thus that for the prophetic circle that issued the oracle, there would be no further need to remain in preparedness for the parousia.

4. The Conflict over Ecstatic Manifestations

That the Thessalonian Christians had experienced the spirit in powerful ways is clear from Paul's description of their conversion in 1 Thess 1:5–6.[47] This has particular significance rhetorically, because the closing words of the thanksgiving and the opening sentence in the long narratio section both refer to the congregation's encounter with the holy spirit in connection with the preaching of the gospel and the ecstatic joy of Christian piety. The wording of 1 Thess 1:5 suggests that powerful manifestations of a miraculous sort had accompanied the initial preaching of the gospel in Thessalonica.[48] In 1 Thess 1:6 the joy that constitutes a decisive part of Christian imitation of the apostles and Christ is identified as coming from the "holy spirit," that is, from a supernatural source manifesting itself in an ecstatic manner.[49]

A passage suggesting troubles related to ecstatic manifestations is 1

---

[44] Cf. Baumgarten, *Paulus und die Apokalyptik*, who concludes on 64 ". . . that with the technical term ἡμέρα κυρίου (Χριστοῦ) the returning as well as the judging Lord (cf. 2 Cor 5:10) can be described. Therefore the concept of the Parousia is ordinarily implied or associated. . . ." Cf. also Beker, *Paul the Apostle*, 135–81.

[45] Aune, *Prophecy*, analyzes the "parenetic salvation-judgment oracles" on p. 326, but actually does not include 2 Thess 2:2 under this category; cf. p. 220.

[46] Cf. Aune, *Prophecy*, 220, who assumes the identity of the Lord as Christ in 2 Thess 2:2.

[47] Cf. Bruce, *Thessalonians*, 14; Collins, "The Church of the Thessalonians," 343; Koenig, "From Mystery to Ministry."

[48] Cf. Marshall, *1 and 2 Thessalonians*, 53f.; Lünemann mentions the impression among ancient Greek commentators of the "miracles by which the power of the preached gospel was attested," although he prefers the less overtly miraculous interpretation that "our preaching of the gospel . . . could only be ascribed to the operation of the Holy Ghost." *Thessalonians*, 27f. In either case, ecstatic manifestations of the spirit would be implied.

[49] Marshall sustains part of this conclusion by suggesting that 1 Thess 1:6 identifies joy as "not merely a human emotion, but . . . ascribed to a divine influence. . . ." He shows that imitation of Jesus' joy in suffering is the point of Paul's reminder in 1:6, citing the ecstatic admonition of the blessed disciples who rejoice and "leap for joy" despite all adversity in Luke 6:22f. *1 and 2 Thessalonians*, 54f.

Thess 5:6–8. Evald Lövestam has pointed out the relation between spiritual enthusiasm and the references to sobriety in this passage, observing that drunkenness is frequently associated with forms of ecstasy that erode self control.[50] There is a much clearer indication of ecstatic conflicts in 2 Thess 2:2, showing that by the time of writing the second letter Paul had become concerned over the kind of ecstatic prophecies that could proclaim the end of time had already arrived.[51] Whether there is additional evidence in 1 Thessalonians of such conflicts is less fully accepted,[52] but I find the argument of Schmithals convincing at this point. He contends that the antithetical wording of 1 Thess 5:19–22 indicates conflicts within the congregation concerning the control and legitimacy of ecstatic gifts.[53] Although he rarely agrees with Schmithals on anything, Marshall basically concurs in this reading of the evidence: "The implication is that there was a tendency in the church to quench the fire of the Spirit. If so, this further implies that it was probably a reaction against what may have seemed to be an over-enthusiastic stress on the Spirit."[54] Marshall goes on to infer from 1 Thess 5:21 that "it can very well be that at Thessalonica the variety and dubious quality of the utterances of some prophets were dragging the phenomenon into disrepute."[55]

A close reading of 1 Thess 5:19–22 confirms the presence of conflicts over ecstatic manifestations in the congregation. On the one side, Paul urges the leaders not to "quench the spirit" or "despise prophesying," which indicates there were tendencies to stamp out such ecstatic expressions entirely.[56] As W. C. van Unnik has shown,[57] the expression "quench the spirit" was used in Greco-Roman literature to connote a subduing of enthusiasm. But on the other side, Paul insists that "everything" be tested

---

[50] Lövestam, "Über die neutestamentliche Aufforderung," 81–87.

[51] Cf. Best, *Thessalonians*, 279: "A 'spirit' [in 2 Thess 2:2] almost certainly refers to an ecstatic utterance or spiritual revelation (apocalyptic prophecy rather than glossolalia) inspired by the Spirit, or possibly from Paul's point of view inspired by a lying spirit." See also Masson, *Thessaloniciens*, 93f.

[52] Cf. Best, *Thessalonians*, 237.

[53] Schmithals, *Paul and the Gnostics*, 172–75; cf. also Aune, *Prophecy*, 191: 1 Thess 5:19–22 reveals that ". . . prophesying had, for whatever reason, become a factor in intramural conflict."

[54] Marshall, *1 and 2 Thessalonians*, 157. For a similar perspective, cf. Friedrich, *1 Thessalonicher 5, 1–11*, 250; cf. also Reese, *1 and 2 Thessalonians*, 65f. and Marxsen, *Der erste Brief*, 72; Albrecht Oepke, *Thessalonicher*, 178.

[55] Marshall, *1 and 2 Thessalonians*, 159; cf. also Friedrich, *1 Thessalonicher 5, 1–11*, 250.

[56] Cf. Aune, *Prophecy*, 219; Neil, *Thessalonians*, 130f.; Plummer, *First Epistle to the Thessalonians*, 99: "But what follows seems to show that, in the general unsettlement at Thessalonica, the special charismatic gifts of the Spirit were being ignored, and the manifestations of them were being repressed." Friedrich draws a similar inference in *1 Thessalonicher 5, 1–1*, 250. Hill, *New Testament Prophecy*, 119f. fails to account for the peculiar warning in 1 Thessalonians about quenching prophecy, although he observes that the Corinthians obviously needed no such admonition.

[57] Unnik, "'Den Geist löschet nicht aus.'"

according to the moral standards of good and evil, which indicates there
were some who felt these ecstatic manifestations were beyond evaluation.[58] Since the discussion of these conflicts is the final topic in the fifth
and final section of the *probatio* of 1 Thessalonians, according to our
rhetorical analysis, it assumes a position of emphasis and particular
congregational relevance for the letter as a whole.[59]

5. THE CRITICISM OF PAULINE LEADERSHIP

The narration of Paul's behavior while in Thessalonica (1 Thess 2:1–12)
is formulated in such a way as to counter charges or suspicions of
illegitimacy. While the language of such an apology was largely traditional as Abraham Malherbe and others have shown,[60] this does not in
any sense prove that the argument was unrelated to the situation in
Thessalonica.[61] The prominent place of this material in the narration of
reasons for Paul's thanksgiving indicates its importance for the morale of
the church which the rhetoric of 1 Thessalonians aims to sustain.

A penetrating analysis of the situational implications of this material
has been worked out by Schmithals, who showed that the statement
concerning Paul's visit not having been "in vain" (1 Thess 2:1) and
consisting ". . . not only in word but also in power" (1 Thess 1:5) reflects
the charge that he had merely proclaimed the spiritual message rather
than demonstrating it. In other words, Paul had not shown himself to be a
"pneumatic"[62] by ecstatic manifestations such as public display of glossolalia or visions. Such a criticism reflects not only the assumption that
spiritual power is directly visible in ecstatic behavior but also a willing-
ness to counter human authority in the name of such power. These
inferences seem justified even if one is disinclined to accept Schmithals'

---

[58] Cf. Cullmann, "Meditation"; also Reese, *1 and 2 Thessalonians*, 66: "This is an important
admonition, especially for radical enthusiasts who may feel they are subject to no restraints."
[59] Cf. Dibelius, *An die Thessalonicher I, II*, 31f.
[60] Malherbe, "'Gentle as a Nurse'"; Dibelius, *An die Thessalonicher I, II*, 7–11; cf. also
Koester, "I Thessalonians," 41f., where the use of the traditional defense of the Greco-
Roman popular philosopher in 1 Thess 2:1–12 is acknowledged but Paul's "non-
conventional" acceptance of the affectionate role "undercuts the authority structure implied
in the tradition of the true philosopher used here." Raymond F. Collins provides an account
of Paul's prophetic, bureaucratic and philosophical language in "Paul, as Seen," 356–64.
[61] Cf. Marshall, *1 and 2 Thessalonians*, 61: ". . . it is difficult to see why Paul, a Christian
preacher, should have gone to such pains to describe himself in terms of the ideal
philosopher if there was nothing in the situation to make him do so. He must have felt that
he was being accused or stood in danger of being accused of behaving like a second-rate
philosopher, and he defended himself by claiming that his standards as a preacher were in
no way inferior to those of the best philosophers."
[62] Schmithals, *Paul and the Gnostics*, 140; cf. also Lütgert, "Die Volkommenen," 616.

gnostic hypothesis; whatever the precise cause, the criticism of Paul's leadership appears to be related to the ecstatic temperament of the congregation.

A critical attitude toward the leadership that Paul had left in charge of the Thessalonian congregation was probably related to this bias in favor of ecstatic expressions of the faith. It is indicated by Paul's unusual admonitions in 1 Thess 5:12–13, to "respect those who labor among you and are over you in the Lord and admonish you." This is the first of several exhortations related to congregational life in the final proof of the letter. The threefold description of the status and duties of congregational leaders hardly seems necessary in an informational sense, because the congregation surely knows what is being done. It rather seems designed to justify the status and action of these leaders in the face of internal criticism.[63] In all likelihood the leaders in question were patrons and patronesses of the house churches in Thessalonica as well as the socially prominent members of the congregation, assuming that the social profile of other Pauline churches is relevant.[64] Resistance against the leadership of such persons was typical of Greco-Roman society as well as for some of the other Pauline churches.[65] But it is noteworthy in the context of these arrangements of subordination to upper-class leaders that Paul refrains from any legal or institutional warrants, urging a willing submission from the good will of the congregation. The leaders are to be esteemed "very highly in love."[66] The peculiar rhetoric of Paul's admonition in these verses has led exegetes to suspect that resistance in this instance was spurred by spiritual enthusiasm.[67] Such an inference may be premature, but it at least seems clear that Paul is being extremely careful not to resort to traditional subordination language in this passage, which reveals a sensitive conflict of some kind. The final admonition in this section, "be at peace among yourselves," has something of the same implication, according to James E. Frame. He suggested "that the workers . . . had been opposed by some of the converts, presumably the idlers . . . with the result that friction between them arose and the peace of the group was ruffled."[68]

---

[63] Cf. Friedrich, 1 Thessalonicher 5, 1–11, 248; Marxsen, Der erste Brief, 71; Marshall, 1 and 2 Thessalonians, 147–50. For a less polemical construal of these verses, cf. Black, "The Weak in Thessalonica," 311f.; note, however, that Black contends on p. 314 that the admonitions "are directly relevant to the situation in Thessalonica."

[64] Cf. Meeks, The First Urban Christians, 51–72; Judge, The Social Pattern; Theissen, The Social Setting, 69–120; Holmberg, Paul and Power, 57–102; Ollrog, Paulus und seine Mitarbeiter, 85–87; Funk, Status und Rollen, 156–89.

[65] Lightfoot, "Church of Thessalonica," 265, links the "tendency to despise lawfully constituted authorities" with the independent political temperament of the Thessalonians.

[66] Cf. Laub, "Paulus als Gemeindegründer," 32.

[67] Laub, "Paulus als Gemeindegründer," 33; Lütgert, "Die Volkommenen," 77.

[68] Frame, Thessalonians, 90.

Marshall observes that Paul refers in this context to peace within the church rather than peace with the outside world: "It would, therefore, seem very probable that there was a real tendency, known to Paul, for some members of the church to disregard the direction given by the church leaders and to oppose them."[69] It seems quite likely that this resistance against local leaders was related in some way to the criticism of Pauline authority.

6. THE PROBLEM OF THE Ἄτακτοι

The task of admonishment mentioned in 1 Thess 5:12 as a key task of congregational leaders is specified with precisely the same term in 5:14 in relation to the ἄτακτοι. Under the influence of evidence from 2 Thess 3:6–15, several earlier commentators selected the option "loafers" to translate this term.[70] Recent commentators such as Best and Bruce and translations such as Moffatt and the *Revised Standard Version* favor this option.[71] But the definitive study of this term by Ceslas Spicq has shown that the basic meaning of the term is standing against the order of nature or of God. The word was typically used in military contexts to depict someone who would not keep step or follow commands. Spicq terms this group the "refractaires,"[72] which should be rendered the "obstinate" or "insubordinate" in English.[73] Resistance against authority is therefore implied by this term, which brings us very close to the resistance against church authorities as inferred in our preceding section. Holland calls attention to the association of this term with περιεργάζομαι in 2 Thess 3:11, which carries ". . . political or religious overtones as an indictment of those who over-reach themselves."[74]

Judging from the details in 1 Thessalonians alone, Marxsen concludes that this group were "enthusiasts who because of the nearness of the parousia are no longer taking seriously the things of everyday life."[75] The wording of 1 Thess 4:11f. and the admonition in 1 Thess 5:22 suggest that

---

[69] Marshall, *1 and 2 Thessalonians,* 149.

[70] Milligan, *Thessalonians,* 152–54; Frame, *Thessalonians,* 197; for a more ample development of this approach, cf. Frame, "Οἱ Ἄτακτοι (I Thess. 5.14)," 194: ". . . οἱ ἄτακτοι in I 5.14 is to be translated straightway 'the loafers.'"

[71] Bruce, *Thessalonians,* 122; Best, *Thessalonians,* 230.

[72] Spicq, "Les Thessaloniciens," 1–13, esp. 12. This view was reaffirmed in *Notes de Lexicographie* 1:159.

[73] Cf. Marshall, *1 and 2 Thessalonians,* 150; Rigaux, *Thessaloniciens,* 582f.; for an earlier statement of this conclusion, see Bornemann, *Die Thessalonicherbriefe,* 236f.

[74] Holland, "Let No One Deceive You," 330.

[75] Marxsen, *Der erste Brief,* 71.

the behavior of this group threatened the reputation of the congregation by violating widely accepted social standards.[76] While it would be premature to decide upon the precise identification of the obstinate persons in Thessalonica as "enthusiasts," Marxsen's linking of this group with those resisting congregational authority in 1 Thess 5:22 is defensible and the effort to associate them with a misunderstanding of the parousia is suggestive.

The picture of the ἄτακτοι as obstinate resisters of authority is confirmed by the evidence in 2 Thess 3:6–15 where it becomes clear that they had given up their occupations and were being supported by other members of the congregation. This is indicated by Paul's argument in 2 Thess 3:6–10 that he had the right to demand support but had refrained in order to give them an example of self-sufficiency.[77] The ἄτακτοι may well have claimed something like apostolic privilege in demanding such support. There is no evidence in this passage that the motivation of their behavior was laziness;[78] this is a false inference, so far as I can tell, from the fact that Paul counterposes his example of self-sufficient labor. The outmoded translation of "loafer" or "idler" provided misleading support for this false inference. The basic meaning of ἄτακτοι as rebellious or insubordinate should still be maintained in this passage.[79]

7. THE CHALLENGE TO SEXUAL ETHICS

The wording of Paul's exhortation concerning marital holiness implies substantial elements of resistance to normal standards, bringing this material into close proximity to the treatment of the ἄτακτοι. The placement of 1 Thess 4:1–8 as the first proof following the extraordinarily long narratio section indicates its significance for the congregation.[80] While Paul acknowledges that the Thessalonian behavior in the sexual area is still consistent with the ethic they had earlier received from Paul (1 Thess 4:1), there is a peculiarly repeated reminder about this previous teaching (1 Thess 4:1, 2, 6) which stands in stark contrast to the warning in 4:8 that "whoever disregards this, disregards not man but God, who gives his Holy Spirit to you." It would appear that Paul is countering an intellectual

---

76 Cf. *Der erste Brief,* 62, 72.
77 Cf. Best, *Thessalonians,* 337.
78 Trilling, *Der zweite Brief,* 143–46.
79 Spicq, *Notes de Lexicographie,* 157–59.
80 Reese observes that "obviously Paul would not have put these warnings in the letter if Timothy had not called attention to problems in the area of sex." *1 and 2 Thessalonians,* 46; cf. also Dobschütz, *Die Thessalonicher-Briefe,* 154; Friedrich, *1 Thessalonicher 5, 1–11,* 236.

challenge to the authenticity of the traditional ethic, insinuating that it derived from humans rather than from God.[81] The pointed reminder that God,who was spurned in this challenge, was the source of the spirit would seem to indicate that Paul felt the challenger did not properly relate morality on this issue to the possession of the spirit.[82]

These details were shrewdly used by Wilhelm Lütgert to suggest that a libertinistic movement in Thessalonica was seeking to show that immorality was forbidden neither by Paul's previous teaching nor by God's command itself.[83] Even though Lütgert's general thesis concerning enthusiasm in Thessalonica requires some correction, he remains the first to grasp the implications of these details in a penetrating and comprehensible manner. The element of resistance against authority that he perceived is sustained by the wording of Paul's command that "no man overreach and take advantage against his brother in this matter" (1 Thess 4:6). This admonition is couched in traditional Judaic terminology for the marriage contract,[84] so that the issue is perceived to be that of forcefully breaking across the legal arrangements of marital fidelity.[85] As Raymond F. Collins has concluded, "Paul maintains a rather traditional attitude, marriage still being perceived in terms of the husband's rights over his wife, and adultery being considered as an offense against the aggrieved husband."[86] Paul appears to be countering an effort in Thessalonica to challenge this traditional view.

---

[81] Cf. Friedrich, 1 Thessalonicher 5, 1–11, 240.

[82] Cf. Malherbe, "Exhortation in First Thessalonians," 251: Paul "must have had a reason for this extraordinary stress on the motivations for the Christian moral life." While Malherbe does not draw specific inferences about the Thessalonian audience, his identification of Paul's distinctive emphasis on the motivation of divine will and vengeance appears congruent with the conclusion I draw. Raymond F. Collins, on the other hand, insists that the language in 1 Thess 4:1–8 ". . . does not demand that the text be understood as Paul's response to a specific problem existing within the community at Thessalonica." "'This is the Will of God,'" 51.

[83] Lütgert, "Die Volkommenen," 619ff.

[84] Cf. Jewett, "The Sexual Liberation," 61f.; also Beauvery, "Πλεονεκτεῖν in I Thess. 4.6a"; Maurer, "σκεῦος," TDNT 7:359–67. For an extensive discussion of the linguistic background of this passage, cf. Rigaux, Thessaloniciens, 500–515. The most recent survey of the thoroughly "Jewish flavour of the Pauline paraenesis" in this passage is provided by Collins, "The Unity of Paul's Paraenesis," 421.

[85] Cf. Baltensweiler, Die Ehe im Neuen Testament, and Baltensweiler, "Erwägungen zu 1. Thess. 4, 3–8," for the arguement that all of 1 Thess 4:1–8 deals with a concrete problem in the congregation related to marriage. But his suggestion that 4:6–8 deal with the problem of Christian adjustment to Roman heiress law seems to require a strained translation of ἐν τῷ πράγματι; Schmithals, Paul and the Gnostics, 156–58 on this point. It is also difficult to reconcile Baltensweiler's theory of extensive involvement with inheritance laws with the intense eschatological expectation visible elsewhere in Thessalonians.

[86] Collins, "The Unity of Paul's Paraenesis," 426.

8. The Problem of the Anthropological Trichotomy

In the benediction of 1 Thess 5:23 there is a curiously atypical reference to three constitutive parts of humankind: "And may the God of peace himself sanctify you [to be] integral, and may your spirit and soul and body be kept complete [in all of its parts] [and] unblemished at the parousia of our Lord Jesus Christ."[87] While the emphasis here on persons remaining holy and undivided until the return of Christ conforms closely to the issues of bodily purity and spiritual ecstasy in Thessalonica, the trichotomy itself is completely atypical for Pauline anthropology.[88] The efforts to solve this dilemma by suggesting Paul did not mean to be taken literally,[89] that "spirit" here refers strictly to the divinely apportioned gift,[90] to the intellectual capacity of humans,[91] or that the benediction should be divided with "spirit" in one half and "body and soul" in the other[92] have not been able to prove convincing to other scholars. There is a theological defensiveness in these efforts to preserve the theology of Paul from potentially heretical implications. None of these suggestions is capable of accounting for the rhetorical relationship to the main argument of the letter, and hence the integral connection with the congregational situation.[93]

When one takes into account the formal use of benedictions like 1 Thess 5:23 to sum up the previous argument in a sermon or letter,[94] the emphasis on the indivisibility of humans may be seen as the crucial point in relation to the Thessalonian problem as Paul understood it.[95] The hapax legomenon ὁλοτελής[96] is used in this sentence with the related term ὁλόκληρος[97] to provide an unprecedented emphasis on wholeness, completeness and indivisibility. But why would Paul have to emphasize

---

[87] Cf. the analysis of the problem in this formulation in Jewett, *Paul's Anthropological Terms,* 175ff. For the translation, see Jewett, "Form and Function," 20.

[88] Cf. Rigaux, *Thessaloniciens,* 596ff.; Dibelius, *An die Thessalonicher I, II,* 32.

[89] Neil, *Thessalonians,* 119; Reese, *1 and 2 Thessalonians,* 69: "The passage then does not offer significant help in clarifying Paul's anthropology." Best, *Thessalonians,* 244: "If Paul has created the verse then he is almost certainly using his terms loosely, perhaps in dependence on popular psychology. . . . We ought not then to use this text as a source for Pauline psychology. . . ."

[90] Frame, *Thessalonians,* 211.

[91] Veloso, "Contenido antropologico de 1 Tesalonicenses 5,23," 134f.

[92] Masson, "Sur I Thessaloniciens V, 23"; also with slight variations, van Stempvoort, "Eine stilistische Lösung."

[93] See the discussion in Jewett, *Paul's Anthropological Terms,* 177–79. A more precise estimate of the rhetorical significance of the benediction is possible when one takes account of the fact that it opens the peroration of 1 Thessalonians, recapitulating major themes in the preceding argument. Cf. Lausberg, *Handbuch,* 236–40; *Classical Rhetoric,* 20.

[94] Cf. Jewett, "Form and Function," 18–34; cf. also Collins, "I Thessalonians."

[95] Frame, *Thessalonians,* 210f.

[96] Bauer, Arndt, Gingrich, and Danker, *A Greek- English Lexicon,* 565.

[97] Cf. Spicq, *Notes de Lexicographie* 2:616f.

this unless there were some tendency either to devalue or to separate some portion from the others? This inference gains plausibility when placed in the context of Greco-Roman anthropology. Eduard Schweizer has noted the widespread use of soul and body in antithesis to spirit in Hellenistic culture.[98] Hans Jonas discovered a definite preference for such a dualistically intended trichotomy in Gnosticism,[99] which has been confirmed by more recent studies.[100] It is certain that such tendencies were present in the first-century period, because the Corinthian Gnostics, or Proto-gnostics, associated "psychic" with "sarkic" as marks of the realm impervious to the "spirit."[101] When one reflects on the argument of the benediction in light of this background, it appears likely that the tendency to downplay the significance of body and soul in comparison with the spirit correlates with several of the other tendencies of the Thessalonians as observed above. The challenge to the traditional sexual ethic (1 Thess 4:1–8) is obviously related to body and soul as understood in the Greco-Roman world, and the tendency to place the spirit beyond ethical or societal norms (1 Thess 5:19–22) would fit with a dualistic construal of the anthropological trichotomy. The most likely explanation of the unprecedented trichotomy, therefore, is that Paul is citing and correcting a doctrine current in Thessalonica.[102] If so, there were dualistic tendencies in Thessalonica that stood close to Gnosticism, viewing the physical side of humans as the source of corruption and contrasting it with a divine portion of the human self.

9. Concluding Reflections

There will inevitably be disagreements between scholars concerning recipient inferences from the literary text of the Thessalonian correspondence. The best one can hope to achieve is a modest measure of objectivity gained by controlling such inferences through a coherent rhetorical analysis of the correspondence and an appropriate use of the exegetical method, guided by the insights of Thessalonian specialists. It is also important to separate as far as possible the assembling of individual inferences from the construction of a final hypothesis. The greatest danger

---

[98] Schweizer, "Zur Trichotomie," 76f.; Schweizer, "Πνεῦμα, πνεματικός," *TWNT* 6:393f.

[99] Jonas, *The Gnostic Religion*, 40, 281ff.

[100] Cf. Pagels, *The Gnostic Paul*, 59–86; Rudolph, *Gnosis*, 88–113.

[101] Cf. Brandenburger, *Adam und Christus*, 73ff.; Wilckens, *Weisheit und Torheit*, 88ff; Schmithals, *Gnosticism in Corinth*.

[102] Cf. the lengthier presentation of this case in Jewett, *Paul's Anthropological Terms*, 175–83, 250f., 347.

is the elimination of important inferences because they do not fit into a preconceived image of the audience situation. No matter how well grounded, audience inferences are insufficient in themselves to create an adequate audience hypothesis. They need to be combined with historical, archaeological, and cultural details concerning the local setting of the Thessalonian churches. And there is a need to select a suitable model to bring such exegetical and cultural details into a meaningful pattern. Our next step is therefore to consider how the literary evidence just sketched can be correlated with the cultural details and an appropriate theoretical model of the congregational situation.

Chapter Seven

THE SETTING IN THESSALONICA

The Setting in Thessalonica
Historical and Cultural Evidence

As we turn to examine the cultural situation in Thessalonica, it is striking to observe how little attention is paid to such matters in recent commentaries and scholarly articles related to the Thessalonian correspondence.[1] Earlier studies by Lightfoot and Burton and the more recent study by Judge deal with details in Acts' account of the Thessalonian ministry but do not draw attention to many details in the letters themselves or from the cultural history of the city.[2] The most substantive discussion is available in a little-used dissertation by Robert M. Evans.[3] The publication of an article by Karl Donfried[4] in the summer of 1985 begins to rectify this omission in scholarly attention. Nevertheless, it is clear that the parameters of the discussion of the Thessalonian problems have already crystallized in such a way as to predispose scholars to view the situation in a kind of cultural vacuum. Those parameters must be enlarged here if the quest for the audience of the Thessalonian correspondence is to be advanced.

There are some risks in postponing the treatment of the cultural background in Thessalonica to this point in the investigation. To do so serves to emphasize that a process of selective perception is involved in the sifting of cultural details from archaeology, ancient history, literature, numismatics, and the history of religion. Although the number of specific details available to us concerning Thessalonica is limited by the fact that

---

[1] The recent commentaries by Marxsen, Marshall, Masson, Best and Bruce provide brief summaries of the political and geographic setting of Thessalonica, but only two of them even so much as mention the availabile studies of the political, economic, and cultural situation or of the peculiar cults of the city in their bibliographies. Best, *Thessalonians,* 1–2, lists the studies by Charles Edson but makes no effort to discuss this material or to incorporate it into his commentary. Bruce, *Thessalonians,* xix–xx, provides a more comprehensive bibliography of historical and cultural studies of ancient Thessalonica, but I find no reference to these works in the text of his commentary. With his characteristic thoroughness, Rigaux discusses some of these studies in his introduction but thereafter they drop out of sight and are not mentioned in the commentary itself, as far as I can observe; *Thessaloniciens,* 13–20.

[2] Lightfoot, "The Church of Thessalonica"; Burton, "The Politarchs"; Judge, "The Decrees of Caesar."

[3] Evans, *Eschatology and Ethics,* 1–86. Even in Collins' exhaustive survey of scholarly work on 1 Thessalonians, which includes no less than fifteen doctoral dissertations written since 1956, the Evans study is overlooked. *Studies on the First Letter,* 70, 387.

[4] Donfried, "The Cults of Thessalonica"; cf. also Donfried, "Thessalonica," 1065f.

the city has never been systematically excavated,[5] there is still a need for meaningful selection. A listing of random details will not advance our quest and unexamined assumptions concerning the congregational situation could easily lead to false assessments of the relevance of historical information. The principles of selection that I intend to employ are provided by the rhetorical analysis of the argument in the two Thessalonian letters, the inferences drawn from the literary evidence concerning the congregational situation, and the array of models that will be discussed in the next chapter. I am looking for cultural details that can be brought into meaningful correlation with the situational details manifest in the Thessalonian correspondence and the models that can be used to interpret these data. The danger, of course, in using this principle of selection is that potentially significant factors may be overlooked.

1. Acts 17 as the Traditional Framework

Since the issue of selectivity has been raised, it is worth observing that previous efforts to relate archaeological, historical, and cultural details to the Thessalonian situation have largely been guided by the framework provided in the Book of Acts. For instance, Lightfoot fuses details from the letters into the account of Acts 17, pointing out the historical accuracy of the reference to the authorities as πολιτάρχαι in Acts 17:6 and assuming a similar accuracy in the problematic account of the siege of Jason's house (Acts 17:5).[6] Carl Clemen was equally optimistic about the feasibility of correlating the evidence in Acts and the Thessalonian letters.[7] Rigaux rests his entire explanation of Paul's precipitous departure from Thessalonica and the subsequent persecution of the church on the detail in Acts 17:7 concerning the alleged proclamation of "another king."[8] Bruce follows a similar course, explaining the public pressure against Paul and the Thessalonian church as resulting solely from the agitators referred to in

---

[5] In 1948 Charles Edson wrote that "few ancient cities of equal importance have been the subject of so little investigation in modern times. Up to now, the inscriptions found in Salonica have all been chance discoveries, almost invariably due to such causes as the demolition of the old city walls . . . the remodelling or removal of older buildings and other construction. . . ." "Macedonia, III," 153. A more recent account of the topographical surveys and partial excavations is available in Vickers, "Towards Reconstruction." The most recent survey is in the dissertation by Hendrix, *Thessalonicans Honor Romans,* esp. 10–13.

[6] Lightfoot, "The Church of Thessalonica"; he expresses skepticism, however, at the implication in Acts 17:2 that the riot occurred after only three weeks of missionizing: "It is plain . . . from the Epistles that the length of his sojourn was much greater. At the close of these three weeks we may suppose that he devoted himself more exclusively to the heathen." 259.

[7] Clemen, "Paulus und die Gemeinde," 140–50.

[8] Rigaux, *Thessaloniciens,* 29f.

Acts 17:5, without alluding to the internal radicalism within the congregation itself as visible in the letters.[9] Although the difficulties in Acts 17 have been pointed out by critical scholars,[10] most commentators allow this framework to shape their view.[11]

Reliance on the Lukan framework also marks most of the historical sketches that have been written concerning Thessalonica.[12] The brief accounts of the beginnings of Christianity in Thessalonica by Unger, Vacalopolous, and Blaiklock are entirely dependent on Acts 17.[13] Even the valuable summary of historical, archaeological and cultural evidence by Robert M. Evans relies primarily on Acts for the picture of the origin of the Christian community, its organization, and the crisis faced by the congregation.[14] The recent, comprehensive survey of archaeological and historical evidence by Winfried Elliger is no exception in this regard: "The report of Acts of the Apostles closely matches the picture drawn here of the political relationships in the capitol city [of Thessalonica]."[15] Elliger concentrates his attention on issues such as the identification of the city authorities in Acts 17:6, the term used for the riotous crowd in 17:5, and the political implications of the allegations in 17:6–7, but does not attempt to describe the congregation's behavior and outlook as revealed in 1 and 2 Thessalonians.[16]

A survey of the assessment of Acts 17:1–9 in recent commentaries will provide the basis for a more critical use of this evidence in the reconstruction of the congregational situation. Ernst Haenchen lays the foundation for the current approach by observing that Acts 17 contains the two

---

[9] Bruce, *Thessalonians*, xxii–xxv.

[10] Cf. Vielhauer, *Geschichte der urchristlichen Literatur*, 82–89; Koester, *Introduction to the New Testament* 2:108, states categorically that "all the individual events of Paul's activity in this city are legendary (Acts 17:1–10)."

[11] Cf. Dobschütz, *Die Thessalonicher-Briefe*, 10–13; Frame, *Thessalonians*, 3–7; Milligan, *Thessalonians*, xxvi–xxxv; Reese, *1 and 2 Thessalonians*, xii; Masson, *Thessaloniciens*, 5; Friedrich, *1 Thessalonicher 5, 1–11*, 203f.; Marshall, *1 and 2 Thessalonians*, 3–6. A conspicuous exception is Ernest Best who carefully compares the accounts in Acts 17 with the details in the letters and other historical information, concluding that all Luke knew was that "Paul visited Thessalonica, that there was trouble after his preaching, that a certain Jason was involved in it and that Paul had to leave abruptly. To this Luke added Paul's preaching in the synagogue with the summarized content of his argument there, the jealousy of the Jews and probably the content of the accusation that was made against Paul." *Thessalonians*, 7. Marxsen, *Der erste Brief*, 15–26, also expresses considerable skepticism about Acts 17.

[12] An exception is Oberhummer, "Thessalonike."

[13] Unger, "Historical Research"; Vacalopoulos, *A History of Thessaloniki*, 17f.; Blaiklock, *Cities of the New Testament*, 46–49.

[14] Evans, *Eschatology and Ethics*, 87–100.

[15] Elliger, *Paulus in Griechenland*, 93.

[16] Elliger, *Paulus in Griechenland*, 94–96. As a valuable but unacknowledged precessor of Elliger's study, Collins has recently called attention to Rossano's study, "Note archeologiche sulla antica Tessalonica."

typical portions of a Lukan account of a founding mission. "What Luke recounts of the missionary efforts of Paul is essentially in each case the story of the founding of the community and then the persecution which forces the apostle away to his next goal."[17] This means that the impression of close proximity between mission and departure on account of persecution results in suppressing details about Paul's necessarily more lengthy period of self-employment as a handworker and the repeated financial support he had received from Philippi (cf. Phil 4:16). The sudden appearance of Jason in Acts 17:5 is explained by Haenchen as consistent with Luke's narrative strategy to keep "the spotlight of interest" exclusively on Paul rather than his coworkers.[18] Haenchen further questions whether the Lukan picture of Jewish persecution is consistent with 1 Thess 2:14, 17; 3:2f., which imply persecution from Gentile sources.

Hans Conzelmann's commentary shares some of Haenchen's critical observations, adding that the charge against Paul is formulated with apologetic motivation.[19] Gottfried Schille also accepts Haenchen's perspective, but rejects the suggestion that the charge was apologetic on the grounds that it was actually undeniable.[20] He stresses the reworking of congregational traditions in the duplicated formulation of the accusation in 17:6 and as well as in the account of Jason's payment of a bond against further disturbances.[21] Jürgen Roloff attempts to resolve several of the anomalies that Haenchen discovered. He suggests that the account in Acts 17:1–9 rests on two unstated premises, that Jason had provided housing for Paul and his missionary colleagues, and that they had departed from Thessalonica before the riot.[22] This would explain why Jason rather than Paul was brought before the magistrates. Roloff concludes that the account rests on a local anecdote concerning the danger faced by a leading congregational member. Luke composed the account of the political allegations in such a way, however, as to make clear to readers that "the true instigators are not Paul and his group, but those who raise the charges against them."[23] This reference to Luke's narrative achievement effec-

---

[17] Haenchen, *The Acts of the Apostles,* 510.
[18] *The Acts of the Apostles,* 513.
[19] Conzelmann, *Die Apostelgeschichte,* 95.
[20] Schille, *Die Apostelgeschichte des Lukas,* 351f.
[21] *Die Apostelgeschichtee des Lukas,* 351: "Did the tradition know of a Christian assembly that was, to be sure, apprehended but no missionaries were present? That would correspond exactly to what 1 Thess assumes! Two accusations surface here: the doublette fully proves the reworking of an older text. In the first accusation the writer is speaking. The words in v. 6b do not fit the people around Jason at all [a citation from Haenchen]. . . . The second accusation on the other hand aims directly against the arraigned (not against the missionaries) and relates precisely to their actions and thinking. . . ."
[22] Roloff, *Die Apostelgeschichte,* 249.
[23] *Die Apostelgeschichte,* 251.

tively settles the question whether the charges were designed to be apologetic or not.

The recent commentary by Gerhard Schneider shows the extent to which the approach of Haenchen has been accepted: "The suggestion appears likely that Luke composed in a schematic manner on the basis of traditional information."[24] In his study of Acts as a popular historical novel, Richard I. Pervo provides a more precise analysis of the compositional schemes underlying Acts 17:1–9. He analyzes the stereotypical quality of this account, which blames the troubles in Thessalonica on Jewish provocateurs and a low class mob. "If one of Luke's two villains is 'the Jews,' the urban rabble is the other."[25] The congregation is depicted as marked by representative leaders from high society (Acts 17:4), matching the typical Lukan emphasis on "the ease" with which Paul moved "in the upper level of society." This reflects the preferred upper-class origins of characters in Greco-Roman novels while downplaying the predominately lower-class origins of Christianity.[26]

These recent studies render the traditional reliance on Acts 17 rather problematic. It appears clear that the earliest tradition available to Luke involved accusations against Paul's patron, Jason, and that Paul and his missionary colleagues were either in hiding or had left Thessalonica by the time this crisis arose. Wherever they might have been, it appears certain that Jason was held responsible for whatever troubles had arisen. Also, it is certain that the departure of Paul and his colleagues was considerably later than three weeks after their arrival, as Acts implies. Several months would have been required for the repeated communications between Thessalonica and Philippi implied in Phil 4:16, as most commentators now agree. Although it is evident from 1 Thess 2:2, 16 that Paul had faced serious opposition while in Thessalonica, probably on this account departing from the city before he was ready (1 Thess 2:17), it seems clear that the behavior of the members of the church meeting in Jason's house had evoked the charge of political subversion in Acts 17:7. The bond he posted apparently had nothing directly to do with Paul's activities, but dealt with the cessation or prevention of certain actions by the church itself. While Acts attempts to place this situation in a positive light, implying that the problem was caused by the false accusations of

---

[24] Schneider, *Die Apostelgeschichte* 2:222.

[25] Pervo, *Profit with Delight,* citation from p. 65.

[26] *Profit with Delight,* 156; Pervo concludes on p. 169 that "the amount of space in Acts 16ff. devoted to describing Paul's status and friends among the elite, the high character of his teaching and practice, the quality of his followers and the baseness of his opposition is truly remarkable and must be appreciated if the nature of Acts is to be understood. Luke affirms, in a most engaging way, that one can be a Christian and still have social aspirations."

Jewish provocateurs who riled up a fickle Gentile mob, there is every
likelihood on the basis of this recent research that objectionable beliefs and
actions of congregational members were significant factors.

Even if there are some scholars who may find this reading of the
evidence unsatisfactory, it should at least be clear that the traditional
picture of the congregation's troubles coming exclusively from the outside
is no longer credible. If the recent advances in our understanding of Acts
17 are taken seriously, the benign vision of the Thessalonian congregation
that Acts intends to present should no longer be used as the framework to
interpret the evidence in 1 and 2 Thessalonians and to assess the relevance
of the archaeological and cultural data.

2. Social and Economic Circumstances

There are some discrepancies between the account of the Thessalonian
ministry in Acts 17 and the details in the Thessalonian correspondence
concerning the racial and cultural makeup of the congregation. When
Paul refers in 1 Thess 1:9 to the converts having "turned to God from
idols," it seems highly unlikely that the audience could have contained a
substantial proportion of Jews. Most commentators prefer to avoid drawing a strict conclusion from this formulation,[27] but several make a case
that Acts must have been at least partially in error. Ernest Best discusses
this issue along with several other discrepancies between Acts and the
Thessalonian letters, showing that Paul neither addresses Jewish Christians at any point nor makes frequent reference to the Hebrew scriptures.
Since the congregation did not contain many former Jews, Best feels the
writer of Acts was responsible for inventing the references to Paul's
preaching in the synagogue.[28] I. Howard Marshall concludes on a similar
note, that "the Gentile element in the church was larger than Acts
indicates and that it included Gentiles who had not been attached to the
synagogue as worshippers of the one God."[29] While advocating such a
conclusion, Dobschütz points out, however, that we know the names of
several Jewish Christians from Thessalonica. A clear example is Aristarchus (Col 4:10–11; Phlm 24; Acts 20:4).[30] In addition, several Acts

---

[27] Frame, *Thessalonians*, 3; Bruce, *Thessalonians*, xxii–xxiii; Masson, *Thessaloniciens*, 5;
Oepke, *Thessalonicher*, 156; Rigaux, *Thessaloniciens*, 22–27; Evans, *Eschatology and
Ethics*, 97–100; Vacalopoulos, *A History of Thessaloniki*, 17.

[28] Best, *Thessalonians*, 4–7.

[29] Marshall, *1 and 2 Thessalonians*, 5; cf. also Marxsen, *Der erste Brief*, 17, for similar
conclusions.

[30] Dobschütz, *Die Thessalonicher-Briefe*, 11.

commentators agree with Dobschütz that the name Jason probably implies a background in Hellenistic Judaism.[31] A third Thessalonian leader, Secundus (Acts 20:4), may reflect Latin rather than Jewish origins but no conclusive inference can be made in this instance.[32] The conclusion to be drawn from these considerations is that the Thessalonian congregation probably consisted of a handful of Jewish Christians and a large majority of Gentile Christians.

The population of Thessalonica was largely of Greek descent, the Macedonians having long been integrated into a rather coherent nation with Greek identity.[33] The city had been founded as an amalgamation of Greek immigrants with the local Macedonian inhabitants of a number of surrounding villages on the site of the ancient city of Therme.[34] The recollection of the origins of the city and the continued settlement of descendents from some of these previous urban centers in specific neighborhoods of the city indicates a measure of continuity in population despite later immigration.[35] During the Roman period there were numerous Italians who had followed the Roman legions into Thessalonica, as well as a few Celts and other minorities.[36] The hordes of barbarians that Cicero had complained about in Thessalonica a century before Paul's arrival[37] were likely well integrated into the Greek population of the city by the time of the Thessalonian correspondence, though some of them were probably the descendents of the Macedonian villagers who retained a measure of distinctiveness down to Cicero's time. Since the only evidence concerning Jewish population in Thessalonica is the account in Acts 17, and since no evidence of Greek synagogues or Jewish inscriptions has been found, it is impossible to estimate their significance in the city. The Acts commentators that I have consulted do not raise questions about the presence of a synagogue in Thessalonica or the likelihood that Paul's mission commenced there. Given the wide dispersion of Jewish popu-

---

[31] Cf. Die Thessalonicher-Briefe, 11, who vaguely identifies Jason as a Jewish Christian. Schille, Die Apostelgeschichte des Lukas, 351, and Schneider, Die Apostelgeschichte 2:224, accept the theory that "Jason" is the Greek adaptation of the Hebrew name, "Joshua" or "Jesus."

[32] Cf. Schneider, Die Apostelgeschichte 2:281 n. 20; but cf. Frey, Corpus of Jewish Inscriptions, 618–26, for examples of Jews with Latin names. Lifschitz discusses the issue on p. 23f.

[33] Cf. Kalleres, Les anciens Macedoniens, 503–31; also Evans, Eschatology and Ethics, 46f.

[34] Cf. Strabo, 7. Fragment 21, which refers to the "synergism" of twenty-six villages. Vickers notes that remains of fifth-century B.C.E. buildings of Therme have been found in modern Saloniki; "Hellenistic Thessaloniki," 164.

[35] Vickers refers in "Towards Reconstruction," 239–51 to the evidence of some of the population from the constituting villages in neighborhoods of ancient Thessalonica.

[36] Evans, Eschatology and Ethics, 47.

[37] Cf. Elliger, Paulus in Griechenland, 89.

lation in the eastern half of the Roman Empire,[38] it is likely that there were substantial numbers of Jews in Thessalonica. The fact that a Samaritan synagogue has been excavated in Thessalonica, dating apparently from the third century B.C.E.,[39] is another indication of the racial and religious diversity in this port city.

A second discrepancy in the account of Acts 17 has to do with the social status of the Thessalonian congregation. We noted above the question raised by Richard I. Pervo concerning the impression intended by the formulation "leading women" in Acts 17:4, namely, the predominance of respectable, upper-class converts. The admonition in 1 Thessalonians 4:11 to work with their own hands indicates, in the words of a nineteenth-century scholar, "that the Thessalonian church was mostly composed of the working class."[40] A more recent commentator infers that "the great majority of the Thessalonian Christians were manual workers, whether skilled or unskilled. . . ."[41] Robert E. Evans suggests the relevance of Paul's remark about the extreme poverty of the Macedonian Christians in 2 Cor 8:2–4,[42] which can be correlated with the picture Ronald F. Hock has recently drawn of the precarious economic status of handworkers in the Greco-Roman cities.[43] Paul refers in 1 Thess 2:9–12 and 2 Thess 3:6–12 to self-sufficient labor in order to earn daily bread, which indicates that the audience consisted mainly of employees or self-employed laborers. But it is difficult to square Paul's remarks with the image in Acts of the Thessalonian congregation as containing an impressive number of upper-class women. And there are no indications, in contrast to the Corinthian congregation, that there were slaves in the Thessalonian church. The paucity of patrons with high status or wealth in the congregation may well have reduced the likelihood of slaves being incorporated into the church as members of the patrons' households. It would be inappropriate to lay too much weight on this argument from silence, however, because at least one patron with wealth, Jason, is linked with the congregation, and as Murphy-O'Connor has shown, the archaeological evidence in the Greek cities renders it essential to assume the presence of a few patrons whose

---

[38] Cf. Stern, "The Jewish Diaspora," 114–17; the only proof he cites on p. 159 of Jewish population in Thessalonica, however, is the reference in Acts 17.

[39] Lifschitz and Schiby, "Une synagoge samaritaine."

[40] Lünemann, *Thessalonians,* 123.

[41] Best, *Thessalonians,* 176.

[42] Evans, *Eschatology and Ethics,* 90f.; note, however, that he correlates this evidence on p. 92 with a rather credulous acceptance of the reference to the rich women in Acts 17:4, resulting in a "full spectrum of class representation" in Thessalonica.

[43] Hock, *The Social Context,* 34–36. For an earlier assessment of the "wretched" economic circumstances faced by workers in Greek cities, cf. Glotz, *Ancient Greece at Work,* 361. The low social status of craftsmen and small merchants is discussed by MacMullen, *Roman Social Relations,* 88–120.

houses were large enough to serve as centers for house churches.[44] The fragments of available evidence therefore point to a somewhat narrower range of social levels in the Thessalonian church than in other Pauline congregations; it appears to have consisted mainly of what Wayne Meeks describes as the "typical" Christian in the Pauline churches, "a free artisan or small trader."[45]

When one brings these details into relation with the evidence of economic growth in Thessalonica, it appears that the converts derived from a stratum of the population suffering from a degree of relative deprivation. The general economic situation in Thessalonica was gradually improving through the first century,[46] despite the evidence of the lingering effects of devastation and depopulation during the civil wars in the preceding century.[47] The evidence concerning immigrants from Greece, Asia, and Rome indicates the presence of economic opportunities.[48] The literary references to the growth and beauty of Thessalonica[49] as well as the evidence of extensive building developments indicate an increasing level of prosperity.[50] The junction between the port and the Via Egnatia[51] made Thessalonica an important trading center for Macedonian food, and mining products and timber as well as for manufactured products to be sold in the Balkan peninsula. The city became a focal point of east-west as well as north-south communications in the empire.[52] Names of prominent Italian as well as Greek merchants have been found on Thessalonian sarcophagi, indicating the Roman orientation of trading prosperity.[53] Wealth was also earned in mining and minting, both of which involved substantial numbers of slave laborers. In general, it could be said that the various sources of wealth were unevenly distributed, with the Roman administration favoring a small elite and economic circumstances holding a large proportion of the non-slave,

---

[44] Murphy-O'Connor, *St. Paul's Corinth,* 153–61.

[45] Meeks, *The First Urban Christians,* 73.

[46] Cf. Rostovtzeff, *The Social and Economic History,* 91–93.

[47] Cf. Larson, "Roman Greece," 422–35. Erik Gren contends that the cities along the southern coast of Macedonia showed no sign of improving economic circumstances during this period, but he does not refer explicitly to Thessalonica, which appears to be an exception; *Kleinasien und der Ostbalkan,* 33.

[48] Cf. Elliger, *Paulus in Griechenland,* 89.

[49] *Paulus in Griechenland,* 89.

[50] Cf. Evans, *Eschatology and Ethics,* 20f.

[51] For a discussion of the original route of the Via Egnatia through Thessalonica, cf. Makaronas, "Via Egnatia and Thessalonike"; a less critical account is provided by Davies, "The Macedonian Scene," 103–6.

[52] Vacalopoulos, *A History of Thessaloniki,* 12; cf. also Papazoglu, "Quelques aspects de l'histoire," 356–57, and for a less substantive assessment, Blaiklock, *Cities of the New Testament,* 46.

[53] Cf. Evans, *Eschatology and Ethics,* 29.

lower-class population in poverty.[54] The Thessalonian Christians appear to have stemmed from this low level of society, witnessing the economic advancement of others, but participating in it only marginally themselves.

In 1928 Samuel Dickey offered some significant reflections on the way the status of poverty would have been understood in the Hellenistic environment of a city like Thessalonica. He pointed out the continuing appeal of the "longing for equality" evoked by ancient democratic ideals, noting that the failure to achieve these ideals evoked the utopian visions of realms of perpetual prosperity and justice.[55] With the burden of high taxation and adverse economic circumstances, the lower classes in the Greek cities during the Hellenistic period had been prevented from achieving these widely shared ideals but the overwhelming preponderance of military power in imperial hands kept protests and social unrest strictly in check. With the coming of Roman rule, Dickey observed, the Greek cities "only passed from one Shylock to another."[56] In the light of the evidence concerning low wages, frequent famines, and the lack of legal recourse for the urban proletariat, Dickey suggested the fundamental appeal of Christian apocalypticism:

> During the first three centuries the general economic status of the laboring classes went from bad to worse. There was no permanent alleviation, and there seemed no hope of it by ordinary processes. Therefore when Christianity entered with its promise of a 'new age' of righteousness inaugurated by divine power, which included 'feeding the hungry with good things' and 'exalting those of low degree,'it could not help get a hearing.[57]

Dickey pointed out in this connection the popularity of fabulous legends of prosperity in the future messianic age in Syrian Baruch 29:5 and 1 Enoch 10:19, similar to those reported from Papias in Irenaeus, *Against Heresies* 5.33–36. He suggested that the rapid triumph of the gospel was due in part to the congruence between Greek utopianism and Jewish messianism, offering an apocalyptic gospel that "appealed especially to the ignorant and exploited masses. It [the gospel] made its way with amazing rapidity, for it expressed in experience and anticipation a multiplicity of their deepest and most universal needs."[58]

Of particular interest to our quest is Dickey's effort to relate these economic circumstances and expectations to the theology of the Thessa-

---

[54] Evans, *Eschatology and Ethics*, 22–26.
[55] Dickey, "Some Economic and Social Conditions," 393.
[56] Dickey, "Some Economic and Social Conditions," 396.
[57] "Some Economic and Social Conditions," 411.
[58] "Some Economic and Social Conditions," 416.

lonian correspondence. He refers to the fact that Paul's Thessalonian letters reveal how literally his own apocalyptic expectations were expressed and "how prone his converts were to take his word even more literally than he intended."[59] In a significant way, this virtually forgotten[60] study by one of the predecessors of the current sociological interpretation of early Christianity prepares the way for the development of a millenarian theory of the Thessalonian situation.

3. The Political Situation

There are some aspects of the political situation that throw additional light on the peculiar behavior of the Thessalonian congregation. The city had been founded by one of Alexander's generals in 316 B.C.E., and became part of a Roman province in 146.[61] It was later involved in the Roman civil war that led to the triumph of Octavian in 42. The city's cooperation with the victor resulted in the declaration of its status as a free city,[62] which apparently meant that a measure of local autonomy, freedom from military occupation, the right to mint coins, and an advantageous tax situation could be enjoyed.[63] Thessalonica remained the residence of the proconsul of the province of Macedonia, which was reorganized in 27 C.E. when the more southerly province of Achaia was created.[64] But within the city itself, the traditional structure of a democratic civil administration was retained. It consisted of a popular assembly—the δῆμος, a council, local magistrates called the "politarchs," the city treasurer and other administrative posts. The real power was apparently held by five or six politarchs who functioned as agents of Roman rule.[65] Although the suggestion has been made that the office of politarch was created in Thessalonica by the Romans, it now appears certain that it was a carryover from earlier governance.[66] Since the politarchs in traditional democratic theory expressed the will of the assembly, the Roman coopta-

[59] "Some Economic and Social Conditions," 414.

[60] Dickey's study is missing in the bibliographies of all of the Thessalonian commentaries I have consulted, in the updated bibliography for the reprinted Dobschütz commentary compiled by Merk, *Die Thessalonicher-Briefe*, 321–33, and also in the exhaustive bibliography recently prepared by Collins in *Studies on the First Letter*, 385–401.

[61] Cf. Morgan, "Metellus Macedonicus," 442.

[62] Edson, "Macedonia, II," 133.

[63] Cf. Evans, *Eschatology and Ethics*, 3f.

[64] Cf. Papazoglu, "Quelques aspects de l'histoire," 325–28.

[65] Cf. Burton, "The Politarchs," 628, who concludes on the basis of numerous inscriptions from Thessalonica that "it is probably safe to assume that it had either five or six [politarchs] in the New Testament period." Cf. also Elliger, *Paulus in Griechenland*, 93f.

[66] Cf. Horsley, *New Documents*, 34.

tion of this system expresses the conservative fiction that was characteristic of the *pax Romana* under Augustus.[67] In fact, as Dieter Nörr
concludes, "It was the successful tendency of Roman politics to keep the
lower classes in the cities as distant as possible from the government."[68]
But the Roman overlordship functioned in Thessalonica under the guise
of conserving democratic ideals.[69]

A recent dissertation by Holland Hendrix shows that the city authorities ascribed the advantages they and the city enjoyed to the benefaction of
Antony and Octavian, building a temple of Caesar where suitable honors
could be paid.[70] As Charles Edson had shown, this cult was probably
established immediately after Octavian's victory at Philippi.[71] A priesthood dedicated to the goddess Roma and to the emperor as a god was
established. The ceremonies were primarily honorific, acknowledging the
political and economic advantages shared by the ruling elite in Thessalonica and thus representing an "ongoing cultivation of the new ruler's
confidence in the city's loyalty to him and his successors."[72] Coins were
struck in which the heads of Augustus and his ancestor Julius Caesar
were identified as divine.[73] Hendrix discovered that the inscriptions
always list the "priest and agonothete of the Imperator" first, indicating a
"strict observance of protocol" in the royal theology that expressed the
high priority that was given to the legitimation of the Augustan dynasty.[74]
Slogans concerning "freedom and harmony" were expressed on the coins
minted in Thessalonica,[75] claiming the traditional virtues of democratic
rule as deriving from this Roman form of benefaction[76] honored in the
civic cult.

The Thessalonian style of honoring Roman benefaction was a distinctive adaptation of what Nilsson describes as the "patriotic religion" of the
earlier Greek polis that thanked the gods and the heroes for "the personal
freedom of her citizens and their self-esteem, the political rights which
they exercised as members of the sovereign democracy, the blessings of
peace . . ." and so forth.[77] These ideals were coopted in Thessalonica to

---

[67] Cf. Evans, *Eschatology and Ethics,* 14.
[68] Nörr, "Zur Herrschaftsstruktur," 5.
[69] Cf. Nörr, "Zur Herrschaftsstruktur," 12–14, for a discussion of the transformation of the Greek concept of political freedom under the manipulation of Roman imperial ideology.
[70] Hendrix, *Thessalonicans Honor Romans,* 62.
[71] Edson, "Macedonia, II," 133.
[72] Hendrix, *Thessalonicans Honor Romans,* 337; Cf. also MacMullen, *Paganism in the Roman Empire,* 102–5.
[73] Hendrix, *Thessalonicans Honor Romans,* 293–95.
[74] *Thessalonicans Honor Romans,* 312.
[75] Evans, *Eschatology and Ethics,* 4.
[76] For an orientation to the rationale of benefaction, cf. Danker, *Benefactor,* 26–46.
[77] Nilsson, *Greek Piety,* 67.

legitimate Roman colonialism, and although the populace of Thessalonica had not experienced any form of democracy for centuries, the force of the ideals remained sufficiently alive to be useful at the propagandistic level. The goal of the imperial cult was to sustain Roman power, so the religious and political ideals it celebrated functioned as an ideology.[78] The victims of this process of ideological cooptation were the economically disadvantaged, indigenous Greek population of Thessalonica—the very class of menial laborers and craftsmen from which the converts to the church were drawn.

These circumstances suggest a way to interpret the historical details that Edwin A. Judge set forth concerning the alleged violation of the "decrees of Caesar" mentioned in Acts 17:7.[79] The oath of personal loyalty to Caesar and his rule made by local magistrates in Paphlagonia and Cyprus could well have been part of the civil religion in Thessalonica. Such an oath would imply the prevention of subversive activities and politically dangerous soothsaying, in which case, Judge argues, the proclamation of 1 and 2 Thessalonians might have a direct bearing because it proclaims the coming of a future ruler. But as we have seen, the charge in Acts 17:7 was aimed against Jason rather than against Paul,[80] so that the key issue is what the congregation meeting in Jason's house made of this apocalyptic message.[81] If members of the congregation understood Paul's proclamation in political terms, involving either the imminent arrival or current reign of Christ as a benevolent world ruler, it is understandable that allegations would be raised by persons loyal to the present regime. Such allegations would be particularly likely if the congregation were composed of disenfranchised laborers who were known to be restive under Roman rule. This might explain what Judge found puzzling, that Paul did not insist on a report to Rome concerning the inappropriateness of the subversion charge, following the precedent of a case in Cyrene.[82] Paul was apparently not present when the crisis concerning the behavior of Jason's household occurred, and the allegation of disloyalty may well have been partially accurate for some portion of the congregation itself.

---

[78] Cf. Kee, "The Imperial Cult," 114–24.

[79] Judge, "Decrees of Caesar."

[80] Judge acknowledges this point in "The Decrees of Caesar," 2.

[81] In Donfried's recent discussion of these issues, the distinction between Paul's original message and the congregation's understanding of it is inadequately drawn, leading to the conclusion that "Paul and his associates could easily have been understood as violating the 'decrees of Caesar' . . ." by proclaiming the presence of a κύριος and attacking the 'peace and security' motto of Roman rule; "The Cults of Thessalonica," 334.

[82] Judge, "The Decrees of Caesar," 6.

4. The Religious Climate

Given the importance of the imperial cult in Thessalonica, it is somewhat artificial to discuss the religious climate in a separate section. There are impressive archaeological remains of the large temple of Roma and many inscriptions concerning the activities of its priesthood. Charles Edson identified four priestly establishments, stemming from periods prior to Paul's arrival: a civic priesthood of the Greek gods from 316 B.C.E., the priest of Zeus Elutherios from 148 B.C.E., the Priest and the Benefactor of Rome in 42–41 B.C.E., and the Priest and Agonothete of Augustus from 27 B.C.E.[83] Following the precedent of viewing the Macedonian king as the son of God[84] or the embodiment of a divine hero,[85] the Thessalonian elite entered into honorific cult of Rome with particular enthusiasm. This involved a celebration of a peculiar Roman form of what the sociologist Werner Stark identified as political "messianism," the Augustan expectation expressed in Virgil's fourth eclogue concerning the dawn of a new age with a future ruler who would "live as a god."[86] The evidence shows that Julius Caesar and subsequent ruling emperors were honored as god.[87] The titles of the emperor employed in the cult of Rome probably included typical terms like "savior," "lord," "son of God," "benefactor," and "god manifest."[88] Religious feelings of awe and thankfulness to the supreme power governing the Mediterranean world were mixed with a generous portion of civic self-interest in the honorific cult in Thessalonica, as we have seen, because Roman rule placed advantages in the hands of a small elite who acted as the chief instigators of the cult.[89] Hendrix points out that honors to Rome ensured further benefaction required for the future prosperity of the Thessalonians,[90] particularly one might add, for the leading Greek families and the Latin friends of Roman administrators.

The mystery religions played an important role in Thessalonica as in other cities of the Greco-Roman world. The cults of Serapis and Dionysus were particularly prominent and well integrated with the civic cult.[91] The cult of Isis appears to be somewhat less well supported by the civic

---

[83] Edson, "Macedonia, II."
[84] Elliger, *Paulus in Griechenland,* 69.
[85] Kalleres, *Les anciens Macédoniens,* 581–89.
[86] Stark, *The Sociology of Religion* 1:106f.
[87] Cf. Elliger, *Paulus in Griechenland,* 97; Hendrix *Thessalonicans Honor Romans,* 108.
[88] Cf. Evans, *Eschatology and Ethics,* 66.
[89] Cf. Hendrix, *Thessalonicans Honor Romans,* 278–82.
[90] *Thessalonicans Honor Romans,* 306f.
[91] Cf. Edson, "Macedonia, III," 154–88.

establishment.[92] There is evidence of shrines in honor of Aphrodite, Demeter, Zeus, Asclepius and other deities. Some of these ceremonies offered regeneration, immortality, forgiveness of sins, a measure of equality and self-respect for an initiate, relief from ills and misfortune, and the promise of sexual fulfillment—concerns reflected in a general way in the Thessalonian correspondence.[93] Karl Paul Donfried calls particular attention to the possible connections between Dionysian sexuality and the situation reflected in 1 Thess 4:3-8: "Paul's severe warnings in this section . . . [are] intended to distinguish the behaviour of the Thessalonian Christians from that of their former heathen and pagan life which is still much alive in the various cults of the city."[94] He goes on to argue that the prevalence of "'high density' paraenetic language" in this section "suggests that Paul is very deliberately dealing with a situation of grave immorality, not too dissimilar to the cultic temptations of Corinth."[95] Although the background of phallic religion helps to explain a predeliction towards promiscuity, it throws an uncertain light on the sudden rise of an intellectual challenge to the traditional sexual ethic in 1 Thessalonians 4. In contrast to the Corinthian situation, the Thessalonians had not yet advanced to the stage of acting on the basis of this predilection, as Paul's admission of their current compliance in 4:1 reveals. Donfried appears to be on more solid ground in noting the parallels between 1 Thess 5:5-7, 19-22 and the mystery religions, because Paul's references to drunkenness and spiritual confusion do imply an orgiastic content to the Thessalonian piety. However, there is no reason to limit this reference to "the excesses of Dionysiac . . . frenzies,"[96] because other cults resident in Thessalonica favored similar orgies.

Although infrequently mentioned in Thessalonian commentaries, the mystery cult of Cabirus was the most distinctive feature of Thessalonian religious life. Cultural historians are agreed on the ubiquity of evidence concerning the Cabiric cult in Thessalonica, indicating it was not only the most distinctive but also the most important factor in the religious environment.[97] In the words of Rex E. Witt, "Without any doubt, this was the cult that during the Empire held the field at Thessalonike. . . . on numismatic evidence, [Thessalonike] was addicted to the cult of what may

---

[92] Cf. Witt, "The Egyptian Cults," 326.
[93] Cf. Anrich, *Das antike Mysterienwesen*, 47-56; Burkert, *Greek Religion*, 276-78; Evans, *Eschatology and Ethics*, 75-79; Donfried, "The Cults of Thessalonica," 337-42.
[94] Donfried, "The Cults of Thessalonica," 342.
[95] "The Cults of Thessalonica," 341f.
[96] "The Cults of Thessalonica," 342.
[97] Cf. Edson, "Macedonia, III," 210; Hemberg, *Die Kabiren*, 106; Evans, *Eschatology and Ethics*, 68; Elliger, *Paulus in Griechenland*, 98; Donfried, "The Cults of Thessalonica," 338.

perhaps be termed Kabeiric monotheism."[98] It is curious that this cult has
not attracted more attention, because the structure of its myths and the
nature of its piety can be more closely correlated with the evidence of the
Thessalonian congregation than any of the other mystery religions. However, the widespread dispersion of the cult of the Cabiri in the Eastern
Mediterranean, the variations in worship and identification of the god or
gods, and the difficulties in tracing plausible lines of influence in syncre-
tistic cults like this present very complex problems in interpreting the
voluminous and contradictory evidence on this subject. The survey by
Charles Edson[99] and the comprehensive monograph by Bengt Hemberg[100] provide the essential foundation for a current understanding of
Cabiric worship in Thessalonica.[101]

The Cabirus figure worshipped in Thessalonica was structurally
similar in some regards to the apocalyptic Christ proclaimed by Paul. He
was a martyred hero, murdered by his brothers, buried with symbols of
royal power, and expected to return to help lowly individuals and the city
of Thessalonica in particular. Whereas in other cities, two or three Cabiri
figures are honored, Hemberg shows that in Thessalonica there was a
concentration of devotion on a single hero.[102] The basic story was that
after being murdered by his two brothers, the head of Cabirus was
crowned, wrapped in a royal purple cloth, and carried on a spear point to
be consecrated and buried at the foot of Mount Olympus so that no one
would ever discover the disgraceful circumstances of his death.[103] A
disputed aspect of the myth is that the fratricides placed the phallus of
Bacchus in a box as they fled to a land far away to establish their cult.[104]
Other centers of Cabiric worship recalled legends of his miraculous birth

---

[98] Witt, "The Kabeiroi," 78. Hendrix refers to the "ascendency of Dioscuri/Cabiros cults at
Thessalonica" by the early first century C.E. as evident in the pilaster reliefs found in the
extant portion of the western portal of Thessalonica; *Thessalonicans Honor Romans*, 154.

[99] Edson, "Macedonia, III."

[100] Hemberg, *Die Kabiren.*

[101] For a synthesis of earlier views, cf. Kern, "Kabeiros and Kabeiroi," and for a depiction of
the bearing on the Thessalonian situation, reflecting the knowledge at the turn of the
century, cf. Lightfoot, "The Church of Thessalonica," 257f. For an orientation to the earlier
discussion of cult of twins which is often confused with the Cabiri, cf. Harris, *The Cult of
the Heavenly Twins.* A sober assessment of Cabiric mysteries, without reference to their
mythical embodiment or distinctive shape in Thessalonica, is available in Burkert, *Greek
Religion*, 281–84. Cf. also Cole, *Theioi Megaloi.*

[102] Hemberg, *Die Kabiren*, 275.

[103] Hemberg, *Die Kabiren*, 207, and Edson, "Macedonia, III," 200–202, piece this myth
together from accounts in Clement of Alexandria *Protrepticus* 2.19.1–4 and Firmicus
Maternus XI. On the latter, cf. Julius Firmicus Maternus, *L'Erreur des Religions
Paiennes*, 100f., 252f. Clement associates the Cabirus legends with Macedonia and Firmicus
Maternus links them explicitly with Thessalonica. Despite the late dating of these
references, Hemberg argues (p. 9) that Cabirus was being worshipped in Thessalonica no
later than 200 B.C.E.

[104] Hemberg, *Die Kabiren*, 207; cf. Witt, "The Kabeiroi," 73.

from the Great Goddess and his prowess with forge and hammer, the latter detail being celebrated on some of the Thessalonian coins.[105]

The heroic Cabirus apparently returns to life, however, at least on an intermittent basis, with his powers fully restored. He is able to aid his devotees by providing in A. D. Nock's words, "safety at sea, good luck in perils and ventures of various kinds, and greater righteousness."[106] Other references associate Cabirus' blessings with helping in the manufacture of iron and the accomplishment of other manual labor requiring axe and hammer, performing magic for the needy, providing freedom for slaves, and offering sexual fulfillment. Cabirus also provided protection of Thessalonica from military oppression, as evident in the third-century C.E. coin in his honor struck after the successful defense against a Gothic attack.[107] For such boons, Cabirus was worshiped as the beardless young man, often with a hammer in one hand and a drinking horn in the other. He was celebrated as the "lord of changeful form, two-natured god, manifold, bloodstained, slaughtered by his two brothers," in the words of an Orphic hymn.[108] A Thessalonian inscription celebrates him as "the most holy ancestral god" of the city.[109]

It also appears to me that the worship of Cabirus exhibits some intriguing parallels to Pauline Christianity. In what appeared to be a Cabiric cult in Samothrace, the initiation of participants involved donning special robes, confessing sins, and cleansing through water baptism and through symbolic immersion in the blood of the martyred god.[110] Another source refers to ceremonial participation in the shed blood of Cabirus by means of blood sacrifices.[111] A. D. Nock inferred from the discovery of a wooden platform in a temple that he believed was devoted to the Cabiric cult in Samothrace that it was used after the confession of sin and the ritual washings to place initiates on a throne around which the ecstatic

---

[105] Cf. Witt, "The Kabeiroi," 70f.

[106] Nock describes these as the ". . . glorious gifts of the Cabiri," portrayed by Orph. *Arg* 2; "A Cabiric Rite," 577.

[107] Cf. Edson, "Macedonia, III," 192. In later centuries, St. Demetrius takes up this role of the military protector of Thessalonica, according to Edson, and the suggestion has been made that the Demetrius legends were influenced by those of Cabirus. Edson, 203f., accepts a limited portion of Gelzer's elaborate theory on this question in "Die Genesis." Gelzer did not refer explicitly to Cabirus, arguing (p. 54) that the Demetrius legends are a personification of the ancient Greek conception of a God as the patron of a city. Cf. also Hemberg, *Die Kabiren,* 210. Rex E. Witt discusses the other scholars who have taken a position on this issue, pointing out that the Byzantine legend identifies two pagan warriors who aid St. Demetrius, one of them names κούβερ. Witt feels that this name was a "reminiscence" of the Cabirus figure; "The Kabeiroi," 79.

[108] Edson cites these lines from the Orphic Hymn 39, lines 5–6, dedicated to the Corybantes, also known as the Cabiri, in "Macedonia, III," 201.

[109] "Macedonia, III," 193.

[110] Cf. Witt, "The Kabeiroi," 72.

[111] "The Kabeiroi," 73.

music and dance of the orgy would take place.[112] Although Nock does not
mention this, the enthronement might well have involved a measure of
divinization, the assumption on the part of the initiate of the identity of the
murdered but now triumphant Cabirus.[113] This suggestion is supported
by Hemberg's observation that priests of Cabirus took the name and the
identity of the god for themselves.[114] It is also sustained by Lehmann and
Spittle's recent study of the frieze of dancing devotees of the mysteries
found at Samothrace. Both the dancers and the musicians are depicted
with costumes indicating that ". . . as participants in ritual actions, they
become assimilated to divinity by wearing the garb that otherwise is
restricted to the gods."[115] The presence of both male and female participants in this scene indicates an egalitarian emphasis that is consistent
with the details Hemberg discovered about the inclusion of slaves and
strangers as honored initiates in various Cabiric temples; slaves dedicated
their chains or their writs of manumission to Cabirus, indicating that he
was the god of the "suppressed population."[116]

Reflection on the parallels between the piety of the Cabiric cult and
early Christianity may throw light on a feature that has baffled
researchers. Rex E. Witt refers to the shocking juxtaposition of the
terrifying rites of symbolic initiation and the "lighthearted, Bacchic, noisy
. . . [and] grotesquely phallic . . ." scenes in Cabiric art. "On the evidence of
what has been discovered at the Theban Kabeireion the worship in pre-
Christian times must have been for much of the time one long joke. . . .
Outwardly, at least, it all seems to have been gaiety, with food and wine,
sport and music making."[117] If the experience of initiation involved
identification with the god, the gift of apotheosis, the achievement of
equality, the relief of guilt, and the promise of the elimination of threats, a
raucous celebration would seem as appropriate as it appeared for Pauline

---

[112] Nock, "A Cabiric Rite," 579. Cole has recently disputed whether the evidence sustains the
presence of a Cabiric cult at Samothrace, in *Theoi Megaloi*, 1–3, 79. There is considerable
literary evidence that the Samothracian gods included the Cabiri, but the archaeological
evidence does not appear to sustain this. The reminder of MacMullen concerning the "lack
of uniformity in cults" needs to be kept in mind in evaluating this evidence; *Paganism in the
Roman Empire*, 101.

[113] For general background on this, cf. Anrich, *Das antike Mysterienwesen*, 37; also Farnell,
Greek Hero Cults.

[114] Hemberg, *Die Kabiren*, 276f.

[115] Lehmann and Spittle, *Samothrace*, 221. Donfried, "The Cults of Thessalonica," 340f., calls
attention not only to this detail but also to the depiction on Thessalonian coins of the laurel
crown of Cabirus. Donfried's interest, however, is not in the matter of divinizing initiates.

[116] Hemberg, *Die Kabiren*, 295f.

[117] Witt, "The Kabeiroi," 72. Witt observes that Hemberg was similarly struck by the presence
of phallic elements; *Die Kabiren*, 203. The prominence of ecstatic elements is perhaps what
led Nilsson to classify the Cabiri with the "seers and oracles" of Greek popular religion;
Greek Popular Religion, 121.

Christians whose violent, apocalyptic theology evoked repentance, regeneration, and joy.

A highly significant development, with a direct bearing on the situation in the Thessalonian church, was the absorption of Cabirus into the civic cult that had occurred during the Augustan period. Charles Edson points to inscriptions in what appeared to be a Cabiric shrine at Samothrace referring to the visit of the Thessalonian priest of the Augustan shrine and other Thessalonian initiates. "One may conclude," he writes "that by the reign of Augustus at the latest members of the city's upper classes were showing interest in the cult of the Samothracian gods."[118] A third-century C.E. inscription found in Thessalonica points in the same direction, honoring a distinguished member of the aristocracy who had served as a politarch as the leader of the Cabiric cult.[119] The depiction of Cabirus on the coins minted in Thessalonica during the Roman period[120] also attests to the incorporation of the cult into the civic establishment. Robert M. Evans offers a significant suggestion about the impact of this fusion of the Cabiric cult into the civic cult of Thessalonica. "By the time of the first century in Thessalonica, the city-cult had meaning only for those most directly interested in the welfare of the city. Thus the transformation is complete. The Cabiri rose to be identified with the city god of Thessalonica, but in so doing lost their religious value and contact with the lower classes."[121] The cooptation of the figure of Cabirus, whose primary role had been to provide equality, aid, and succor for Greeks whose livelihood came from manual labor, left the craftsmen and laborers of Thessalonica without a viable benefactor. The process of propagandistic cooptation of the democratic civic ideals that we noted earlier is here matched by the exploitation of the laborers' hero by the ruling class in Thessalonica. This cooptation would also have entailed a measure of moralistic domestication, because the orgiastic components of the Cabiric cult would surely have been curtailed by the Augustan establishment. A religious and social vacuum was thereby created, which may have made possible the remarkably rapid acceptance of a particular type of Christian proclamation and piety that offered in a new and more viable form many of the features that had been provided in the now discredited Cabiric cult. This might also help to explain why some of the distinctive excesses of the Thessalonian church were adumbrated by the outlines of the coopted Cabiric piety.

A further consequence of the incorporation of the Cabiric cult into the civic cult of Thessalonica was that a mystery religion deity previously

---

[118] Edson, "Macedonia, III," 190; the inscriptions are discussed on p. 189f.
[119] "Macedonia, III," 192–94.
[120] "Macedonia, III," 190–92.
[121] Evans, *Eschatology and Ethics*, 71.

functioning on an individualistic basis had now become politicized. The figure of Cabirus was thereby automatically infected with an element of the pagan messianism that was part of the cult of Rome. An unwelcome and certainly unintended result, from the perspective of the Thessalonian politarchs, was that if a figure like the heroic Cabirus were perceived to have returned in behalf of the laborers of the city in a form not under the control of the civic cult, it would pose a threat of revolutionary dimensions. The παρουσία of any religious figure structurally similar to Cabirus would therefore naturally be perceived as subversive to Roman rule. The unique concentration on Cabirus and his cooptation by the civic authorities may therefore help to explain why the charge of violating the "decrees of Caesar," unparalleled in any of the other centers of Pauline missionary activity, was raised against Jason and his colleagues. In Thessalonica it was perceived to be politically provocative to believe that a new age had dawned outside of the jurisdiction of the civic cult, that a new savior was present, and that the frustrated yearnings for a genuine benefactor for the poor were now fulfilled. As we shall see, the situation was ideal for the rise of a millenarian movement that took such beliefs with a literalism and immediacy not evident elsewhere in Pauline churches. It was a movement arising from the very members of the working class in Thessalonica that had suffered the loss of their redeemer figure.

Chapter Eight

PREVIOUS MODELS OF THE
THESSALONIAN CONGREGATION

Previous Models of the Thessalonian Congregation

There is a tendency in the studies considered thus far to present pictures of the Thessalonian congregation based on relatively uncritical models derived either from the Book of Acts or from modern church experience. We have encountered references to the Thessalonian Christians as "Gnostics," or "enthusiasts" influenced by "prophets" or "eschatological fanatics." We have observed that some scholars appear to view the congregation as similar to "a modern Christian congregation." Modern social science has alerted us to the significance of such models, particularly when cross-cultural comparisons have to be made between groups and circumstances in the ancient and modern worlds.[1] For the most part the models that have been employed in the Thessalonian debate are vaguely formulated or uncritically assumed. Only rarely are they even named. Significant advantages can be gained in becoming more precise and critical about the selection and use of audience models: "Models bring hitherto unconscious levels of thought into awareness. They also enlarge our conscious control over the ways in which we handle data."[2]

In the sections that follow, I will be following Thomas F. Carney's preference for homomorphic,[3] descriptive,[4] "cross-cultural models" based on a comprehensive assembling of clues brought to light by previous research. Since models provide cognitive filters that rule out irrelevant information, there is always a danger that such assembling of clues will be foreshortened so that a "strategic mischoice" is made.[5] I believe this has sometimes occurred in the quest for the audience situation in Thessalonica when apologetic interests became attached to socially or theologically acceptable models of the congregation with the result that some of the more disreputable details were denied and eliminated. While there is no final guarantee of objectivity available to researchers, I have at least

---

[1] Carney, *The Shape of the Past,* xiii–xviii, 1–38.
[2] Carney, *The Shape of the Past,* 6.
[3] Carney defines "a homomorphic model" as "one in which only the gross similarities, and not all the detail of the thing modelled are replicated." *The Shape of the Past,* 10. The contrast is with "isomorphic models" which are perfect replicas or scale models.
[4] Carney defines "descriptive models" as providing "organizational frameworks for systematically gathering information about large and nebulous topics. . . ." in contrast with "normative models" or "static models." *The Shape of the Past,* 11.
[5] *The Shape of the Past,* 35.

attempted to address this problem by assembling the literary, historical and cultural evidence prior to discussing in this chapter which model should be selected. Finally, by a comparison of the adequacy of various congregational models to match the evidence assembled through a variety of means, I hope to bring the selection process out into the open so that it can be evaluated by subsequent researchers. The goal in an essentially experimental procedure like this, of course, is not to discover the "true" model of the Thessalonian situation, which would presuppose that the original congregation were immediately and directly accessible for us to replicate, but rather the most "useful and appropriate" model to interpret the fragmentary evidence at hand.[6]

1. TRADITIONAL MODELS

Since the traditional models of the Thessalonian situation used by commentators are usually not sharply profiled or explicitly named, we are faced with the awkward task of inference. It seems to me that the models fall into three broad types, each of which appears to have its primary analogue in contemporary European and North American church experience.

(a) A Revivalistic Congregation

That the Thessalonians were experiencing minor problems deriving from too much charismatic fervor is the picture drawn by the influential commentator, James Everett Frame.[7] He uses language ordinarily associated with a successful religious revival in Protestant churches of England and North America to describe the piety of the Thessalonians. They exhibited a "vital and enthusiastic religious life," marked by "spontaneous" and "intense" expressions of the spirit.[8] Frame describes the way the "contagious power of the same spirit" that Paul had exhibited "infected the listeners," much in the way an inspired evangelistic preacher moves congregations in a revival meeting.[9] The problems that Paul deals with in 1 and 2 Thessalonians are called "imperfections . . . [which] were not serious,"[10] which sounds like a Wesleyan moralist working in a revival to tidy up the loose ends.

---

[6] *The Shape of the Past,* 9.
[7] Frame, *Thessalonians,* 5–7.
[8] *Thessalonians,* 5.
[9] *Thessalonians,* 5.
[10] *Thessalonians,* 7.

All three of the minor problems faced by the congregation, Frame asserts, came from the "intensity of their religious fervour."[11] (1) The Thessalonians had a lack of moral seriousness, implying just a hint of the mild antinomianism that sometimes accompanies a modern revival. (2) The congregation's concern about the day of the Lord was really a matter of "worry about their salvation,"[12] which sounds very much like the theme of assurance in modern Wesleyan or Baptist revivals. (3) Some members of the congregation "became excited" and gave up their daily work, which appears to be understood in terms of a revivalistic yearning to remain in a state of religious ecstasy to the detriment of everyday responsibilities.

This model provides an admirable acceptance of the charismatic piety of an early Pauline congregation, but the difficulties faced by the congregation and the impact of the pagan religious environment are downplayed. Since the revivalistic model appears to be so unconsciously applied, Frame provides no discussion of how the immense cultural distance between ancient and modern forms of religiosity is to be bridged. There is no explanation in this model for the surprise the congregation felt at the death of congregational members or the continuation of persecution. The criticism of Pauline leadership is muted and the intellectual challenge of Paul's traditional sexual ethic is overlooked. That the ἄτακτοι are merely an insignificant fraction of "excited idlers" who are too caught up in their conversion to perform their daily work seems incongruous if, as Frame argues, 2 Thess 3:6–15 is a "main point of the letter."[13]

A more sophisticated use of the revivalist model has been worked out by Elpidius Pax, OFM.[14] Arguing on the basis of epistolary theory that the situation of the audience is a crucial factor in shaping the statement of the writer, Pax describes the climate of conversion to Jewish monotheism in the Greco-Roman world. Rather than resorting to modern church parallels, he builds his case on the descriptions of proselytes in Judaism. Among the religious consequences of Gentiles submitting to divine election was the obligation of holiness: "With conversion, moreover, a person enters into the status of holiness . . . , since it is God's will that we be holy. . . . The central concept of the Bible, that God's people must be as holy as God is, picks up strongly eschatological aspects in Christianity. . . ."[15] The ethical admonitions in 1 Thessalonians 3 and 4 are thus understandable responses to the new experience of separation from the unholy, pagan

---

[11] *Thessalonians,* 6.
[12] *Thessalonians,* 7.
[13] *Thessalonians,* 297–300.
[14] Pax, "Beobachtungen"; Pax published a more succinct version of his argument in "Konvertitenprobleme."
[15] Pax, "Beobachtungen," 235.

world. Further consequences of this separation are economic and familial difficulties and a critical sense of inferiority.[16]

Pax recognizes some differences between the situation of Jewish prose-lytes and Christian converts in the warmth with which they were received, the style of ethical formation, and the use of Christological language.[17] The encounter with Paul's warm and decisive personality is identified as the decisive motivation for conversion, while his departure exacerbated the sense of isolation.[18] The unacknowledged weight of the European, Roman Catholic church experience surfaces, however, in Pax's failure to mention the distinctively charismatic quality of early Christian conversion or to provide any explanation of the peculiar criticism of church leaders that arose in Thessalonica. The further weaknesses in the conversion model that Pax proposes are the lack of explanations for the apocalyptic confusion in Thessalonica, for the concern over the death of congrega-tional members, or for the disruptive activities of the ἄτακτοι. While Pax is indisputably on the right track in emphasizing the importance of conversion for the Thessalonian situation, the lack of sociological insights about the sectarian qualities of the converted community, which seem to be blocked by the unacknowledged weight of established church assump-tions, erodes the usefulness of his work.

(b) A Decent but Impractical Congregation
with an Overly Literal Eschatology

In Ernst von Dobschütz's classic commentary, the Thessalonian church is depicted as admirable in every regard except for an overly intense eschatology that led to some rather impractical consequences. He infers from Paul's extensive thanksgivings that the congregation had exhibited a "joyous enthusiasm" even in face of persecution, an "active faith that worked successfully in spreading the gospel," a "self-giving brotherly love" and a "confident hope that yearned for the coming of the Lord."[19] There were no moral difficulties or challenges to the sexual ethic, because in Dobschütz's view, 1 Thess 4:1–8 is purely traditional catechesis, unrelated to the congregational situation.[20] The picture sounds like an ideal, European Protestant congregation of the nineteenth century— sturdy, attentive to duties, and loyal to the proper theological principles of faith and hope.

Rather strangely, however, the Thessalonian congregation developed a

---

[16] "Beobachtungen," 243.
[17] "Beobachtungen," 250–57.
[18] Pax, "Konvertitenprobleme," 30–35.
[19] Dobschütz, Die Thessalonicher-Briefe, 12.
[20] Die Thessalonicher-Briefe, 169.

quirky belief in an overly intense eschatology that led to an impractical abandonment of jobs, an unrealistic expectation of an end to earthly troubles, an inappropriate concern for governmental affairs that were none of their business, an otherworldly distraction from proper responsibilities, and resultant poverty. Dobschütz explains the behavior of the "disorderly" as follows:

> It is thus the tense expectation of the end that misled Christians to this disorderly life style, that is, rather than pursuing a regular earning of bread they did not concern themselves with earthly matters, trusting that all relationships would soon be transformed, and therefore speaking much about God and his anticipated powerful deeds while projecting such eschatological speculations boldly into the public arena, promoting there a buzz of propaganda. Why concern oneself about earthly possessions and subsistence when the end of the world and therewith the end of all needs is at hand? Are there no more important things to do? . . . The excitement for the new fad absorbs people and their energies. The natural consequence was rapid impoverishment. . . . [21]

The model for this fringe group was the occasional cell of pietists in European churches that took apocalyptic predictions and their own salvation experiences too seriously and began handing out tracts and meddling in the affairs of state churches and bureaucracies. Dobschütz conceived the problem largely in theological terms: wrong belief—in this instance, overly literal belief—was the source of socially offensive actions. As to why such a decent and otherwise sensible congregation could spawn such beliefs, no explanation is offered. The social function of apocalyptic thought and its connection with the charismatic experience of early Christianity are overlooked in the traditionally condescending scope of Dobschütz's explanation. In the view of mainline university professors and churchmen such as Lünemann, Bornemann, Schmiedel, Lightfoot and Moore who develop this model, apocalypticism appears intellectually incomprehensible and wildly impractical.[22]

The strength in this model is that it calls attention to the centrality of apocalyptic confusion in the Thessalonian situation, even if it fails to

---

[21] *Die Thessalonicher-Briefe*, 182.

[22] Lünemann, *Thessalonians*, 167f.; Dobschütz, *Die Thessalonicher-Briefe*, 183, lists Schmiedel, Bornemann, and Lightfoot as following this line. While I have difficulty confirming this from the first two, Lightfoot, "The Church of the Thessalonians," 264f., fits in well. Dobschütz states that Lightfoot compared the enthusiasts in Thessalonica with Anabaptists, a tendentious point that I have been unable to confirm. Moore, *1 and 2 Thessalonians*, 99f., 115, appears to follow this line in discussing the "realized eschatology" of the Thessalonian "idlers."

understand or sympathize with it to any appreciable degree. But there is nothing in this model that explains the shock felt by the congregation as a whole at the continuation of adversity. The effort of Paul to sustain preparedness for the parousia would have been particularly ill-suited for a congregation whose problem was overly literal anticipation of the return of Christ. The conflicts in the congregation over the relevance and control of ecstatic manifestations and the problem of sexual rebellion are seemingly unrelated to what this model conceives as the core of the problem. Nowhere in 1 or 2 Thessalonians does Paul undercut a literal belief in the parousia, which would have been absolutely necessary if the diagnosis of Dobschütz and his cohorts were correct.

(c) An Average Congregation Facing Minor Confusions and Outside Pressures

The most frequently used model among Thessalonian commentators is vaguely formulated and more difficult than the others to label. It is the typical British, Continental or North American congregation of the twentieth century, generally marked by low spiritual intensity, an amorphous doctrinal and moral legacy, and exhibiting no serious internal problems while standards of decency are being resolutely maintained and outside pressures resisted. If model (a) was marked by recent revivalistic experiences, this one has not been touched by a revival in a long time. None of the marks of recent conversion and neither the passion nor the divisiveness of sectarianism are visible. This model is presented in classic form by Ernest Best, who argues that Paul "is not angry or indignant" at anything in the congregation, but to the contrary "is very pleased with them." The congregation is "on the right path; what they chiefly needed was stimulation and direction."[23] After writing the first letter, the situation deteriorates slightly in relation to confused eschatology and "idleness,"[24] but there is nothing to suggest the presence of major problems.

Best is particularly concerned to show that there were no sharply profiled groups or problems in the congregation. His concluding argument reveals the basic premise of what I am calling "an average congregation," based on the experience of a particular type of modern British Protestant church that Best assumes his readers share:

Anyone who has served for any length of time as a pastor in a congregation will know that there are many groups whose criticisms, fair and unfair, have to be met, and that it is totally unjust to apply Occam's

---

[23] Best, *Thessalonians*, 15.
[24] *Thessalonians*, 59.

razor and say that because one hypothesis is better than many therefore it is to be assumed that all the groups are basically motivated in the same way. Human situations, let alone church situations, are rarely susceptible of such clear-cut solutions. Instead therefore of looking for one definite group which Paul was attacking in Thessalonica we must see present a number of ideas from the Hellenistic atmosphere which . . . Paul had to refute; but it is not necessary to suppose one group consciously held together all these ideas and advocated them; whatever unity the ideas have comes from the prevailing culture and not from a definite set of people. There were also many wandering teachers and the Thessalonians had to be warned that Paul was not of their type; in addition to this there will have been pressure from the Jews. . . .[25]

The kind of parish that Best refers to here is one in which even the memory of sectarian strife or apocalyptic and charismatic intensity has vanished. It is a low intensity, Protestant church, marked by mild, internal democratic pressures but no well defined parties. An amorphous boundary between the church and the society is assumed, and whatever difficulties these pflegmatic Christians face is surely caused by the culture, which appears to be much more coherent than the church. Above all, this is a model in which excitement of any kind is deemed inappropriate. As Best remarks about Paul's Thessalonian correspondence, "there is no passion as there is in so many of Paul's other letters because there is no group against which Paul can be passionate."[26] With minor variations, this model is assumed by Findlay, Milligan, Schmidt, Schlier, Bruce, Kaye, Marshall and others,[27] which indicates that the assumption of an amorphous, modern congregation as the norm is found in places other than Great Britain.

Of the three traditional models, this has the least to commend it. The impression of normality in the Thessalonian correspondence is made by the peculiar strategy of Paul's argument embedded in thanksgivings, not by the content of the argument itself. No attention is given to the appropriateness of using modern, low-intensity congregations to construct the model for a charismatic, apocalyptic congregation in the Greco-Roman culture that had experienced a world-shaking conversion from paganism. At the same time, none of the internal difficulties faced by the congregation is appropriately explained by this model. Instead, the preference

---

[25] *Thessalonians*, 22.
[26] *Thessalonians*, 22.
[27] Findlay, *Thessalonians*, 35–39; Milligan, *Thessalonians*, 31–35; Schmidt, *Der erste Thessalonicherbrief*, 96–100; Schlier, *Der Apostle und seine Gemeinde*, 11–13; Bruce, *Thessalonians*, xxxv–xxxix; Kaye, "Eschatology and Ethics," 56f.; Marshall, *1 and 2 Thessalonians*, 20.

for decent, middle-class normality tends in these commentaries to be
applied unconsciously to downplay the evidence of radicalism or peculiarity in the congregation.

(d) Conclusions

Despite occasional insights, the application of these traditional models
has been relatively unproductive of scholarly progress. These models
allow hidden premises to operate in decisive but unacknowledged ways.
Because the traditional models are for the most part unnamed and inex-
plicit, they are hard to evaluate. The burden of proof is always placed on
the critic, not only to find the flaws but also to infer from tenuous hints
what model is actually being employed. The vagueness of these hypotheses also makes them difficult to evaluate. Although the lack of scholarly
specificity is preferred on grounds of avoiding extreme hypotheses or
overinterpreting the evidence, it also has an apologetic side effect of not
allowing any picture to arise that might discredit the reputation of the
early church. In the long run, it seems to me, the lack of clarity in the
selection of models acts as a block to scholarly advances. There is a
peculiar dearth of scholarly progress in the Thessalonian commentators
who employ these traditional models. The same implicit models with the
same flaws are being advanced in studies written a generation apart from
each other, without any discernable advance in critical perspective or
scholarly precision. This is not likely to change until the risk of constructing and evaluating explicit models of the congregational situation is
taken by a larger number of commentators. For this reason, it seems to
me, the creative leap forward in the historical-critical quest for the
Thessalonian situation occurred with the work of Wilhelm Lütgert. He
broke away from the traditional approaches for the first time and proposed an explicitly acknowledged, new model of Greco-Roman enthusiasm for the situation in the Thessalonian congregation.

2. The Enthusiastic Model

Although there are occasional references to enthusiasm in earlier investigations of the Thessalonian situation,[28] this model was fully developed for
the first time by Wilhelm Lütgert. His study in 1909 of the Thessalonian
situation[29] was one of a series of monograph-length investigations of the
Pauline letters, beginning with Corinth in 1908 and ending with Gala-

---

[28] For example, cf.Clemen, "Paulus und die Gemeinde," 158–62.
[29] Lütgert, "Die Volkommenen."

tians in 1917.[30] In an admirable expression of scholarly flexibility he created a differentiated model for each congregation, using some materials about Greco-Roman religion uncovered by the History of Religion school and categories from later church history. His general theory was that the troubles in Pauline churches were caused by radicalization of Paul's teachings, caused by unique but mysterious local circumstances. He did not, however, investigate the cultural situation in the various centers of the Pauline mission to explain this distortion. In the case of the Thessalonians, Lütgert perceived a group of leaders who vied with Paul's authority by offering a superior level of charismatic freedom and power.[31] He showed that the congregation's concern over the fate of those dying before the parousia implied the belief that such persons were somehow eliminated from the new age.[32] On the basis of evidence from 2 Thessalonians, Lütgert went on to analyze the strange link between the confusion over ecstatic manifestations, the assertion that the parousia had already come, and the lack of a traditional resurrection hope. Lütgert concluded that the Thessalonian Christians identified the gift and manifestations of the spirit that they had experienced with the strange "parousia" of which Paul spoke. If they possessed the spirit, the parousia of Jesus must have come to them. And if the parousia had already arrived, it followed that the resurrection would be viewed as already having taken place. This would explain why the separation of a congregational member through death was felt to be permanent. Lütgert stated the kernel of his idea this way: "If the day of the Lord is already present, it follows that what one expected as resurrection has already occurred. There is therefore no more resurrection to be expected."[33]

Lütgert went on to connect this insight with several other details of the Thessalonian situation. He suggested that the activities of the ἄτακτοι were motivated by spiritual enthusiasm. But he associated the "busybodies" of 2 Thess 3:11 with modern sectarian evangelists, suggesting they were proselytizing like some ancient members of Watchtower Society or the like,[34] which hardly comports with their opposition against order and authority. There is little doubt, in fact, that the ἄτακτοι were opposed to any form of regular work, of which evangelism would certainly be a variety. As noted above, both letters provide a positive rationale for self-supporting labor, which appears to counter such tendencies.[35] Thus an

---

[30] Lütgert, "Freiheitspredigt"; "Gesetz und Geist"; "Der Römerbrief."
[31] Lütgert, "Die Volkommenen," 618–23.
[32] "Die Volkommenen," 632.
[33] "Die Volkommenen," 637f.
[34] "Die Volkommenen," 628, 641.
[35] Cf. 1 Thess 1:3; 2:9; 3:2, 5; 4:9–12; 5:12, 13; 2 Thess 1:11–12; 2:17; 3:6–16.

alternative way of relating this idleness to the ecstatic perspective of the ἄτακτοι should have been sought if the Lütgert approach was to remain viable. At this point it is interesting to note that other enthusiastic movements in the first century tended to encourage the view that labor was unnecessary for the ecstatic.[36] In the spirit, one was assumed to have transcended the mortal plague of work, an understandable feeling in light of the Hellenistic belief that labor was a demeaning sign of bondage to the treadmill of fate and necessity.[37] There are also precedents in the Greco-Roman world for the spirit-filled leader to demand monetary compensation from the less enlightened admirers as an acknowledgement of transcendent superiority.[38]

Several scholars who were relatively uninterested in apologetics were willing to follow Lütgert's model that fused the disreputable term applied by the Reformers to the left wing fanatics, "Schwärmer," with the term from Greco-Roman religion, "enthusiasm." Bo Reicke used the former to describe the Thessalonian radicals: "The enthusiastic stance of some Thessalonians was basically related to a twisting of eschatology."[39] Although the tendency toward idleness was manifest at the time of the first letter, the shift to a realized eschatology that occurred before the writing of the second letter caused a further radicalization and social disorientation, bringing the church into the mode of the typical ". . . social and political opposition movements in the Greek cities."[40] Although the category of "Schwärmerei/Enthusiasm" comes from church history, Reicke's research anchored it in the agitation that marked the life of guilds and corporations in the Greco-Roman world. Franz Laub and Gerhard Friedrich use the same categories without dealing explicitly with this cultural background.[41]

Additional clarification of the Greco-Roman background of radical enthusiasm as perceived by Lütgert and others in the Thessalonian congregation was provided by Josef Pieper. He reconstructed the shape of religious mania from evidence in Plato's *Phaedrus*,[42] in which the believer is filled with god, made capable of prophecy, relieved from troubles, and possessed by an eros that defies conventional standards. Walter Burkert discusses the range of this religious mania, showing it was conceived either as a "pathological frenzy" provoked by the anger of a god, or as a

---

[36] Cf. Reicke, *Diakonie*, 243–47, 308–14.
[37] Cf. Hauck, "Arbeit"; Hauck, "Erwerb."
[38] Cf. Georgi, *Die Gegner des Paulus*, 234ff.
[39] Reicke, *Diakonie*, 244.
[40] *Diakonie*, 246; cf. also Reicke, "Thessalonicherbriefe."
[41] Laub, *Eschatologische Verkündigung*, 121, 137, 145f.; Friedrich, *Der erste Brief*, 205.
[42] Pieper, *Enthusiasm and Divine Madness*, 50–81.

"transfigured consciousness" that brings "fulfillment" by the ecstatic in-dwelling of deity, or as "a sober emotion which overtakes . . ." prophets, miracle workers, poets and rhapsodes.[43]

The frequency with which this model has been employed without referring explicitly to the Greco-Roman background indicates its source in the tradition of Christian radicalism. Without specifying the cultural sources, James M. Reese uses the category of "radical enthusiasts" to describe the Thessalonians who advocated the "over realized eschatology" to the effect that the parousia had already occurred.[44] Without referring to the research of Reicke or Pieper, Christopher L. Mearns develops the theme of Thessalonian "enthusiasts who felt oversure that they enjoyed the present possession of the Kingdom of God, with its accompanying charismatic powers."[45] He argues that Paul had originally advocated a thoroughly realized eschatology, reminiscences of which are still visible in the phrasing of 1 Thess 1:10, 3:13, 5:5 and 2 Thess 1:7, but that he shifted to a more futuristic position in the argument of 1 Thessalonians, and finally to a deferred apocalyptic in the second letter. The alteration of Paul's eschatology was necessitated by the shock suffered in Thessalonica at the death of congregational members who were presumably saved and beyond mortality, by the emergence of a piety marked by boastful pos-session of salvation, and by imminent expectations caused by the Caligula episode in C.E. 40.[46] A less elaborate theory is offered by Bruce, who refers to "an over-enthusiastic expectation of the imminent advent of Christ . . ." that arose because Paul's teaching was "imperfectly digested."[47]

Not everyone who employs this model accepts realized eschatology as a crucial component in the Thessalonian piety. Ernest W. Saunders refers to the "distorted views of spiritual perfectionism" and the "heady enthu-siasm" of the Thessalonian church, without developing a theory of realized eschatology.[48] Gerhard Friedrich uses the term "Schwärmer" without resorting to realized eschatology, suggesting that some of the Thessalonians. took Paul's eschatological proclamation so seriously that they gave up their daily occupations in preparation for the future par-ousia. These "schwärmerische Pneumatiker" wanted to rearrange the affairs of the congregation according to endtime standards, possibly also threatening the sexual ethic and disrespecting congregational leaders.

---

[43] Burkert, *Greek Religion,* 110f.
[44] Reese, *1 and 2 Thessalonians,* 90.
[45] Mearns, "Early Eschatological Development," 141.
[46] "Early Eschatological Development," 157.
[47] Bruce, "St. Paul in Macedonia," 333. Black takes a similar position in "The Weak in Thessalonica," 315.
[48] Saunders, *1 Thessalonians,* 2f., 41.

They were opposed by others who rejected the disorderly behavior on principle, threatening the unity of the congregation.[49] Although he was less sensitive to the social consequences in the congregation, Willi Marxsen uses the more appropriate category, "enthusiastisch," to describe the Thessalonian radicals who responded to Paul's intensification of apocalyptic preaching after the conflict with Peter at Antioch.[50] By proclaiming Christ as the one who provides salvation from the wrath to come, Paul offered a theoretical kind of present salvation that was accepted eagerly by the Thessalonians. "Salvation is no longer simply a goal but a present possibility. . . . So they require no further anxiety about an uncertain future: the one in whom God has already prepared salvation will soon return."[51] Despite the wording of this passage, Marxsen thinks of the Thessalonians as sharing a modern kind of existential neo-orthodoxy rather than a realized eschatology, because the day of the Lord remains a future event. Hence the congregation was shocked at the death of congregational members simply because it occurred before the anticipated parousia.[52]

My own previous work on the Thessalonian situation rested on the premise of enthusiasm involving realized eschatology that was developed by Lütgert.[53] Some of the clues about the Thessalonian situation that he had overlooked or misconstrued I attempted to fit into the hypothesis. The opposition against the conservative sexual ethic fit in well with the belief in having been freed from earthly ties or limitations that Lütgert had identified. For the Hellenistic enthusiast who had attained immortal life in the spirit, bodily relationships would be viewed with hostility and the strictures of the moral law would seem irrelevant. The shocked reaction at the continuance of persecution was also capable of being fit into this hypothesis. Since persecution carried with it the threat of death, it would reveal that mortal contingency had not altered by possession of the spirit, and thus it would cast doubt on the authenticity of the new faith. This doubt extended to the effectiveness of Paul's apostolate itself. It was recalled that he had not manifested the transcendent spirit through public displays of ecstasy. This was taken as evidence that the gospel lacked the power to set people free from the encumbrances of "soul" and "body." Finally, this sort of enthusiasm would lead quite naturally to disrespect for the leaders of the congregation. Each enthusiast would consider himself or herself a leader in an unqualified sense of the term. The radical

---

[49] Friedrich, *Der erste Brief*, 205.
[50] Marxsen, *Der erste Brief*, 21.
[51] *Der erste Brief*, 22.
[52] *Der erste Brief*, 26.
[53] Jewett, "Enthusiastic Radicalism."

denial of order and authority ensuing from such enthusiasm made conflict inevitable.

There were several substantial weaknesses in my adaptation of Lürtgert's model. Inadequate account was taken of the Greco-Roman background and no reference was made to the unique cultural circumstances in Thessalonica. A further weakness of Lütgert's model lies in the tenuous connection between the parousia and the spirit. The apocalyptic character of the Thessalonian faith, as described in Paul's references to the Thessalonians' conversion, was not integral to Greco-Roman enthusiasm. This shortcoming was disguised in some adaptations of Lütgert's theory by the use of the anachronistic term, "Schwärmer," whose antecedents in the Reformation period included apocalypticists. But this actually did nothing to strengthen the connection between eschatology and enthusiasm in the Thessalonian setting. Both in Lütgert's and my work, the connection between charismatic experience and realized eschatology remained on the level of an inappropriate mental association by Greco-Roman minds grappling with Paul's strange references to the parousia of Christ. The lack of an appropriate social theory that coordinates the belief in a new age with manifestations of the spirit is painfully obvious. Consequently, the indications of a collapse of apocalyptic faith caused by the unexpected onset of persecutions and the death of congregational members remained hard to explain. Although my earlier effort to revise the Lütgert approach attracted some interest,[54] it remains flawed and inadequate. While it seems likely that some of the widely shared assumptions about religion manifest in Greco-Roman enthusiasm were present in Thessalonica, this model alone hardly suffices to explain the full range of convictions and problems manifest in the Thessalonian situation.

3. The Gnostic Model

A gnostic identification of the Thessalonian piety was suggested by Walter Schmithals as part of the elaborate partition theory discussed above in chapter 3. It is difficult to disentangle the support for the gnostic model from the rather implausible reconstruction of the four letters that Schmithals posits, with their complicated interaction with the congregational situation. Nowhere in his lengthy study is the gnostic hypothesis set forth systematically,[55] with the result that it is less compelling than

---

[54] Cf. Reese, *1 and 2 Thessalonians,* 90f.; Mearns, "Early Eschatological Developments," 142; for an extensive critique of this approach, cf. Best, *Thessalonians,* 19–22.

[55] Schmithals, *Paul and the Gnostics,* 123–218.

Schmithals' work on the Corinthian situation. It is instead assumed on the basis of Schmithals' earlier studies advocating a pan-gnostic interpretation of the other Pauline congregations. For instance, Paul's defense of his apostolicity in 1 Thess 1:5, 9; 2:1–12 is interpreted in light of similar passages in other letters as responses to "typical Gnostic charges."[56] Schmithals interprets 1 Thess 4:1–8 as a response to "Gnostic libertinism," but fails to explain Paul's admission in 4:1 that the congregation had not yet broken from traditional fidelity, which differentiates this situation so drastically from that in Corinth.[57] He relies on Lütgert's study of 1 Thess 4:13–18 to show that an "enthusiastic movement of Gnosticism" was present, fusing the two models together without further argument, but straining the evidence considerably by positing "doubts of the Thessalonians about the resurrection as such. . . ."[58] He makes an equally awkward case that the argument in 1 Thess 5:1–11 aims to counter a gnostic "rejection of all earthly expectation of the end, whether one calls it Parousia, resurrection, or judgement."[59] It is much easier to incorporate 2 Thess 2:2 into the gnostic model as Schmithals links it with 2 Tim 2:18 where Gnostics are claiming the resurrection had already occurred.[60] Also the admonition to respect church leaders in 1 Thess 5:12–13 is assimilated to later gnostic struggles against church authority.[61] A major premise in the entire construction, however, is that gnostic missionaries from other churches are causing the difficulty in Thessalonica,[62] a contention for which not a shred of credible evidence within the correspondence itself is available. We discussed in chapter 4 the correlative thesis about the composition of the Thessalonian letters on the so-called "Third Missionary Journey" when evidence becomes available for missionaries evoking threats in other Pauline churches.

Wolfgang Harnisch expands and offers minor corrections to Schmithals' suggestions about the gnostic background of 1 Thess 4:13–5:11.[63] He accepts the contention that 4:13–18 responds to a denial of the resurrection but suggests that 4:15b is Paul's citation of the gnostic thesis concerning ". . . an absolute superiority of the living in relation to the dead. . . ."[64] Since the dead have fallen prey to the realm of $\sigma\acute{\alpha}\rho\xi$, only the living can participate in the resurrected life of the $\pi\nu\epsilon\hat{\upsilon}\mu\alpha$, according to

---

[56] *Paul and the Gnostics,* 140.
[57] *Paul and the Gnostics,* 156–58.
[58] *Paul and the Gnostics,* 159–64.
[59] *Paul and the Gnostics,* 166.
[60] *Paul and the Gnostics,* 166f.
[61] *Paul and the Gnostics,* 168f.
[62] *Paul and the Gnostics,* 175.
[63] Harnisch, *Eschatologische Existenz.*
[64] *Eschatological Existenz,* 27.

gnostic doctrine.[65] The trouble with this suggestion is that the key verb in 4:15b, $\phi\theta\acute{\alpha}\sigma\omega\mu\epsilon\nu$, has a temporal rather than a qualitative, comparative sense, and must be translated "we shall not *precede* those who have fallen asleep."[66] This would make no sense in the allegedly timeless perspective of gnostics wishing to express ontological superiority over the dead. He goes on to argue that the motto, "peace and security" in 1 Thess 5:3 is a direct quotation of a gnostic boast in the possession of salvation,[67] so that 5:1–3 needs to be understood as an attack on pneumatic self-consciousness.[68] This is a plausible but not a compelling suggestion, since the words would make equal sense if Paul were criticizing enthusiasts by reasserting his apocalyptic theology.

The gnostic model derives its strength from the same evidence that sustains the enthusiastic model. But it is certainly not an improvement because there are several distinctive features of Gnosticism that are conspicuously absent in Thessalonica: dualism of flesh and spirit, christological speculation, the speculative use of Genesis 1–3, or the enactment of libertinistic behavior. Furthermore, the abandonment of temporary categories in the gnostic system assumed by Schmithals and Harnisch makes the details of Paul's argument very difficult to interpret at face value.

4. The Divine Man Model

A portion of my earlier study of "Enthusiastic Radicalism" dealt with the bearing of the so-called "apology" in 1 Thess 2:1–12 on the reconstruction of the congregational situation.[69] I argued for a dialectic in this section against a pattern of behavior that was strongly reminiscent of what Dieter Georgi had analyzed in his study of the divine man movement in 2 Corinthians.[70] Although this argument was rather inconclusive and the model that Georgi posited has been severely criticized, the dialectic has some significance for reconstructing the Thessalonian situation. The discovery of a significant divinization component in the Cabiric cult at Thessalonica throws new light on this material.

Given the widely diverging interpretations of the evidence in 1 Thess 2:1–12, it seemed methodical to assign it a subordinate role in developing

---

[65] *Eschatological Existenz,* 28.
[66] Bauer, Arndt, Gingrich, and Danker, *A Greek-English Lexicon,* 856f.; Rigaux, *Thessaloniciens,* 540; Bruce, *Thessalonians,* 99.
[67] Bruce, *Thessalonians,* 81.
[68] Bruce, *Thessalonians,* 160.
[69] Jewett, "Enthusiastic Radicalism," 208–15.
[70] Georgi, *Die Gegner des Paulus.*

the picture of the congregational situation. To consider this material in
isolation, however, was to open the door to arbitrary interpretation. It had
led Frame, Neil and others to suggest, for example, that the congregation
had inexplicably fallen prey to vicious Jewish propaganda about Paul's
character and motivations.[71] The very same evidence led Schmithals to
posit an attack by Gnostics similar to those found in Corinth.[72] Others
sought to avoid the dilemma by suggesting these verses simply expressed
Paul's defensive mood[73] or was unrelated to any specific problems in the
congregation.[74] One approach was to interpret the passage strictly on the
basis of the background and source of the terminology Paul used. Thus
Denis made a case from the use of messianic and servant terminology from
the Old Testament that Paul was asserting his role as a messianic prophet
to the Gentiles.[75] Horbury limited the background to the Old Testament
discussion of true and false prophecy, failing to develop the hint that Paul
might be responding to "Jewish opposition."[76] Malherbe has pointed to
the Cynic philosophical tradition as the source of Pauline language and
arguments in 1 Thessalonians 2, concluding that since Dio and others
were not necessarily responding to personal attacks, Paul was not making
a "personal apology" at all.[77] Palmer compares the items in Paul's
ostensible self-defense with those in Cynic diatribes and concludes that
". . . Paul is specifically relating his choice of themes to the Thessalonian
situation."[78] These diverse interpretations reflect the complexity of the
material and the shape of the methodical issue.

I am not satisfied with the methodical antithesis between seeking to
uncover Cynic or Old Testament background on the one hand or seeking
congregational relevance on the other. No matter what the source of
material Paul uses in 1 Thessalonians 2, the exegetical question is how
the material in its present form fits into the structure of the letter, which
must be viewed rhetorically as a portion of the dialogue between Paul and
his audience. The valuable parallels discovered by Denis, Malherbe,
Horbury and others may contribute to this essential exegetical quest but
can never obviate it.

My approach therefore was to analyze the pattern of positive and
negative contrasts between Pauline behavior and some other pattern of

---

[71] Frame, *Thessalonians*, 13f.; Neil, *Thessalonians*, 192.; Plummer, *First Epistle to the Thessalonians*, 17f.
[72] Schmithals, *Paul and the Gnostics*, 135–76.
[73] Dobschütz, *Die Thessalonicher-Briefe*, 106f.
[74] Masson, *Thessaloniciens*, 25ff.
[75] Denis, "L'Apôtre Paul," 245–318.
[76] Horbury, "I Thessalonians," 507.
[77] Malherbe, "'Gentle as a Nurse,'" 203–17.
[78] Palmer, "Thanksgiving, Self-Defence, and Exhortation," 30.

behavior, and to relate this argument in some comprehensible manner to the rhetorical situation as defined from the rest of the letter. It seemed likely that 1 Thessalonians 2 constitutes an important step in the argument against the false understanding of faith and leadership by developing a contrasting concept of apostolic leadership. By describing the shape of the apostolic example, Paul clarifies the character of the new age and at the same time indirectly criticizes the ἄτακτοι whose behavior stood in such contrast to his own. In working through this evidence, a number of details seemed distantly reminiscent of the divine man ideology whose presence was hinted at in the discussion of the problem of apostolic remuneration.

(a) Negative Correlations with Features of Undesirable Leadership

By examining the antitheses between Paul's behavior and that of the radical ἄτακτοι, a series of details came to light which could be correlated to some degree with the profile of the divine man movement as investigated in the past. Several of the crucial themes appeared to be introduced in 1 Thess 2:3.

(1) Paul insisted that his proclamation had not derived from πλάνη, a term that reappears in 2 Thess 2:11 in connection with the discussion of the Thessalonians' mistaken conception of the parousia. In the latter context Paul placed the very eschatological delusions current in Thessalonica under the rubric of the divine consignment to wrath. The shape of this delusion was also discernable in the first letter, particularly in 5:1–11 where Paul castigated the false sense of "peace and security" current in the congregation. He argued that such confidence did not take adequate account of the coming judgment. Thus whereas the radicals in Thessalonica seemed to have based their stance on the delusion of transcendence over world and history, Paul's message took sober cognizance of eschatological reality.

(2) The reference to ἀκαθαρσία in 1 Thess 2:3 seemed to point to sexual immorality, judging from the connotations of this term elsewhere in the Pauline corpus.[79] This term appears in the summary of Paul's discussion of the marriage ethic: "For God has not called us for uncleanness, but in holiness." (1 Thess 4:7) Thus in insisting that his proclamation did not derive from "uncleanness," Paul seemed implicitly to be condemning the denial of the validity of the traditional ethic. Similarly the reference in 1 Thess 2:10 to the apostles' "blameless . . . behavior" was related to this holiness theme, being associated very closely in 1 Thess 3:13.

---

[79] Cf. the use of this term in Rom 1:24; 6:19; 2 Cor. 12:21; Gal 5:19; also the use in Eph 4:19; 5:3 and Col 3:5. Hauck points to this connotation in "καθαρός, κτλ," *TWNT* 3:432.

(3) The reference to δόλος in 1 Thess 2:3 seemed to relate most closely to the discussion of monetary compensation in the later verses of the "apology." Paul denied in 2:5 that he and his colleagues had sought such compensation under a "cloak for greed,"[80] by using "words of flattery" on the congregation about the great honor they would do themselves in supporting such exalted apostles. Instead, Paul insisted in 2:9, "we worked night and day, that we might not burden any of you," presumably in the sense of gaining monetary compensation.[81] These details appeared to relate quite directly to the successful maneuverings of the ἄτακτοι in getting the less enlightened members of the congregation to pay them something like apostolic compensation (2 Thess 3:6–13).

(4) A negative correlation was also suggested in the discussion of domineering versus gentle behavior in 1 Thess 2:6–7. In denying that the apostles had sought "glory from men" even though they had a perfect right to "claim a status of importance as apostles,"[82] Paul implicitly condemned the proud, domineering behavior of the ἄτακτοι. The allusion to Paul's gentle behavior, "like a nurse taking care of her children" (1 Thess 2:7), appeared to point in the opposite direction from the domineering demeanor of persons with divine man pretensions.[83] Likewise the reference in 1 Thess 2:6 to the "affectionate desire" for the well-being of the congregation on the part of Paul and his associates was seen to stand in contrast to the exploitative use of the congregation by the "disorderly ones."

(5) A final negative correlation was visible in Paul's claim of "pious and upright . . . behavior" (1 Thess 2:10). This is the only use in the Pauline corpus of the typical Hellenistic expression for propriety ὁσίως καὶ δικαίως.[84] The use of conventional pagan terminology seemed to indicate a situation where public respectability needed to be preserved. This appeared to correlate with the pattern of scandalous libertinism practiced by the ἄτακτοι, alluded to in 1 Thess 4:11f. where the "respect of outsiders" is at stake.

---

[80] Delling,"πλεονέκτης," TWNT 6:273; Dibelius, An die Thessalonicher I, II, 7f.
[81] Cf. Masson, Thessaloniciens, 29; Neil, Thessalonians, 40 and the parallels in 1 Cor 9:14 and 2 Cor 11:7–9.
[82] The use of βάρος in 1 Thess 2:7 indicates "gewichtigen und absichtlichen Sich-zur-Geltung-Bringen" according to Schrenk, "βάρος, κτλ." TWNT 1:554. This interpretation is supported by Dobschütz, Dibelius and Neil. The latter follows Moffatt's translation, "as apostles of Christ we had the power of claiming to be men of weight." The First and Second Epistles, 39.
[83] Cf. 2 Cor 11:20; Georgi, Die Gegner des Paulus, 220ff.
[84] Cf. Hauck, "ὅσιος, κτλ," TWNT 5:489–91.

(b) Connections with Divine Man Behavior in Corinth

Several of the points of correlation noted above were shown to have close connections with the divine man agitation in Corinth, as set forth in investigations by Dieter Georgi and others.[85] The motif of "deceit," or "guile," was reflected in Paul's charge that these superlative missionaries invading Corinth were "deceitful workers" (2 Cor 11:13) in that they, like the Thessalonian ἄτακτοι, seemed primarily interested in gaining monetary compensation (2 Cor 11:7–9; 12:13). In both instances, the maneuvering took the form of demanding recognition by the congregation of the superior ecstatic gifts of the divine men, so that in the Corinthian case, Paul's adversaries argued that his refusal to accept such apostolic compensation proved he was not a true apostle.[86] Consequently Paul had to defend himself in 2 Corinthians against the suspicion that he gained his status with the congregation by means of some superior form of "guile" (2 Cor 4:2; 12:16). This connection between "guile" and monetary compensation was a typical feature of the model of divine man controversies in the Greco-Roman world developed by Georgi on the basis of earlier research by Weinrich, Bieler and others.[87] I also pointed to the parallels in the Corinthian situation to the antithesis between the "gentle" behavior of the apostles and the domineering actions of their opponents. Paul opened his discussion in 2 Cor 10:1 with entreaties "by the meekness and gentleness of Christ" and went on to castigate the congregation for tolerating it "if a man makes slaves of you, or preys upon you, or takes advantage of you, or puts on airs, or strikes you in the face. To my shame, I must say, we were too weak for that!" (2 Cor 11:20f.) This abusive pattern of behavior was an expression of the claim to be "superlative apostles" (2 Cor 12:11) whose spiritual superiority was manifested in ecstasy, brilliant rhetorical gifts, wonder-working powers, and domineering demeanor.[88]

(c) Competitive Correlations with Divine Man Ideology

In addition to these antithetical correlations, there appeared to be several claims in 1 Thess 2:1–12 that brought Paul into a kind of com-

---

[85] Georgi, *Die Gegner des Paulus*; Schulz, "Die Decke des Moses"; Friedrich, "Die Gegner des Paulus."

[86] Georgi, *Die Gegner des Paulus*, 234–41.

[87] Older studies of the divine man movement that note the charge of guileful embezzlement are Kahrstedt, *Kulturgeschichte*, 310f.; Nock, *Conversion*, 77–98; Weinrich, "Antikes Gottmenschtum," 633–51, esp. 648. For a more idealistic picture of the divine man in the Greco-Roman era, cf. Bieler, ΘΕΙΟΣ ANHP 1:145. Several other studies relevant to this issue are Betz, *Lukian von Samosata*, and Habicht, *Gottmenschentum*, 160–242. For additional bibliography, cf. n. 104 below.

[88] Georgi, *Die Gegner des Paulus*, 229ff.

petitive correlation with specific features of a divine man ideology. Paul claimed a bold "courage" for himself in 1 Thess 2:2 which was similar to the confident missionizing of the divine men in 2 Corinthians.[89] Paul's claim in 1 Thess 2:4 to be "approved by God" was shown to be couched in the same terminology as his rebuttal of the self-approving divine men in 2 Cor 10:18: "For it is not the man who approves himself that is accepted, but the man whom the Lord approves." This controversy was reflected in the other uses of the terms δοκιμή and δόκιμος in 2 Cor 13:3-7,[90] the use of the letters of approval by the invading missionaries in Corinth (2 Cor 3:1-3; 10:12; 12:11, etc.),[91] and the debate over divinely bestowed "ability" in 2 Cor 2:14-17; 3:5 in which Paul claimed to be "commissioned by God."[92]

Finally I suggested a potential competitive correlation with Paul's claim in 1 Thess 2:8 that he had been "ready to impart to you not only the gospel of God but also our own selves." Since the Corinthian missionaries claimed that the power of Christ was visible in their own lives, they "preached themselves" (2 Cor 4:5) as the perfect embodiments of the transforming power of the spirit, making them into divine men equal to Christ in dignity.[93]

(d) General Similarities between the Thessalonian Radicals and Divine Men

On the basis of earlier research, it appeared that the divine man movement tended to concentrate on ecstasy as proof of the presence of the divine in the person of the missionary.[94] In the Corinthian situation, for example, the invading missionaries boasted about their experiences of ecstatic visions, mystical silences and heavenly journeys as proof of spiritual prowess (2 Cor 12:1-13).[95] This emphasis on ecstasy, understood in a Hellenistic fashion, led to the claim of actual divinity on the part of the missionary. Many instances of this claim had been discovered in Greco-Roman culture.[96] The Book of Acts appeared to reflect this cultural

---

[89] *Die Gegner des Paulus*, 211, 220ff.

[90] *Die Gegner des Paulus*, 228, 232.

[91] *Die Gegner des Paulus*, 241ff.

[92] *Die Gegner des Paulus*, 220ff.

[93] *Die Gegner des Paulus*, 285ff.

[94] Cf. Nock, *Conversion*, 83ff.; Nock, *Early Gentile Christianity*, 87ff.; Weinreich, "Antikes Gottmenchtum," 633ff.; Kahrstedt, *Kulturgeschichte*, 374.

[95] Georgi, *Die Gegner des Paulus*, 296ff.; cf. also Betz, "Eine Christus-Aretalogie," 288–305, esp. 304.

[96] Nock, *Conversion*, 83, summarizes the typical claim: "It is easy and usual for each to say, I am God, or the Son of God, or a divine spirit. I have come, for the world is already perishing and you, O men, are going to destruction because of iniquities. I wish to save you. . . ." This citation from Celsus is paralleled at many points by materials gathered in the studies by Bieler and Weinreich.

assumption with Cornelius falling down to worship Peter (Acts 10:25f.) and the crowds at Lystra saying of Paul and Barnabas, "The gods have come down to us in the likeness of men!" (Acts 14:11f.) The terms θεῖος ἀνῆρ and θεῖοι ἄνθρωποι that were current in the Hellenistic era seemed to give apt expression to this idea which appeared to be rather close to the consciousness of the ἄτακτοι of having transcended time and trouble in their ecstatic experiences. This led at times to the belief that a divine man would in some sense transcend death,[97] and there are examples of their either proclaiming they would never die, or of their purportedly returning back to their believers after death.[98]

These assumptions about the immortal divine man seemed to fit quite closely with the Thessalonian sense of shock that death was still a possibility for those who had received the divine spirit of the new age. Similarly, there was an expectation in Thessalonica that recipients of the spirit would transcend troubles and human frailties. This aspect of the ideology was also in evidence in 2 Corinthians, where the missionaries boasted of their superior strength, beauty, ability, and transcendence.[99] A further example of this expectation had been detected in the divine man movement in the early church at Ephesus which criticized Paul because of the mortal weakness manifested in his imprisonment, a weakness that allegedly jeopardized the success of the mission.[100] This appeared to relate to a major problem addressed by 1 Thessalonians, the surprise and despair that persecution could still mark the life of a new community in the apocalyptic triumph of the spirit.

(e) Evaluation

In part because of the peculiar history of the "divine man" debate, the effort to restate this model makes a rather dated impression. The primary

---

[97] Betz, *Lukian von Samosata,* 124, describes the typical divine man death reports as follows: "In all accounts the wise man is depicted as standing completely above the events. Moreover, the scheme includes the prediction of death, a last word, death in extraordinary circumstances, accompanying miracle, resurrection and apotheosis in different form, reaction of observers."

[98] Bieler, ΘΕΙΟΣ ANHP, 44–49, notes that although the typical divine man dies, the death is unusual, often in the form of martyrdom, and often connected in the legends with a great farewell scene. There are usually signs that the divine presence has passed from the scene: earthquakes, eclipses, miracles of all sorts. The corpse is wonderfully preserved or buried by the gods. And very frequently there are reports of resurrections and bodily appearances among the living. "To have overcome death is the final crowning of an extraordinary life," is Bieler's conclusion on p. 48. He cites *Acta apostolorum apocrypha* 1:240, 146, 202, 224f. as examples of the general tendency in the case of Simon Magus. Reitzenstein also spoke of divine men reappearing as "spirits" to their followers in *Die hellenistischen Mysterienreligionen,* 316f.

[99] Georgi, *Die Gegner des Paulus,* 220–34.

[100] Cf. Jewett, "Conflicting Movements," 364–71.

investigation of the relevance of this model for a Pauline congregation by Dieter Georgi has been much delayed in its English translation, although the extensive critiques by Tiede,[101] Holladay,[102] and others[103] have long been available. Many of the basic investigations of the divine man phenomena in the Greco-Roman world have been available only in German.[104] In a sense the antithesis has been more widely known than the thesis itself as far as the wider, English-reading public was concerned. One of the results of this curious anomaly was that many scholars came to the conclusion that the model was fundamentally indefensible, even for 2 Corinthians. It is to be hoped that the American edition of Georgi's book will allow a renewed sifting of the issue. But even this is unlikely to make the divine man model plausible as a comprehensive explanation of the Thessalonian situation.

The major difficulty is that the divine man model can be correlated only with 1 Thess 2:1-12 and a few other references to the behavior of the ἄτακτοι. It throws no light on the apocalyptic confusion or the peculiar challenge of the sexual ethic. This model is also inappropriate as a comprehensive explanation of the Thessalonian situation because there are substantial components of the divine man movement evident elsewhere in early Christianity that are not reflected at all in Thessalonica. There is no evidence here of invading missionaries proving their superiority over Paul by displaying letters of recommendation listing miracles and ecstatic visitations. Unlike the situation in 2 Corinthians, there is no indication here of an emphasis on eloquence or a particular strain of allegorical interpretation of inspired writings. The background in Hellenistic Judaism that Georgi posited for the Corinthian missionaries is also problematic for the Thessalonian congregation, consisting almost exclusively of former pagans.

Nevertheless, this model does provide material to fill in the profile of the ἄτακτοι and offers some fascinating parallels to the divinization of initiates of the Cabiric cult, as discussed in the last chapter. Paul's efforts to warn against the dangers of the behavior popularized by this model

---

[101] Tiede, *The Charismatic Figure.*

[102] Holladay, *THEIOS ANER in Hellenistic-Judaism.*

[103] Cf. Oostendorp, *Another Jesus*; Kee, "Aretology and Gospel"; Liefeld, "The Hellenistic 'Divine Man'"; Thrall, "Super-apostles."

[104] Cf. n. 87 above. The most recent presentation of the evidence concerning the divine man concept is Betz' article, "Gottmensch," cols. 234–312, esp. 296–305. An infrequently cited article in English is Knox, "The 'Divine Hero' Christology"; the most accessible study in English is Hadas and Smith, *Heroes and Gods*; a succinct summary of the profile of the Greco-Roman "divine man" is available in Betz, "Jesus as Divine Man." The only statement of Georgi's position that I know in English is the brief article, "Second Letter to the Corinthians," 184f. A brief, critical presentation of the evidence in the Greco-Roman era is available in Kee, "Divine Man."

indicates his impression that there were some components of the Thessalonian situation with these traits. This would not have been visible without the experimental application of the divine man model, which confirms the usefulness of using an explicit model in an exegetical investigation, even when that model proves inadequate to explain all the evidence. A viable model of the Thessalonian situation should be able to take these traits into account.

Chapter Nine

THE MILLENARIAN MODEL

Given the inadequacies of previous hypotheses, the appeal of the millenarian model is that it promises to encompass not only the apocalyptic components of the Thessalonian piety but all of the other relevant features of the congregational situation. In light of the work of Yonina Talmon,[1] the general congruence of this model with the Thessalonian situation is apparent. She uses the term "millenarian" to describe religious movements that expect the total transformation of this world to occur in connection with a cataclism in the near future.[2] The characteristics of such movements include a sense of impending crisis, a this-worldly orientation, a tendency toward ecstatic, antinomian behavior, and competition between inspired prophets and local organizers. "The majority of millenarian movements are *messianic*," Talmon observes, involving the appearance of a "god-ordained representative of the divine," a "long departed warrior hero who comes to life again and rescues his people," or a "culture hero or a departed leader who had been persecuted and put to death by the authorities."[3] Moveover, such movements are typically led by charismatic leaders who are distinct from the messianic, redeemer figure.[4]

Millenarian groups differ in the weight given to historical as compared with mythical time, but in most cases there is "a flight from history to a mythical *Endzeit*."[5] Some groups dwell on the extension of tribulations that will precede the millennial age, while others expect the catastrophe to be a prompt prelude to that age. When the anticipated catastrophy does not arrive on schedule, these movements sometimes fall into despair or disintegration, but in some instances respond to the disappointment with intensified missionary activities and new prophetic oracles. In many

---

[1] Talmon, "Pursuit of the Millennium"; "Millenarian Movements"; "Millenarism."
[2] Talmon writes that "The millenarian conception of salvation is *total* in the sense that the new dispensation will bring about not mere improvement, but a complete transformation and perfection itself. . . . The believers will be liberated from all ills and limitations of human existence. . . . The millennial view of salvation, also is *revolutionary* and *catastrophic*. The world has broken away from the divine and is the incarnation of negativity, a counter-creation. . . . The transition from the present intensified missionary activity and new into the ultimate future is . . . a sudden and revolutionary leap into a totally different level of existence. The transition is usually accompanied by terrible tribulations which are the birth pangs of salvation." "Millenarian Movements," 166f.
[3] Talmon, "Millenarian Movements," 169.
[4] "Millenarian Movements."
[5] Talmon, "Millenarism," 352.

instances, an apocalyptic rejection of the social order results in "cessation of economic activity."[6]

Since Talmon shows that Judaism was the channel through which the millenarian tradition was passed to Christianity and Islam, and thence to the modern world,[7] there is a *prima facie* relevance for a situation like Thessalonians where Jewish-Christian apocalyptic was so central. She contends that Christianity

> . . . derived its initial elan from radical millenarism. It is by its very name a form of messianism. . . . The most important aspects of the development of the messianic doctrine in Christianity are the mythologization of the figure of the Messiah, the universalization of the concept of redemption, and the elaboration of the 'suffering servant' motif. Jesus is conceived of as the incarnation of God, and not just as a God-ordained representative of the divine. The concept of the golden age becomes trans-national and meta-political. . . . Jesus and his followers expected an imminent inauguration of the Kingdom of God and lived in tense expectation of the beginning of the golden age. . . . The subsequent institutionalization of the churches and the influence of Greek philosophy and theology led to the denunciation of millenarism as a Jewish heresy.[8]

Although the subsequent discrediting of millenarism in Christian theology[9] leads to a disinclination on the part of Christian scholars to use this category as an analytic tool,[10] it contains significant explanatory potential for understanding the Thessalonian situation.

1. The Comparative Use
of the Millenarian Model

The question is whether the general congruity between the Thessalonian situation and millenarian movements elsewhere provides sufficient warrant to select this model. Articles by Norman Cohn[11] and George

---

[6] "Millenarism," 354.

[7] Talmon, "Millenarian Movements," 159–65. Hobsbawm draws a similar conclusion, "that classical millenarian movements occur only, or practically only, in countries affected by Judeo-Christian propaganda." *Primitive Rebels,* 57.

[8] Talmon, "Millenarism," 162.

[9] Cf. Sandeen, "Millennialism," 104–7; cf also Sandeen, "The 'Little Tradition,'" and *The Roots of Fundamentalism.* Cf. also Harrison's distinction between respectable, intellectually sophisticated "millennialism" and the more disreputable "folk millenarianism" in *The Second Coming,* 5.

[10] A conspicuous exception is the pathbreaking study by Gager, *Kingdom and Community.*

[11] Cohn, "Medieval Millenarism," 31–43.

Shepperson[12] agreed that Jewish messianism[13] influenced all of the later millenarian movements and that a prophetic or messianic leader was essential in each movement. Nevertheless, the assessment of Yonina Talmon seemed justified at that time in concluding that the "comparative analysis of millenarian movements is at its inception, and attempts to construct a systematic typology are partial and not very satisfactory."[14] There are some indications that the current stage of the discussion allows a larger measure of confidence in comparative studies.[15]

In his study of Jewish messianic movements, Stephen Sharot has recently summarized the prevailing approaches of social scientists to millenarian movements.[16] Some have viewed these movements primarily as protests of the dispossessed against the prevailing political and social order.[17] Some interpret millenarism as a response of vulnerable and oppressed peoples to historical and natural disasters.[18] Others stress the existence of social anomie and relative deprivation as the essential precondition to the rise of millenarian movements.[19] Another approach is to study factors such as societal tension, peculiar kinds of religious orientation and the dynamics of recruitment.[20] Social and political institutions have also been studied in terms of their incapacity to channel protests in traditional avenues, thus giving rise to millenarian movements.[21] The symbolic or intellectual approach views the myths and the social role of millenarian leaders as efforts to replace disfunctional ideologies and social

---

[12] Shepperson, "The Comparative Study."

[13] For a general orientation, cf. Scholem, *The Messianic Idea,* 1–36.

[14] Talmon, "Millenarism," 352. For a more sanguine assessment of the possibilities of comparative studies of millenarian movements at the time of the 1960 conference reflected in Thrupp's collection of essays, cf. her introduction in *Millennial Dreams in Action,* 11–27.

[15] Allen explicitly aims at constructing the foundation for a comparative analysis in "A Theory of Millenialism." He uses relative deprivation theory, stressing the loss of a sense of worth as the key factor in the rise of the Irvingites (p. 299). He shows that the rise of a millenarian movement requires a "millennial heritage," which was present in that case (p. 301). Cf. also Lienesch, "The Role of Political Millennialism."

[16] Sharot, *Messianism, Mysticism, and Magic,* 18f.

[17] Worsley discusses millennial beliefs as "The Religion of the Lower Orders" in *The Trumpet Shall Sound,* 225–27; he argues (p. 243) that the requirement for an active form of millenarism is a "situation of dissatisfaction with existing social conditions and of yearnings for a happier life." Cf. also Lanternari, *The Religions of the Oppressed,* 301–15.

[18] Barkun, *Disaster and the Millennium,* 34–61, provides a more detailed specification of the kind of "stress" identified as essential for the rise of revitalization movements. "Millenarian movements almost always occur in times of upheaval, in the wake of cultural contact, economic dislocation, revolution, war, and natural catastrophe" (p. 45). Cf. Wallace, "Mazeway Disintegration," 23–27; "Mazeway Resynthesis, 626–38; "Revitalization Movements," 264–81.

[19] Aberle, "A Note on Relative Deprivation Theory"; O'Dea and Poblete, "Anomie and the Quest for Community"; Glock, "The Role of Deprivation"; Gurr, *Why Men Rebel,* 59–91.

[20] Lofland and Stark, "Becoming a World Saver"; Lofland, *Doomsday Cult,* 65–189; Beckford, *The Trumpet of Prophecy,* 181–95.

[21] Adas, *Prophets of Rebellion,* 43–91.

systems, offering resolution to problems like cognitive dissonance.[22] A version of this symbolic approach stresses the congruity between social control and organization on the one hand and religious beliefs on the other hand.[23]

Sharot's analysis of a wide range of Jewish millenarian movements indicates the need for a multifaceted approach that can be combined with the historical method. In this sense, his work represents an advance over the study by Sheldon R. Isenberg, who concentrated on a single factor in suggesting that first-century millenarian movements in Palestine were caused by relative deprivation suffered by non-establishment groups whose "access to and/or control over the redemptive media" of law and temple had been blocked.[24] Both Sharot and Isenberg, however, provide significant impetus for our study of the Thessalonian situation, because they use the historical method to study movements in close cultural proximity to the early Christian communities. While many scholars are likely to remain skeptical of the relevance of distant cultural parallels such as twentieth-century cargo cults, these studies of ancient Jewish messianism provide plausible analogues to the Thessalonian situation.

Sharot contends that both the "remedy-compensation perspective" and the theories of "symbolic congruency" throw light on some Jewish millenarian groups, but the previous religious development of a particular tradition also appears to play a crucial role. His conclusion provides a significant basis for our study of an early Christian movement whose ideology was expressed in symbols closely associated with Jewish messianism:

> No one cause or particular combination of causes can account for all the [Jewish messianic] movements. . . . Although each religious movement may to some extent be considered unique, their similarities appear to be greater than the various combinations of causes that gave rise to them. This does not mean that every set of circumstances was so unique and fortuitous as to make comparisons pointless and uninteresting; the important alternative causes were relatively few, and certain combinations of causes were found to occur with some frequency. Nevertheless, the diversity of social experiences appears greater than the variety of religious symbols in which they were expressed. This points to the power of messianic and mystical symbols and beliefs to encompass, to

---

[22] Wilson, *Magic and the Millennium*, 484–504; Wilson, *Religion in Sociological Perspective*; Festinger, Riecken and Schachter, *When Prophecy Fails*, 174–215.
[23] Douglas, *Natural Symbols*; Douglas, "Social Preconditions."
[24] Isenberg, "Millenarism in Greco-Roman Palestine," 32.

condense, and to provide a focus for, the complexities of the human condition.[25]

The coherence of recurrent millenarian symbols and practices in Jewish messianic movements provides a basis for understanding some of the peculiar features of the Thessalonian situation, particularly the implications of the apocalyptic gospel that Paul proclaimed. Even though the direct evidence is entirely literary and relatively sparse as compared with millenarian movements studied by modern anthropologists or historians of mass movements, the details fit with considerable precision in this framework of messianic millenarism. Yet we must keep in mind that the social background of the Thessalonian congregation was almost entirely pagan rather than Jewish. This means that the peculiar social and historical circumstances of the Thessalonian urban environment must be taken into account and correlated with the profile of other non-Jewish millenarian movements that have been studied by modern research.

2. Cultural Conditions Conducive to Millenarism

Several theories about the social conditions that contribute to the rise of millenarian movements offer correlations with the unique environment of Thessalonica, as set forth in chapter 7. The revitalization[26] and mazeway[27] theories developed by Anthony Wallace suggest that when a society's religious system is perceived to fail to provide a coherent explanation of life and an adequate resolution of problems in face of external pressures, the circumstances are at hand for a millenarian movement. Wallace and others had in mind particularly the pressures of economic dislocation, political powerlessness, and forms of colonial exploitation, all of which were present in some form in Thessalonica. The cooptation of the Cabiric cult in Thessalonica and its integration into the civic cult resulted in emptying it of the power to provide solace for handworkers facing economic and social pressure under Roman rule. The religious "mazeway" providing a cognitive map for some of the former devotees was discredited, leaving a vacuum that the proclamation of the apocalyptic Christ could fill. The expectation of a returning Cabirus who would aid the poor and defend them against their oppressors was transformed and revitalized in the new and more compelling form of Christ who was present in the congregation as their redeemer and the source of

---

[25] Sharot, *Messianism, Mysticism, and Magic,* 253.
[26] Wallace, "Revitalization Movements," 264–81.
[27] Wallace, "Mazeway Disintegration," 23–27; "Mazeway Resynthesis," 626–38.

their ecstacy, and who was also proclaimed as coming again in wrath against the wicked.

The participants in the Thessalonian church fit the description of "the oppressed" that Lanternari described, victims of foreign occupation who yearn for "freedom and salvation."[28] As we observed in chapter 7, the church in Thessalonica did not contain members of the civic elite. It consisted largely of persons facing the straightened circumstances of handworkers and day laborers. Deprivation theory lends precision to this observation. David F. Aberle defines relative deprivation as "a negative discrepancy between legitimate expectation and actuality. Where an individual or a group has a particular expectation and furthermore where this expectation is considered to be a proper state of affairs, and where something less than that expectation is fulfilled, we may speak of relative deprivation."[29] He observes that groups experiencing such relative deprivation often express a "sense of blockage," a conviction that "ordinary action" will no longer suffice, which encourages the rise of millenarism.[30] The incapacity of lower-class Greeks in Thessalonica to change their social circumstances in the face of Roman power and the cooptation of their political and religious heritage by an elite working with the Roman authorities constitutes a situation of blockage matching Aberle's definition. Similarly Mary Douglas shows that when social structures are too weak to sustain a coherent cosmology in the face of adverse circumstances, a "passive, benign cosmology" can turn into a "revolutionary millennialism."[31]

Charles Y. Glock discusses five kinds of deprivation, all of which were represented to one degree or another in Thessalonica.[32] We have already referred to the evidence concerning what Glock calls "economic deprivation" and "social deprivation." "Organismic deprivation" is a matter of being cut off from the source of mental or physical health, and "ethical deprivation exists when the individual comes to feel that the dominant values of the society no longer provide him with a meaningful way of organizing his life. . . ."[33] The discrediting of Cabirus as the source of aid for the poor, along with the empty rituals of the civic cult that had debased the earlier democratic ideals of equality and justice could have contributed to the feeling of deprivation on both of these levels. Finally, Glock refers to "psychic deprivation" which is close to "ethical deprivation," a sense of the

---

[28] Lanternari, *The Religions of the Oppressed,* 301.
[29] Aberle, "A Note on Relative Deprivation Theory," 209.
[30] "A Note on Relative Deprivation Theory," 212.
[31] Douglas, *Natural Symbols,* 150.
[32] Glock, "The Role of Deprivation," 27–29.
[33] "The Role of Deprivation," 28.

loss of meaning and philosophical coherence, which would have been particularly acute in Thessalonica because of the fusion of the chief religious cults into a repressive civic establishment. Glock contends that the type of deprivation suffered by a particular group will influence the kind of movement or sect that is likely to arise. In the Thessalonian situation, the formation of a Christian community with a strongly sectarian, millenarian character responded to several types of deprivation simultaneously.

In her study of messianic movements in Brazil and elsewhere, Pereira de Queiros discusses a number of "conditions which appear to us necessary" for their emergence.[34] She mentions the presence of what Max Weber had called a "pariah people" that feels oppressed and is incapable of achieving redress of its grievances, a system of deepening social polarization and stratification, often in connection with colonialism, and socioeconomic disruption often caused by some crisis. She lays particular emphasis on the importance of a social structure that prior to its polarization had been marked by family lineage and extended families.[35] This presents an intriguing parallel to the Thessalonian situation, because the city had been created by joining a number of native villages that kept their identity in the neighborhoods of the city for centuries after the founding. It is likely that the medium of continuity was the extended families and clans that made up those original villages, and it is likely that precisely in such traditional Greek groups the primitive expectation of the redeeming Cabirus was alive. Some of these families were disadvantaged with the arrival of Roman bureaucrats, Latin immigrants, and ambitious Greek immigrants from other parts of the empire, and insofar as they were unable to gain access to Thessalonian elite, would have constituted the type of "pariah people" that Pereira de Queiros describes.

None of these social conditions can be correlated, with a high level of predictive certainty, with the rise of a millenarian movement. The discussion of this issue over the past several decades indicates the there are many instances where some of these conditions are present and no movement arises. There is no point in arguing here that since some of these conditions were present, the Thessalonian situation was necessarily millenarian. A wide range of responses to such conditions can be documented from the history of religion. But on the other hand, one cannot argue in face of this evidence that the Thessalonian situation could not possibly have been millenarian because the typical conditions were absent. In fact, compared with the circumstances of the other Pauline congregations for

---

[34] Pereira de Queiros, "Messianic Myths and Movements," 97.
[35] "Messianic Myths and Movements," 95–97.

which information is available, nowhere else are there so many parallels to the historical and cultural background of definitive millenarian movements. It is therefore appropriate to conclude that the circumstances which have been identified as formative factors in cross-cultural studies of later millenarian movements were uniquely present in Thessalonica.

3. Millenarian Symbols and Beliefs in Thessalonica

The reconstruction of millenarism in Thessalonica must begin with a review of the widely acknowledged evidence that the congregation accepted an apocalyptic theology from Paul. The narration of the basis of Paul's thanksgiving opens with a description of the nature and results of the Thessalonians' conversion (1 Thess 1:6–10). Nowhere in the later Pauline letters does one encounter so thorough a concentration on the apocalyptic future as the center of faith. It was public knowledge, Paul claimed, that the Thessalonians had "turned to God from idols, to serve a living and true God, and to wait for his Son from heaven, whom he raised from the dead, Jesus who delivers us from the wrath to come." The apocalyptic world view implied by this language has been intensively investigated by recent studies.[36] The function of Jesus in this framework was to provide safety for the elect during the period of the apocalyptic tribulation that would result in the destruction of the principalities and powers as well as their earthly adherents. With the dawn of the new age after the completion of the tribulations, Christ was expected to inaugurate an era of millennial bliss. The congregation had accepted this anticipatory form of salvation, Paul reports, having "received the word in much affliction, with joy inspired by the Holy Spirit." They had experienced the violent transition between the old age and the new with the kind of apocalyptic joy that is typical for millenarian movements elsewhere, and they expected the prompt culmination of history.

It is important to grant priority to the millennial ideology itself, rather than assuming that it would automatically arise whenever the conditions for a millenarian movement are present. As Roy Wallis points out, "Historically, the evidence surely points to the prior existence of millennial ideas around which a movement formed in the case of such groups as the Doukhobors, Hutterites, Millerites, Jehovah's Witnesses and numerous others."[37] A structurally similar idea present in Thessalonica prior to

---

[36] Cf. Baumgarten, *Paulus und die Apokalyptik*; Beker, *Paul's Apocalyptic Gospel*; Hellholm, ed., *Apocalypticism*; Rowland, *The Open Heaven*; Russell, *Apocalyptic*.
[37] Wallis, *Salvation and Protest*, 52; cf. also Zygmunt, "Prophetic Failure," 927–33.

Paul's arrival was that Cabirus would return, granting blessings to his true devotees. Disjointed from this expectation but part of the Thessalonian milieu were the utopian yearnings for the return of a golden age and the hope for the recovery of the classic freedom and dignity promised to Greek members of the polis. When one takes into account the background of the Cabiric cult in Thessalonica, with the frustrated expectation that he would return as the benefactor of the poor, one is struck by the degree to which Paul's proclamation of the apocalyptic Christ conformed to the role identified by Periera de Queiros as characteristic of millenarian movements. She refers to the modeling myths of "the arrival of a 'Son of God,' of the reappearance of a cultural hero-figure, or of the return of ancestors" that appear to be present when millenarian movements arise.[38] Without the appearance of such a figure, she observes, all of the necessary conditions for the creation of a millenarian movement may be present with no movement arising. She speaks therefore of "the importance of the Messiah."[39]

The peculiar thing about early Christianity, of course, was that the Messiah figure was perceived to be physically absent to the community, while present spiritually in the form of charismatic experience, and in the person of his emissaries like Paul. Only with his παρουσία at the end of history, when he establishes his global rule, would he be physically present. But this, again, matches the coopted, Cabiric expectations to a degree. Cabirus was perceived to be present but not visible in the orgies of the cult community; his blessings were received and celebrated; and his devotees assumed his identity and shared his divinity, even though he was expected to return at some later time when the community needed his aid once again. The politicization of Cabirus rendered likely the possibility that some people in Thessalonica yearned for a return of Cabirus as a defender and avenger who would reverse their fortunes by establishing a new political order to replace that of Rome.

An important kind of living symbol in the Thessalonian correspondence is that of apostolic leadership. Meeks has shown that Paul ". . . filled at least in part the role of a 'millennial prophet,'" providing the apocalyptic world view and a closely knit sense of community.[40] The clarification of the apostolic example in 1 Thess 2:1–12 seeks to differentiate Paul's model from that of spirit-filled, divinized leaders who flatter and exploit their devotees. There were some in Thessalonica who apparently criticized Paul for not conforming to the more overtly ecstatic and orgiastic

---

[38] Pereira de Queiros, "Messianic Myths and Movements," 90, 97.
[39] "Messianic Myths and Movements," 97.
[40] Meeks, "Social Functions of Apocalyptic Language," 701.

style of leadership. 1 Thess 5:12–13 appears to defend the leaders that Paul left in charge of the congregation against similar criticisms. While conflicts over leadership are characteristic for millenarian movements, it is possible to evaluate more precisely the role that Paul filled in Thessalonica on the basis of the paradigm of the successful charismatic leader worked out by T. K. Oommen. In the context of a nascent millenarian movement, such a leader would succeed in achieving the following:

1. Creating awareness among the people of the social problems and unfolding the possibilities of problem resolution, therefore championing the "felt need";

2. Evolving a new means of solving the problem at hand;

3. Voicing commitment to a pursuance of a goal widely acclaimed by the group;

4. Expressing the message in such a manner as to appeal to a substantial portion of the population under reference.[41]

While Paul had evidently been successful on the first and last points, it is apparent that both he and the congregational leaders were perceived as falling short on the others. Some of the congregation were critical that Paul was not manifesting a sufficient degree of sovereign power so as clearly to manifest the divinity of the redeemer figure in his own person. If the priests of Cabirus had traditionally shared the divine power and freedom of the god, why did Paul fail to give proof of the full recovery of phallic powers in the ecstatic rituals of the congregation? Why was he unable to counter the hostile measures of the authorities and assure the devotees of the protection and blessing of the new benefactor, Christ? Was his precipitous departure under the pressure of the politarchs not evidence of a lack of divine power? And if Jason complied with the authorities' demand to put up bond against a continuation of the Christian orgies, was this not proof that he and other congregational leaders were feckless? Where was the assurance that the goal of salvation was being achieved, that the "peace and security" of the new age were manifest in face of opposition? In these regards, as our study of the "divine man" implications of 1 Thess 2:1–12 revealed, some members of the congregation apparently believed that the ἄτακτοι were more appropriate embodiments of the apostolic role. Their behavior certainly conformed more closely to the culturally favored model of the traditional priests and devotees of the Cabiric cult whose orgies gave proof of their divinization.

In summary, the indications of a tendency on the part of some members of the congregation to drop out of economic activity and civil obligations, and the formulation of Paul's description of their current status as

---

[41] Oommen, "Charisma," 96.

"wait[ing] for his son from heaven" (1 Thess 1:10) indicate that the Thessalonian movement matches what Hobsbawm describes as "the 'pure' millenarian movement."

> Its followers are not makers of revolution. They expect it to make itself, by divine revelation, by an announcement from on high, by a miracle. . . . The part of the people before the change is to gather together, to prepare itself, to watch the signs of the coming doom, to listen to the prophets who predict the coming of the great day, and perhaps to undertake certain ritual measures against the moment of decision and change, or to purify themselves, shedding the dross of the bad world of the present so as to be able to enter the new world in shining purity.[42]

The first letter was written in response to perceived threats to this kind of apocalyptic certainty. The goal of the demonstrative rhetoric of 1 Thessalonians, as we have seen, was to clarify the apocalyptic ethos that was jeopardized by external events and conceptual confusions. The congregation was surprised and shaken by the presence of persecution and the continued possibility of the death of congregational members. The church had evidently interpreted Paul's message about being saved from the wrath to come as the beginning of permanently altered conditions of immortality and bliss. Congregational members were therefore resisting Paul's previous urging of preparedness for a future apocalyptic event. To use Kenelm Burridge's summary, "the millennium is equivalent to salvation and to redemption itself. . . . A new earth merges into the new heaven."[43] In this instance, the experience of salvation in Thessalonica brought with it the expectation that earthly afflictions were no longer possible. The apocalyptic logic of this dilemma is captured by Jouette Bassler: "If one is convinced that the Day of the Lord has come, the Day that brings with it the resolution of all inequities, and if the church nevertheless continues to suffer affliction, then God's justice is immediately and seriously called into question."[44] Although the explicit claim that "the Day of the Lord has come" was not articulated until after the writing of 1 Thessalonians, this kind of conviction is implicit in the peculiar collapse of morale that had been reported to Paul prior to the first letter. Like the movement among the Comanches instigated by Ishatai in the 1870's when the claim of immunity to bullets and raising the dead led to the abortive attack on the U. S. army post at Adobe Wells, the sudden evidence of mortality caused the millenarian overconfidence to collapse.[45]

---

[42] Hobsbawm, *Primitive Rebels*, 59; citation from the 1959 2d ed.
[43] Burridge, *New Heaven, New Earth,* 165.
[44] Bassler, "The Enigmatic Sign," 508.
[45] Wilson, *Magic and the Millennium,* 274f.

4. Millenarian Practices in Thessalonica

At a number of points, behaviorial expressions of a millenarian mass
movement were manifest in Thessalonica. A characteristic trait of millenarian consciousness, Burridge's words, is "a condition of being in which
humans become free-movers, in which there are no obligations. . . ."[46] The
challenge to the sexual ethic in Thessalonica represents an initial phase of
conformity to this pattern: claiming as a right the violation of traditional
sexual mores on grounds that the new age is present. "Copulation goes
with revolution; virile prophets show their followers the way."[47] In the
case of the Thessalonian radicals, the principle of revolutionary promiscuity, rather than its actual enactment, was at issue. This seems to fit in a
general way the pattern that Peter Worsley discovered of "ritual breaking
of taboos" in the cargo cults, relating to a stress on a "new morality" in
which the traditional forms of sexual bonding was challenged. He concludes that "sexual communism and sexual asceticism, both so common in
millenarian movements, are thus two sides of the same coin—the rejection
of outworn creeds."[48]

The desire to shatter creeds and taboos allows us to place our earlier
suggestion of a connection between the ἄτακτοι and the sexual rebellion
on a much more solid basis. As we have suggested, these radicals conformed more closely to the cultural expectation of Cabiric priests and
devotees in the pre-Augustan period than did Paul and his appointed
leaders. They apparently believed that the παρουσία of the redeemer that
they experienced in ecstatic worship should in principle free them also for
the expression of full sexual freedom. The basic rationale seems to be
similar to the Cologne Beghards of the fourteenth century as described by
Howard Kaminsky. The goal of the initiate was

> . . . to allow the divine nature and truth to work in him . . . which was
> the highest liberty and it involved absolute indulgence of the prompt-
> ings of the presumably new nature: he could, for example, take money
> from anyone, deceive anyone, have sexual intercourse with anyone, at
> any time he wished. The only danger was that he might submit to some
> restraint and hence 'fall away from the freedom of the spirit. . . .'[49]

Similarly, the Sabbatian Movement in the seventeenth century provided
believers a sense of freedom stemming from "a world made pure again."[50]

---

[46] Burridge, *New Heaven, New Earth*, 165.
[47] *New Heaven, New Earth*, 167.
[48] Worsley, *The Trumpet Shall Sound*, 250f.
[49] Kaminsky, "The Free Spirit," 167.
[50] Scholem, *The Messianic Idea*, 87f.

The new commandment taught by Sabbatai Zvi involved "the holiness of sin" which expressed itself particularly in violating sexual codes.[51]

In the Thessalonian church, this kind of freedom was being argued in principle, but it was not yet being carried out. But the logic from the Thessalonian religious tradition was apparently compelling for a small minority: if the replacement of Cabirus is at hand, can the sacred phallus still be buried and under the control of his murderers? Should not the repression that marked both the Augustan cooptation of the orgiastic cult and Paul's traditional ethical teaching be abandoned? The challenge against the sexual ethic, which we detected in Paul's rhetoric of 1 Thess 4:1-8, is thus historically as well as anthropologically comprehensible.

The abandonment of daily occupations by the ἄτακτοι, which was apparently being supported by some members of the congregation, has many parallels in millenarian movements. As Talmon shows, the typical result of "total rejection of the social order . . . [is] radical withdrawal and noncooperation. Cessation of economic activity, political nonparticipation . . . are frequent concomitants of millenarism."[52] The basic idea is that work as a symbol of the old, fallen age should be replaced with innocent play when the new age arrives or is celebrated. For instance, the Taborites in Hussite Bohemia taught that when the millennium began, the conditions of paradise would be restored. "Those elect still living will be brought back to the state of innocence of Adam in Paradise, like Enoch and Elijah, and they will be without any hunger or thirst, or any other spiritual or physical pain."[53] Those who joined the movement abandoned their occupations, pooled their property, and enjoyed love feasts in a communal life, anticipating the arrival of the thousand year kingdom.

The Old Believers in Nizhny Novgorod followed this pattern of behavior in a different cultural setting. They abandoned their fields and homes in response to the prophecy that the millennial trumpet would sound in 1669.[54] The voluntary killing of cattle by the Xhosa tribespeople in 1856, entailing their abandonment of their main economic pursuit, was described by Bonnie Keller as "an almost 'pure' millenarian response" to external pressure.[55] A prophetic vision informed the tribe that they could prevail over invading white settlers if they renounced witchcraft and killed their cattle, which would be restored in the millennium. The date for its arrival was set in the summer of 1856, with the expectation that it would reunite the tribe with its ancestral spirits, provide a restoration of youth,

---

[51] *The Messianic Idea,* 110–13; cf. also Scholem, *Sabbatai Sevi,* 792–820.
[52] Talmon, "Millenarism," 354.
[53] Kaminsky, "The Free Spirit," 170.
[54] Stark, *The Sociology of Religion* 2:218f.
[55] Keller, "Millenarianism and Resistance," 98.

and a guarantee of paradisical plentitude. In preparation, the tribespeople also consumed their stores of grain and refused to plant their fields, all of which caused a disastrous famine when the millennium failed to arrive.

The cessation of economic activity in the Melanesian cargo cults was closely associated with ecstatic celebration, throwing light on the correlation between work denial and ecstatic celebration among the radicals in Thessalonica. Mircea Eliade provides this vivid description:

> . . . the period of waiting for the catastrophe which will precede the Golden Age is marked by a series of actions expressing an absolute detachment from ordinary values and behavior. Pigs and cows are slaughtered in a holocaust; all savings are spent in order to have done with European money . . . cemeteries are put in order and decked with flowers and new pathways are made; then all work ceases and the people await the dead around banquet tables. . . . The young men and the young women live in a common house; in the daytime they bathe together and they pass the night in dancing.[56]

The manifestation of ecstatic behavior, threatening the reputation of the congregation in Thessalonica, is therefore also a typical expression of millenarian eschatology. Worsley observes that millenarian movements are usually "highly emotional," suggesting that hysterical, irrational behavior expresses the social tensions caused by previous conditions as well as relief at the presence of the new age.[57] Talmon makes the generalization that "millenarian movements tend to be ecstatic. In most movements the ritual involves wild and often frenzied emotional display. We encounter in many millenarian movements cases of hysterical and paranoid phenomena, mass possession, trances, fantasies, and in others ecstatic dance figures prominently."[58] Michael Barkun devotes an entire chapter to the "sources and functions of ecstatic behavior,"[59] which is so omnipresent and varied in its expression in millenarian movements that no single explanation seems adequate. In the final analysis, he contends that ecstasy is "motivated by nostalgia" to regain the utopian state beyond the threat of current circumstances.[60] As in the celebrations of the Cabiric cult, the relief from danger and the initiation into communion with the god gives devotees a momentary sense of sharing the divine power, with all

---

[56] Eliade, "'Cargo Cults' and Cosmic Regeneration," 141f. Cf. Segal, "Eliade's Theory of Millenarianism," for a critique of the idea that millenarism is the regain contact with primordial time. This critique relates to the interpretive framework used in Eliade's study of the cargo cults, but does appear to affect his description of their rituals.

[57] Worsley, *The Trumpet Shall Sound*, 248–50.

[58] Talmon, "Millenarism," 351.

[59] Barkun, *Disaster and the Millennium*, 129–65.

[60] *Disaster and the Millennium*, 165.

its freedom and joy. Hence the ecstasy evident in Thessalonica seems intrinsically linked with the ἄτακτοι's sense of participating already in a divine reality that opposed in principle the limits of earthly existence.

A widespread tendency to overturn everyday patterns of behavior, similar to the basic stance of the ἄτακτοι, was discovered by Steven Sharot in Jewish millenarian movements. For instance, the Frankist Movement in the eighteenth century taught that "the road to life was through nihilism, the rejection of all religions and morals. . . . Men had not only to abandon all religion and laws but also to perform 'strange deeds,' which were intended to negate man's self-respect. Sin became sacred, and among the Frankists, as among other antinomian groups, this principle was expressed in deviant sexual behavior and orgiastic rites."[61] Frank urged his followers, "Throw away what you have learned! Trample on all the laws you have obeyed and obey only me."[62] The Frankist rites involved ecstatic songs and dances and celebrated the presence of the spirit by sexual orgies.[63] Such devaluing of bodily ethics and absolutizing of the spirit is reminiscent of the scope of the anthropological trichotomy that Paul cited in a clarified apocalyptic context in 1 Thess 5:23, insisting that humans are to be kept intact until the parousia.

The structure of the conflict over leadership evident in Thessalonica conforms to the typical pattern of millenarian movements. Talmon describes the typical bifurcation between charismatic and routine leaders: "Leadership tends to be charismatic. The intense and total commitment required by millenarism is summoned forth by leaders who are considered to be set apart from ordinary men and endowed with supernatural power. Often there is also not just one charismatic leader but a multiple leadership . . . we find in a number of instances a division of leadership between the inspired prophet and the organizer who is concerned with practical matters."[64] The evidence that we have examined in 1 Thess 5:12–13 indicates that sober organizers and patrons left in charge of the congregation by Paul were being challenged by charismatics who opposed subordination on principle.[65] The challenge also included a critique of Pauline leadership on grounds that he had not demonstrated charismatic qualities, in which arena the critics apparently claimed special gifts. It is likely that the resistance to authority and the preference for charismatic boldness

---

[61] Sharot, *Messianism, Mysticism, and Magic,* 137.

[62] Mandel, *The Militant Messiah,* 40.

[63] *The Militant Messiah,* 41f.

[64] Talmon, "Millenarism," 351.

[65] Cf. Meeks' discussion of a similar feature in the Corinthian situation, in *The First Urban Christians,* 120: "The Spirit is no respecter of persons . . . such power does not usually flow only in the normal channels of authority created by society, with its roles and statuses."

were linked with the ἄτακτοι whose very identification connotes such traits. The continued activity of this group is evident in 2 Thess 3:6–15, and the prophetic oracle refuted in 2 Thess 2:2 probably also stemmed from this circle.

5. Conclusion:
Millenarian Radicalism in Thessalonica

The description of the Thessalonian situation as marked by "millenarian radicalism" is preferable to the alternatives that have been suggested such as "enthusiastic" or "gnostic." In contrast to the Corinthian situation where such terms appear quite appropriate, there is no evidence in 1 or 2 Thessalonians that the congregation tended to identify knowledge or wisdom with spirit, nor that they favored a docetic Christology. Incipient forms of gnostic dualism may be visible in the anthropological trichotomy of 1 Thess 5:23 as well as the rejection of the sexual and work ethics, but such dualism was widely prevalent in the Greco-Roman world. The crucial element in the Thessalonian situation was the apocalyptic orientation that some radicals interpreted in the direction of realized eschatology. Paul's proclamation of the apocalyptic Christ was understood by these radicals along the lines of the discredited Cabiric cult, in which the benefactor was expected to return in defense of laborers to establish a realm of freedom and bliss. Divinization was expected to result from the ecstatic celebration of the παρανσία of the new redeemer figure, Christ, so that death and misfortune would no longer be possible. This radical form of millenarism was embodied by the ἄτακτοι, who resisted on principle the structures of everyday life including the work ethic, the sexual ethic, and the authority of congregational leadership. They refused to prepare for a future παρουσία of Christ because in principle they were experiencing and embodying it already in their ecstatic activities.

When persecution flared up and members of the congregation died, the inflated millenarian consciousness suffered a crisis of morale. In this regard, the Thessalonian situation is rather atypical of other millenarian movements. As Gerlach and Hine observe, "by its very nature, opposition can facilitate the spread of a movement. Without opposition from the established order, there would be no risk, no bridge-burning, and hence no commitment required for participation."[66] This generalization holds for millenarian movements of the pre-millennial type, because opposition to the future kingdom is anticipated as part of the tribulation period

---

[66] Gerlach and Hine, *People, Power, Change*, 183.

before the dawn of the millennium. But the situation would be very different once the millennium is perceived to have dawned. The recurrence of suffering would then jeopardize the claim of the recovery of paradisical conditions. In the case of the Thessalonians, the radicality of the realized eschatology rendered them vulnerable to collapse when death and persecution arose. The benefaction of the new redeemer figure and the divinization claimed by the radicals in behalf of the congregation proved ineffective. Doubts were expressed about the legitimacy and efficacy of the new faith and criticisms were made about the incapacity of Paul and the leaders he had left in charge of the congregation to embody a sufficient amount of divine power to protect the congregation, ensuring the presence of the new age.

Paul responded to the crisis of a radicalized and hence vulnerable millenarism by writing 1 Thessalonians. But for some reason the letter provoked the radicals to intensify their activities in directions that countered the thrust of Paul's intended argument. They refused to return to their normal occupations or to curtail their ecstatic activities as suggested by the letter. They rejected the interventions of the congregational leaders that were suggested in 1 Thessalonians, increasing their commitment to countercultural activities. In this situation of deepening radicalism, the ecstatic message was suddenly proclaimed by the ἄτακτοι that the Day of the Lord had arrived. For some reason Paul's teaching and letter as well as the ecstatic spirit of the radicals were used to support the legitimacy of this exciting claim of millenarian inauguration (2 Thess 2:2). What had hitherto been merely implicit in the activities of the radicals was now stated in final form: the millennium has come. Paul responds in irritation and disbelief to this incredible report by writing 2 Thessalonians, whose rhetoric centers on a refutation of the false new doctrine, and whose tone is vastly different from 1 Thessalonians.

It is difficult to determine the extent to which the radical self-consciousness of the ἄτακτοι, with their belief in the present possession of immortal existence in the spirit, their challenge to the work and sexual ethics, and their obstinant resistance to authority, was shared by the congregation as a whole. It is clear that the ἄτακτοι were a distinct group within the congregation and that they alone had ceased working for their daily bread. By the time of writing 2 Thessalonians, their resistance against the admonitions of the congregational leaders and the counsel of Paul's letter led to the command that they should be ostracized (2 Thess 3:6).[67] Yet in 2 Thess 3:12 Paul exhorts the ἄτακτοι "in the Lord Jesus Christ" to take up their occupations again, so that one must assume they remained a part of

---

[67] Cf. Neil, *Thessalonians,* 192.

the congregation. The fact that they were supported financially by the congregation indicates that their behavior and theology were approved by a sizable and influential segment of the membership. Another indication of solidity and support between the radicals and other congregational members is visible in 2 Thess 2:2, because the ecstatic word that the parousia had come appears to have been accepted by the congregation as a whole. A similar impression is gained when one reflects on the form of argument employed in 1 Thessalonians, thanking God that the Thessalonians had indeed experienced faith, hope and love in response to the powerful message concerning the new age. This argument countered the collapse in morale suffered by the entire congregation that was provoked by the presence of unexpected persecution and the death of congregational members. There is no indication in the opening chapters of 1 Thessalonians that only a portion of the congregation was affected by these problems. The collapse of overinflated expectations of a trouble free life in the new age appears to have affected the congregation as a whole as well as the ἄτακτοι. In several regards, therefore, the radicals and the congregation as a whole appear to have shared much the same general outlook. Perhaps the best way to describe the situation is that while a large portion of the congregation tended toward millenarian radicalism, only a small minority of its members carried these tendencies to the extent of dropping out of their normal occupations and developing a stance of resistance against congregational leaders and traditional morality.

Chapter Ten

THE RECEPTION OF 1 THESSALONIANS
& THE PROVENANCE OF 2 THESSALONIANS

The Reception of 1 Thessalonians
and the Provenance of 2 Thessalonians

The resources are now at hand to cope with the puzzling question of why 2 Thessalonians was written so soon after 1 Thessalonians and why it contains such odd references to an earlier letter. The rhetoric of both 1 and 2 Thessalonians in the interaction with a congregation marked by millenarian radicalism needs to be taken into account in dealing with these puzzles. A major question is how the Thessalonian radicals could possibly have made a case that Paul's earlier teaching and his first letter sustained the claim that the millennium was present. After discussing the theories explaining the curious references to a previous letter, I turn to the passages in 1 Thessalonians that could possibly have been misunderstood in precisely the direction intimated in 2 Thess 2:2. The evidence sustains the hypothesis that a misunderstanding of 1 Thessalonians which is comprehensible in the context of a millenarian movement called forth the writing of 2 Thessalonians in its present form.

1. Approaches to the Previous Letter

The obvious place to begin this investigation is with the references to a previous letter in 2 Thess 2:1–2 and 3:14 and with Paul's unmistakable signature appended in 2 Thess 3:17–18. There are three basic approaches that have been taken to explain the peculiar features of these references. The first is forgery, which we dealt with in chapter 1. Despite my conclusion that the evidence does not sustain this alternative, it remains an effective and forthright approach that takes some of the implications of these verses with full seriousness. The logical inference to be drawn from 2 Thess 2:2 is that the advocates of the false doctrine are calling upon Paul's first letter to the Thessalonians as their authority. Hence Marxsen concludes that the forger of 2 Thessalonians refers to the letter "as from us" in order to deny the legitimacy of adducing the authority of 1 Thessalonians.[1] Wolfgang Trilling concurs in taking "as from us" as actually written by Paul, so that the reference is probably to the imminent

---

[1] Marxsen, *Der zweite Thessalonicherbrief*, 80.

expectation expressed in 1 Thess 4:15 and 17, which the forger wishes to oppose.[2]

This approach has somewhat more difficulty in achieving a consistent explanation of 2 Thess 2:15, where the author exhorts the congregation to hold fast to the Pauline tradition "either by word or by letter." If this is a reference to a virtually canonical authority of the Pauline letters, as Trilling argues,[3] it seems contradictory to the forger's purpose to sustain what he had sought to discredit in 2 Thess 2:2. Marxsen is forced to argue that the singular "letter" really stands for a plural "letters," meaning the Pauline letter corpus, minus 1 Thessalonians which 2 Thessalonians is designed to replace. But the wording reveals that the author of the forgery is not really interested in encouraging support of the other Pauline letters, Marxsen acknowledges. As a final admission in this zigzag series of inferences, Marxsen says it was not in fact easy for the author to carry through consistently with the pseudonymity.[4] It is apparently even more difficult to incorporate the details of this verse into a consistent hypothesis *about* pseudonymity!

The reference to Paul's signature in 2 Thess 3:17 seems at first glance to fit smoothly into the forgery hypothesis. The claim of authenticity is understandable in a forgery, as Schmidt, Wrede, Trilling, and Marxsen have shown.[5] But it is awkward that the forger expressed this claim with the assertion that "this is the mark in *every* letter of mine; it is the way I write," particularly if this kind of signature is allegedly not at the end of every Pauline letter. The advocates of the forgery hypothesis deny that this could be a reference to the closing greeting or admonition that Paul sometimes places in his own hand, because this would undermine the case for pseudonymity. But this in turn requires a clumsy hypothesis about what precisely is intended by the word "every." Marxsen offers two rather contradictory explanations at this point, for example. On the one hand the forger wished to insist that in any comparison between the eschatology of his forgery and that of 1 Thessalonians, it is 2 Thessalonians which must be viewed as authentic. On the other hand the forger sought to raise his letter to a rank of primacy in the already published Pauline letter corpus.[6] Since Marxsen frankly states that the first explanation reflects a counter-forgery strategy on the part of the writer of 2 Thessalonians,[7] it appears to

---

[2] Trilling, *Der zweite Brief,* 75–77.

[3] *Der zweite Brief,* 127–29.

[4] Marxsen, *Der zweite Thessalonicherbrief,* 94.

[5] Schmidt, in Trilling, *Untersuchungen,* 161; Wrede, *Die Echtheit,* 54ff.; Trilling, *Untersuchungen,* 101–8; Marxsen, *Der zweite Thessalonicherbrief,* 104f.

[6] Marxsen, *Der zweite Thessalonicherbrief,* 105.

[7] Cf. Brox, *Falsche Verfasserangaben,* 24f., 34f.; Lindemann, "Zum Abfassungen," 40.

contradict the authority of Paul's other writings that are recommended as authoritative in 2 Thess 2:15. This would also seem to run counter to the hope that 2 Thessalonians would be viewed as having primacy in an already authoritative letter collection. Trilling avoids some of these discrepancies by rejecting the counter-forgery approach, but this leaves him with no real explanation of the reference to Paul's mark in "every letter," except that it represents a "massive" claim to authenticity.[8] Massivity is hardly an appropriate description of a motif which is actually contradictory to a theory of pseudonymity in this case. Trilling fails to address the puzzle that the author expresses himself in such a way as to invite immediate comparisons with the other letters, where in fact, according to Trilling, such signatures are not present. A more sensible and straightforward inference was drawn by George Milligan in 1904: if 2 Thess 3:17 ". . . had been the work of a forger, he would surely have been more careful to follow St. Paul's general usage. . . ."[9]

One is led to conclude, therefore, that the forgery hypothesis as worked out thus far does not provide a satisfactory account of the peculiar shape of the evidence in 2 Thessalonians concerning its relation to the earlier Thessalonian letter. While there is a clear implication at several points in 2 Thessalonians that a forgery was suspected by its author, it appears impossible to provide a consistent and convincing account of the peculiar contours of these three references. The details in 2 Thess 2:2 and 3:17 appear to contradict those in 2 Thess 2:15, and the reference to Paul's mark in "every letter" remains a conundrum.

A second approach to this evidence is to deny the implications of the suspicion of forgery in 2 Thessalonians. This may be illustrated by Ernest Best's argument that "if Paul had thought they had been deceived in this way he would have made his denunciation of the forgery much clearer."[10] He goes on to conclude "that Paul himself does not know where the Thessalonians received their misleading information, and so he lists three possibilities. . . ."[11] But it is interesting that Best is forced by the wording of 2 Thess 3:17 to open up the possibility that he had denied in relation to 2 Thess 2:2: "This does not however imply that forgeries were actually in existence, but on the vague chance that there may have been some this provides reassurance. . . ."[12] The admission of this possibility reveals why it is impossible to dismiss the reference in 2 Thess 2:2 as a completely groundless supposition on the author's part; when a writer returns to the

---

[8] Trilling, *Der zweite Brief,* 160.
[9] Milligan, "The Authenticity," 450.
[10] Best, *Thessalonians,* 278.
[11] *Thessalonians,* 279.
[12] *Thessalonians,* 347.

forgery theme as he does in 2 Thess 3:17 with a solemn reference to an authenticating signature, this lends obvious weight to the wording of the earlier passage. These details lead one to doubt the cogency of Best's opening contention. That Paul should have proceeded in a more denunciatory manner than he did in 2 Thess 2:2 if the suspicion of forgery was a real one in his mind is a facile contention that Best does not even attempt to document; it is a common sense argument that presumes what a modern exegete finds reasonable must have been reasonable for Paul. The attempt to downplay the precise contours of the wording of these two verses is related to Best's preference for connecting "as from us" in 2 Thess 2:2 with all three of the substantives, "spirit, word or letter." This has the effect of diluting the forgery possibility, but it faces the serious disadvantage of implying that the spirit the Thessalonians had experienced came from Paul and his coworkers.[13] This option was widely debated in nineteenth century commentaries, with Bornemann drawing the logical conclusion by 1904: "The reference to μήτε διά πνεύματος is surely excluded, because the πνεῦμα here is clearly thought of in the context of prophetic, ecstatic speech, and this cannot be derived from Paul."[14]

It seems clear that the option of denying the suspicion of forgery is far less successful in explaining the references to the earlier letter than the more forthright forgery hypothesis. Rather than explaining the evidence as it stands, this approach attempts to pare it back and make it more palatable for modern apologetics. But the reiteration of the forgery motif in 2 Thess 3:17 robs this approach of any plausibility. And the effort to show that the reference to the ecstatic spirit of 2 Thess 2:2 is to Paul's own spirit seems so inconsistent with Pauline theology and usage that it is not even argued in detail by current representatives of this option.

A third approach is that Paul's argument in 1 Thessalonians was being seriously misinterpreted by some members of the congregation. The advocates of the idea that "the day of the Lord has come" had called on the authority of Paul's letter as well as perhaps his word and the ecstatic spirit that had empowered their prophecy. Thus when Paul speaks of the letter "as from us," he is denying that any letter he and his colleagues had written contained such a doctrine. As developed by Dobschütz, Dibelius, Frame and others,[15] this approach takes the wording of 2 Thess 2:2 at face value. It also allows the reaffirmation of the forgery suspicion in 2 Thess 3:17 to determine the degree of seriousness with which Paul appears to have taken the possibility in 2 Thess 2:2. F. F. Bruce provides a fair

---

[13] Best, *Thessalonians*, 278; cf. also Marshall, *1 and 2 Thessalonians*, 186f.
[14] Bornemann, *Die Thessalonicherbriefe*, 361.
[15] Dobschütz, *Die Thessalonicher-Briefe*, 266f.; Dibelius, *An die Thessalonicher I, II*, 44; Frame, *Thessalonians*, 247; Oepke, *Thessalonicher*, 158.

statement of one aspect of this position: "The particle ὡς does not definitely deny the writer's authorship of the epistle in question: the misunderstanding may or may not have arisen from an epistle, and if it has so arisen, the epistle may or may not be authentic. If the reference is to an authentic epistle (and the genuineness of 2 Thessalonians itself be accepted), we should have to think of a misunderstanding of 1 Thessalonians."[16]

The open-endedness of the expression "as from us" in 2 Thess 2:2 allows a range of possibilities that can be narrowed by 2 Thess 3:17, where it becomes clear that a misunderstanding had arisen from a letter purporting to be from Paul, but that such a misunderstanding or such a forgery should be discarded in light of the indisputable Pauline handwriting that he now appends. J. T. Ubbink's study of the phrasing of 2 Thess 2:2 confirms this construal, suggesting that the eschatological excitement of the congregation caused the misinterpretation of both his preaching on the first visit and his letter in the sense that the end of time had arrived.[17] This misinterpretation was so gross, however, that Paul could not comprehend how it might have come from his letter. A misunderstanding on this scale raised the serious possibility in his mind of an actual forgery.

The assertion of authenticity in 2 Thess 3:17 fits in smoothly with the misunderstanding hypothesis. Since Paul is referring to his own awkward writing (cf. Gal 6:11) at the end of the letter as the "sign" of authenticity, there is no need to resort to elaborate theories about this letter displacing others or claiming primacy. The handwriting could simply be checked against the first letter to determine whether in fact a forgery was present. There is no need in this approach to deny that other Pauline letters, including 1 Thessalonians, contained final greetings or postscripts in Paul's hand, typical features of Greco-Roman letter writing.[18] There is in fact evidence of such a personal handwriting by the author at the end of 1 Thessalonians. The sudden change to first person style in 1 Thess 5:27 indicates "that Paul took over the pen at this point and added the adjuration and the concluding benediction with his own hand. . . ."[19] One of the advantages of this hypothesis is that checking the handwriting at the end of 2 Thessalonians would likely have been a possibility at the time suggested for the alleged forgery, because the autographs of several of Paul's letters would have still been available. In short, the wording of 2 Thess 3:17 would have entailed very real risks for a forger, but would

---

[16] Bruce, *Thessalonians*, 164.
[17] Ubbink, "ὡς δι' ἡμῶν (2 Thess 2,2)."
[18] Cf. Koskenniemi, *Studien zur Idee*, 169.
[19] Bruce, *Thessalonians*, 135, referring to the study by Askwith, "'I' and 'We.'"

have been very natural and unproblematic if the author of the second letter were the same as the author of the first.

Finally, this approach allows a perfectly consistent construal of 2 Thess 2:15, where Paul reaffirms the authority of his first letter. To speak in the past tense of the letter in which "you were taught by us" would be unnatural as a reference to a letter now being written, so it cannot easily refer to 2 Thessalonians itself.[20] In the rhetoric of 2 Thessalonians, this exhortation follows the clarification of the eschatological doctrine that had been misconstrued from Paul's earlier letter. His intent in this verse as well as in the other two references to the letter is to distinguish between his teaching in 1 Thessalonians as it was originally intended and a misinterpretation or forgery.

On the basis of this examination of the alternatives, it seems clear that the evidence is most easily explained by the hypothesis of a serious misunderstanding of Paul's first letter on the part of its recipients. The question is whether there are passages in 1 Thessalonians that could have been subject to a misconstrual on so large a scale that Paul could have suspected a forgery. This question needs to be retained in its sharpest form as we investigate some of the details in 1 Thessalonians from the perspective of the millenarian piety that we have reconstructed.

2. Passages Susceptible to Misunderstanding

Earlier advocates of the misinterpretation theory have suggested several passages in 1 Thessalonians that could have led to the mistaken idea that the parousia had already come or was so imminent that it might occur immediately.[21] On the basis of more recent exegetical developments, a comprehensive list of such passages may now be discussed. The first three instances could have evoked the impression in Thessalonica that the parousia was so imminent that no intervening events would have to occur before the end of time arrived. The last three could have been misused by radicals in Thessalonica to claim that Paul himself had written that the day of the Lord had already arrived.

(a) 1 Thess 2:18a

Paul's reference to his urgent and repeated[22] wish to visit the Thessalonians again could have been construed as an expression of his fear that

---

[20] Dobschütz, *Die Thessalonicher-Briefe,* 301; Bruce, *Thessalonians,* 193.
[21] Cf. Dobschütz, *Die Thessalonicher-Briefe,* 266–68.
[22] Cf. Morris, "KAI APAX KAI DIS."

the end would come before he would be able to provide what was lacking in their faith (1 Thess 3:10). The fact that Paul viewed his own missionary task from an apocalyptic perspective would lend weight to such inferences.[23] Even if Paul did not teach that he was "the restrainer" of 2 Thess 2:6 as Oscar Cullmann and others have suggested,[24] he certainly interpreted his task as that of eschatological advocate of divine righteousness who was called by God's mercy to save the elect from the coming wrath. Given this definition of Paul's role, it may well have appeared logical for some of the recipients of 1 Thessalonians to infer that if Paul was so anxious about returning before the parousia, and had finally been frustrated in doing so, the intervening weeks may well have included the date of the parousia itself.

(b) 1 Thess 2:18b

This reference to the hindrance of Satan might have been susceptible to fallacious inferences because Paul had taught the traditional apocalyptic doctrine that an increase of demonic activity was a sign of the end of the world (cf. 2 Thess 2:3–12). Satan was expected to engage the forces of light in an intensified struggle for control of the world, a struggle that would be ended by Satan's defeat in the parousia.[25] Paul pictures the devil as intending to snatch away his "crown" at the last minute before the day of judgment by means of the "hindrance" (1 Thess 2:18–19) and the "temptations" faced by the congregation (1 Thess 3:5). This imagery might have intensified the impression in the congregation that the end was so imminent that only an announcement of its arrival was now required.

(c) 1 Thess 5:1–5

The reference to the return of Christ as a "thief in the night" could easily have encouraged an overly heated expectation of an imminent event. Dobschütz remarks that this passage "awakens the impression that Paul wanted it [the expectation of the parousia] even heightened."[26] As Graydon F. Snyder observes in his study of endtime sayings, "By taking away signs of the end and comparing the end to a thief in the night, the church placed a heavy threat of immediacy on the hearer. . . ."[27] Viewed from our distance as those who do not share the millenarian expectations of Paul and his hearers, we assume that Paul communicated the impres-

---

[23] Cf. Denis, "L'Apôtre Paul," 315–18.
[24] Cullmann, *Christ and Time*, 164–66; Munck, *Paul and the Salvation*, 36–39; for an alternative viewpoint and a review of the interpretive options, cf. Otto Betz, "Der Katechon."
[25] Cf. Best, *Thessalonians*, 127; Kallas, *The Satanward View*, 23.
[26] Dobschütz, *Die Thessalonicher-Briefe*, 203.
[27] Snyder, "Sayings on the Delay," 32.

sion that the parousia was yet in the future (1 Thess 5:2). But did the Thessalonians also understand "will come" in this sense? The implication of stealthy arrival and the warning to keep constantly ready could well have been understood in the sense that the Day of the Lord would occur immediately. Might this not have given someone the basis to say, 'Since the day when Paul wrote the letter to us, the parousia has indeed come'?

The predilection toward apocalyptic immediacy that Johannes Munck detected in the Thessalonian congregation lends credence to this suggestion: he showed that the Christians "had endured their sufferings in the assurance that Christ would end their tribulation by coming soon." They had felt that theirs was to be "the last persecution immediately before the Second Coming."[28] This misperception was consistent with the generalization that Munck makes about other apocalyptic references in the Thessalonian correspondence, namely ". . . how difficult it must have been for former gentiles really to understand the new gospel that Paul brought them."[29]

(d) 1 Thess 3:11–13

The wording of this benediction is such that hearers might have drawn the conclusion that the παρουσία was a present reality. The optative verbs of request, "Now may God . . . direct . . . increase . . . abound . . . establish," have an open time frame that preserves in the blessing form the sense that God is currently acting to provide what is requested.[30] There is no future verb in this benediction to maintain the intended future sense of the "presence of the Lord Jesus with all his saints."[31] Unless the recipients were fully acquainted with Paul's Hebraically conceived apocalyptic system, they might not have caught the future intention. The other reference to the parousia in the context of a benediction (1 Thess 5:23) contains the same possibility of misunderstanding. There are even examples of modern scholars inferring from Paul's wording in such verses as these that the parousia should be conceived as presently in the process of coming.[32] If Christopher L. Mearns is correct in inferring that Paul had taught a realized eschatology during his founding visit to Thessalonica,[33] this kind of inference would have been sustained by Paul's "word" as well

---

[28] Munck, "1 Thess i. 9–10," 100.

[29] "1 Thess i. 9–10," 109.

[30] Cf. Jewett, "Form and Function," 23f., 34.

[31] Note that the RSV seeks to provide what is missing in this benediction by translating παρουσία as "coming" rather than "presence." Marxsen, Der erste Brief, 52, avoids this by translating this term with the technical term "Parousie."

[32] Cf. Ware, "The Coming of the Lord," 109–20, esp. 116: "For Paul the Parousia was imminent: It could be felt to be in the process of happening."

[33] Mearns, "Early Eschatological Developments," 137–57.

as his "letter" (2 Thess 2:2). The fact that intense experiences of realized eschatology were often associated with early Christian worship[34] lends weight to the possibility of this misconstrual of benedictory formulas that probably originated in homiletic settings.[35] As we have already established in our reconstruction of the cultural background of the Thessalonian ἄτακτοι, they were predisposed to celebrate the presence of the divine benefactor in the person of his ecstatic devotees. Even if the recipients did not infer that the parousia was being experienced while the benediction itself was declared in the reading of the letter, the basis was laid for an expectation of such imminence that the ecstatic announcement of 1 Thess 2:2 might have appeared plausible.

(e) 1 Thess 2:16

That God's wrath "has come upon" the Jews "at last" is one of the most controversial contentions in 1 Thessalonians, which as we have seen in chapter 3 (pp. 36–45), has given rise a series of interpolation theories. Although the authenticity of this passage remains likely despite these vigorous arguments to the contrary, the awkwardness both in terms of anti-Judaic implications and eschatological urgency cannot be denied. The latter point is intensified by the fact that in 1 Thess 1:10 Paul had described the salvation of the congregation in terms of being "delivered from the wrath to come." In the context of an apocalyptic world view, wrath implies an intensification of the final drama of world history, in which the evil age is entering into its violent retribution because the bowl of its transgressions is full to overflowing. The new age arrives in its fullness when the bowl of wrath finally spills over to destroy the old age and its wicked inhabitants.[36] Given this conceptual framework which Paul not only believed but also shared with the Thessalonians, the possibilities of drawing radical conclusions from 1 Thess 2:16 were very real: 'If the wrath has already arrived, then the hinge event between the old and the new ages must have occurred, and we must now be in millennial blessedness.'[37]

---

[34] Cf. Aune, *The Cultic Setting,* 134f.
[35] Cf. Jewett, "Form and Function," 29–34.
[36] Cf. Marxsen, *Der erste Brief,* 49f.
[37] Cf. Dobschütz, *Die Thessalonicher-Briefe,* 266f.; Krodel draws similar conclusions, while assuming that 1 Thess 2:13–16 had been interpolated prior to the period when he believes 2 Thessalonians was forged: "If the wrath of God has already come upon the Jews . . . and the Christians already experience the messianic woes in their suffering (2 Thess. 1:4), then the conclusion could be drawn that 'the Day of the Lord is present' (2:2c)." *2 Thessalonians,* 87.

(f) 1 Thess 5:6–10

There is a well-known confusion in Paul's use of the metaphor of sleep in this passage. While καθεύδω refers to biological sleep in verses 6 and 8, it appears to many commentators to refer to death in verse 10.[38] Recently Thomas R. Edgar has made a case against this majority view, suggesting that 1 Thess 5:10 uses "sleep" to refer to biological sleeping and thus metaphorically to a lack of vigilance.[39] He points out that the verb for sleep in 5:10, καθεύδω, is different from that used in 1 Thess 4:13, κοιμάω, which undermines the connection many exegetes have alluded to in this context. It is precisely the same verb as Paul uses to refer to biological sleep in 5:6 and 8. I do not find Edgar's explanation in terms of metaphorical vigilance too convincing for 5:10. I believe it more likely that Paul meant to deal with a potential misunderstanding of the "sleep/awake" rhetoric, namely that you do not have to go to bed anxious every night assuming that if Christ returns while you are asleep you are irrevocably lost. Paul did not really intend to support Christian insomnia, so he sought to allay such fears. But some of the Thessalonian congregation may have misinterpreted Paul's argument in this verse precisely in the sense that Edgar recommends, inadvertently undermining the case for vigilance.

What is most intriguing about Edgar's article from the perspective of the current topic is that a consistent use of "sleep" to refer to vigilance opens the door for libertinism; Paul would thus be perceived to say in 5:10 that whether you are vigilant or not, whether you are asleep or awake, your position with the Lord is secure. Edgar tries his best to close this ample loophole which quite obviously undermines Paul's entire argument about the inability of humans to gain "security" in face of the impending day of the Lord. Edgar's stress on relying upon grace is admirable, but hardly succeeds in eliminating the dangerous possibility that previous scholars have been so quick to eliminate. But what if we relate the outlook of millenarian radicalism to this text precisely as Edgar construes it? Would it not then suggest that no matter what Christians do, whether they sleep or wake, whether drunk or sober, they are securely "with the Lord"? Would it not imply that the παρουσία of the Lord was a present reality which even sleep or drunkenness do not displace? Is it not likely that the ἄτακτοι would have appreciated and exploited this loophole that moralistic commentators have tried so resolutely to close in Paul's behalf?

---

[38] Cf. Best, *Thessalonians*, 218; Marshall, *1 and 2 Thessalonians*, 141; Bruce, *Thessalonians*, 114; Frame, *Thessalonians*, 189f.; Reese, *1 and 2 Thessalonians*, 58.
[39] Edgar, "The Meaning of 'Sleep.'"

And is Paul's bafflement not understandable in this case especially? In his effort to avoid the impression that his use of "sleep" implied Christians should never close their eyes at night, he had inadvertently opened the door to the radicals in Thessalonica to cite his own letter to the effect that the parousia had already come.

(g) Summary

Some of these suggested misunderstandings may appear to be more plausible than others. None of them, in my opinion, is sufficiently plausible that a theory of misunderstanding could be based on evidence within 1 Thessalonians alone. But given the fact that the evidence in 2 Thessalonians so clearly implies the occurrence of such a misunderstanding, these examples demonstrate the live possibilities for an early congregation whose piety included a predisposition in the direction of millenarian radicalism. To conclude from 1 Thessalonians that "the day of the Lord has already come" required a high level of selective listening on the part of the Thessalonians. It involved either a stubborn refusal or an innate incapacity to accept the apocalyptic logic of 1 Thess 4:13–5:11. In either case, the predisposition of the congregation would have been decisive. But from Paul's apocalyptic perspective, it is understandable that he would have been so amazed and appalled at the scale of the reported misunderstanding of 1 Thessalonians that he literally suspected that a forgery had been written in his name.

3. THE MOTIVATION FOR WRITING 2 THESSALONIANS

In conclusion, given the millenarian fever current in the congregation, there are ample possibilities in 1 Thessalonians for a major misunderstanding of Paul's position. Not being in a position to discover precisely what had led to such misconstruals of what he had intended to say, it was logical for him to suspect forgery. But since the millenarian radicals in Thessalonica were quoting Paul's teaching and writing to support their contention that the Day of the Lord had already come, Paul was forced to write again to clarify his argument and his intentions. He summarized his earlier argument, quite naturally with a noticeable difference of tone. The exasperation is visible throughout the letter, leading analysts to the understandable conclusion that it could never have been written by the same person to the same audience within a short space of time.

The addition of new material in 2 Thessalonians, designed to clarify the nature of the eschatological signs that must precede the parousia, does not indicate a changed eschatological perspective on the author's part but rather the urgent need to demolish the belief that the parousia could be present while this evil age is still so clearly in evidence. Having made this case, Paul goes on in 2 Thessalonians to urge that the ἄτακτοι should be disciplined by the church. The radicalized situation in Thessalonica in the wake of the reception of his first letter thus called for a second letter that was both a condensation and an expansion of the earlier letter. This is precisely the shape of the "replacement character" of 2 Thessalonians that Holtzmann and others have discerned, a quality that only Paul is likely to have been able to impart to it.

Bibliography

1. Exegetical and Historical Studies
of 1 and 2 Thessalonians

Adeney, Walter F. *The Epistles of Paul the Apostle to the Thessalonians and Galatians.* New York: Oxford University Press, 1902.

Askwith, Edward Harrison. "'I' and 'We' in the Thessalonian Epistles." *Expositor,* Series 8.1 (1911): 149–59.

_____. *An Introduction to the Thessalonian Epistles: Containing a Vindication of the Pauline Authorship of both Epistles and an Interpretation of the Eschatological Section of 2 Thess. ii.* London and New York: Macmillan, 1902.

Aus, Roger D. "God's Plan and God's Power: Isaiah 66 and the Restraining Factors of 2 Thess 2:6–7." *Journal of Biblical Literature* 96 (1977): 537–53.

_____. "The Liturgical Background of the Necessity and Propriety of Giving Thanks according to 2 Thess 1:3." *Journal of Biblical Literature* 92 (1973): 432–38.

_____. "The Relevance of Isaiah 66:7 to Revelation 12 and 2 Thessalonians 1." *Zeitschrift für die neutestamentliche Wissenschaft* 67 (1976): 252–68.

Bailey, John A. "Who Wrote II Thessalonians?" *New Testament Studies* 25 (1978–79): 131–45.

Bailey, John W. *The First and Second Epistles to the Thessalonians.* The Interpreter's Bible 11. Nashville: Abingdon Press, 1955.

Baltensweiler, Heinrich. "Erwägungen zu 1. Thess. 4, 3–8." *Theologische Zeitschrift* 19 (1963): 1–13.

Bassler, Jouette M. "The Enigmatic Sign: 2 Thessalonians 1:5." *Catholic Biblical Quarterly* 46 (1984): 496–510.

Baur, Ferdinand Christian. "Die beiden Briefe an die Thessalonicher, ihre Unechtheit und Bedeutung für die Lehre der Parusie Christi." *Theologische Jahrbücher* 14 (1855): 141–68; trans. A. Menzies, pp. 314–40 in Ferdinand Christian Baur, *Paul, the Apostle of Jesus Christ, his Life and Work, his Epistles and his Doctrine: A Contribution to the Critical History of Primitive Christianity,* edited by E. Zeller. vol. 2. 2d ed. London: Williams & Norgate, 1876.

Beare, Frank W. "The First Letter of St. Paul to the Thessalonians." *Canadian Journal of Theology* 8 (1962): 4–11.

Beauvery, R. "Πλεονεκτεῖν in I Thess. 4.6a." *Verbum Domini* 33 (1955): 78–85.

Best, Ernest. *The First and Second Epistles to the Thessalonians.* London: A. & C. Black, 1972.

Betz, Otto. "Der Katechon." *New Testament Studies* 9 (1962–63): 276–91.

Black, David Alan. "The Weak in Thessalonica: A Study in Pauline Lexicography." *Journal of the Evangelical Theological Society* 25 (1982): 307–21.

Blake, Buchanan. "The Apocalyptic Setting of the Thessalonian Epistles." *Expositor,* Series 9.3 (1925): 126–39.

Boers, Hendrikus. "The Form Critical Study of Paul's Letters: I Thessalonians as a Case

Study." *New Testament Studies* 22 (1975–76): 140–58.

Bornemann, Wilhelm. *Die Thessalonicherbriefe, völlig neu bearbeitet.* Göttingen: Vandenhoeck & Ruprecht, 1894.

Braun, Herbert. "Zur nachpaulinischen Herkunft des zweiten Thessalonicherbriefes." *Zeitschrift für die neutestamentliche Wissenschaft* 44 (1952–53): 152–56; reprinted, pp. 205–9 in Herbert Braun, *Gesammelte Studien zum Neuen Testament und Seiner Welt.* 2d ed. Tübingen: Mohr-Siebeck, 1967.

Bruce, Frederik F. "St. Paul in Macedonia: 2. The Thessalonian Correspondence." *Bulletin of the John Rylands University Library in Manchester* 62 (1980): 328–45.

———. *1 and 2 Thessalonians.* Waco: Word, 1982.

Burkeen, W. Howard. *The Parousia of Christ in the Thessalonian Correspondence.* Ph.D. diss., Aberdeen University, 1979.

Cavallin, H. C. "Parusi och uppstandelse. 1 Th. 4:13–18 som kombination av twa slags eskatologi." *Svensk teologisk kvartalskrift* 59 (1983): 54–63.

Chadwick, Henry. "I Thess. 3.3, Σαίνεσθαι." *Journal of Theological Studies* 1 (1950): 156–58.

Clemen, Carl C. "Paulus und die Gemeinde zu Thessalonike." *Neue Kirchliche Zeitschrift* 7 (1896): 139–64.

Collins, Raymond F. "A propos the Integrity of I Thes." *Ephemerides theologicae lovanienses* 55 (1979): 67–106.

———. "The Church of the Thessalonians." *Louvain Studies* 5 (1974–75): 336–49.

———. "Paul, as Seen Through His Own Eyes. A Reflection on the First Letter to the Thessalonians." *Louvain Studies* 8 (1980–81): 348–81.

———. *Studies on the First Letter to the Thessalonians.* Louvain: Louvain University Press, 1984.

———. "I Thessalonians and the Liturgy of the Early Church." *Biblical Theology Bulletin* 10 (1980): 51–64.

———. "'This is the Will of God: Your Sanctification' (1 Thess 4,3)." *Laval théologique et philosophique* 39 (1983): 27–53.

———. "Tradition, Redaction, and Exhortation in 1 Th 4,13–5,11." Pp. 325–43 in *L'Apocalypse johannique et l'Apocalyptique dans le Nouveau Testament,* edited by J. Lambrecht. Louvain: Louvain University Press, 1980.

———. "The Unity of Paul's Paraenesis in 1 Thess. 4.3–8. 1 Cor. 7. 1–7, a Significant Parallel." *New Testament Studies* 29 (1983): 420–29.

Coppens, Joseph. "Miscellanées bibliques. LXXX. Une diatribe antijuive dans I Thess., II, 13–16." *Ephemerides theologicae lovanienses* 51 (1975): 90–95.

Cullmann, Oscar. "Der eschatologische Charakter des Missionsauftrages und des apostolischen Selbstbewusstseins bei Paulus. Untersuchung zum Begriff des κατέχον (κατέχων) in 2 Thess. 2, 6–7." Pp. 305–36 in Cullmann, *Vorträge und Aufsätze 1925–1962,* edited by K. Frölich. Tübingen: Mohr-Siebeck, 1966.

———. "Meditation (I Thess. 5:19–21)." *Concordia Theological Monthly* 39 (1968): 6–9.

Day, Peter. "The Practical Purpose of Second Thessalonians." *Anglican Theological Review* 45 (1963): 203–6.

Delling, Gerhard. "ἀπαρχή." Pp. 483–84 in *Theologisches Wörterbuch zum Neuen Testament,* edited by G. Kittel et al., vol. 1. Stuttgart: Kohlhammer, 1933.

———. "πλεονέκτης, κτλ." P. 266–74 in *Theologisches Wörterbuch zum Neuen Testament,* edited by G. Friedrich, vol. 6. Stuttgart: Kohlhammer, 1959.

Demke, Christoph. "Theologie und Literarkritik im 1. Thessalonicherbrief: Ein Diskussionsbeitrag." Pp. 103–24 in *Festschrift für Ernst Fuchs,* edited by G. Ebeling, E. Jüngel and G. Schunack. Tübingen: Mohr-Siebeck, 1973.

Denis, Albert M. "L'Apôtre Paul, prophète 'messianique' des Gentiles: Etude Thématique de I Thess II, 1–6." *Ephemerides theologicae lovanienses* 33 (1957): 245–318.

Dewailly, L. -M. *La jeune Église de Thessalonique: Les deux premières Épîtres de Saint*

Paul. Paris: Editions du Cerf, 1963.

Dibelius, Martin. *An die Thessalonicher I, II.* Tübingen: Mohr, 1937.

Dobschütz, Ernst von. *Die Thessalonicher-Briefe,* edited by F. Hahn. Reprint of the 1909 edition with a bibliography by O. Merk. Göttingen: Vandenhoeck & Ruprecht, 1974.

Donfried, Karl Paul. "The Cults of Thessalonica and the Thessalonian Correspondence." *New Testament Studies* 31 (1985): 336–56.

_____. "I Thessalonians 2:13–16 as a Test Case." *Interpretation* 38 (1984): 242–53.

_____. "Thessalonians, the First Letter of Paul to the." Pp.1063–64 in *Harper's Bible Dictionary.,* edited by P. J. Achtemeier et al. San Francisco: Harper & Row, 1985.

_____. "Thessalonians, the Second Letter of Paul to the." Pp. 1064–65 in *Harper's Bible Dictionary,* edited by P. J. Achtemeier et al. San Francisco: Harper & Row, 1985.

_____. "Thessalonica." Pp. 1065–66 in *Harper's Bible Dictionary,* edited by P. J. Achtemeier et al. San Francisco: Harper & Row, 1985.

Eckart, Karl-Gottfried. "Der zweite Brief des Apostels Paulus an die Thessalonicher." *Zeitschrift für Theologie und Kirche* 58 (1961): 30–44.

Edgar, Thomas R. "The Meaning of 'Sleep' in I Thessalonians 5:10." *Journal of the Evangelical Theological Society* 22 (1979): 344–49.

Edson, Charles. "Macedonia, II. State Cults in Thessalonica." *Harvard Studies in Classical Philology* 51 (1940): 127–36.

_____. "Macedonia, III. Cults of Thessalonica." *Harvard Theological Review* 41 (1948): 153–204.

Egenolf, Hans-Andreas. *The Second Epistle to the Thessalonians,* trans. W. Glen-Doepel. New York: Herder & Herder, 1969.

Evans, Robert M. *Eschatology and Ethics: A Study of Thessalonica and Paul's Letters to the Thessalonians.* Ph.D. diss., Basel University, 1967; Princeton: McMahon Printing Company, 1968.

Faw, Chalmer E. "On the Writing of First Thessalonians." *Journal of Biblical Literature* 71 (1952): 217–25.

Findlay, George. G. *The Epistles of Paul the Apostle to the Thessalonians.* Cambridge, MA: Harvard University Press, 1904.

Frame, James E. *A Critical and Exegetical Commentary on the Epistles of St. Paul to the Thessalonians.* New York: Charles Scribners', 1912.

_____. "Οἱ Ἄτακτοι (I Thess. 5.14)." Pp. 189–206 in *Essays in Modern Theology and Related Subjects: Gathered and Published as a Testimonial to Charles A. Briggs.* New York: Charles Scribners', 1911.

Friedrich, Gerhard. *Der erste Brief an die Thessalonicher.* Göttingen: Vandenhoeck & Ruprecht, 1976.

_____. *Der zweite Brief an die Thessalonicher.* Göttingen: Vandenhoeck & Ruprecht, 1976.

_____. "1 Thessalonicher 5,1–11, der apologetische Einschub eines Späteren." *Zeitschrift für Theologie und Kirche* 10 (1973): 288–315.

Fuchs, Ernst. "Meditation über 1 Thess 1,2–10." *Göttingen Predigt-Meditationen* 18 (1963–64): 299–303.

Giblin, Charles H. *The Threat to Faith: An Exegetical and Theological Re-examination of 2 Thessalonians 2.* Analecta Biblica 31. Rome: Pontifical Biblical Institute, 1967.

Gillman, John. "Signals of Transformation in 1 Thessalonians 4:13–18." *Catholic Biblical Quarterly* 47 (1985): 263–81.

Graafen, J. *Die Echtheit des 2. Thessalonicherbriefs.* Münster: Aschendorff, 1930.

Gregson, R. "A Solution to the Problem of the Thessalonian Epistles." *Theologische Quartalschrift* 38 (1966): 76–80.

Grimm, Carl Ludwig Wilibald. "Die Echtheit der Briefe an die Thessalonicher gegen D. Baur's Angriff vertheidigt." *Theologische Studien und Kritiken* 23 (1850): 753–813.

Hadorn, W. "Die Abfassung der Thessalonicherbriefe auf der dritten Missionsreise und der Kanon des Marcion." *Zeitschrift für die neutestamentliche Wissenschaft* 19 (1919–20): 67–72.

_____. "Die Abfassung der Thessalonicherbriefe in der Zeit der dritten Missionsreise des Paulus." *Beiträge zur Förderung christlicher Theologie* 24 Hefte 3./4. (1919): 157–284.

Harnack, Adolf von. "Das Problem des zweiten Thessalonicherbriefes." *Sitzungsbericht der Preussischen Akademie der Wissenschaft zu Berlin, philosophisch-historischen Classe* 31 (1910): 560–78.

Harnisch, Wolfgang. *Eschatologische Existenz: Ein exegetischer Beitrag zum Sachanliegen von I. Thessalonicher 4,13–5,11.* Göttingen: Vandenhoeck & Ruprecht, 1973.

Hendrix, Holland L. *Thessalonicans Honor Romans.* Ph.D. diss., Harvard University, 1984.

Hilgenfeld, Adolf. "Die beiden Briefe an die Thessalonicher, nach Inhalt und Ursprung." *Zeitschrift für wissenschaftliche Theologie* 5 (1862): 225–64.

Holland, Glenn S. "Let No One Deceive You in Any Way: 2 Thessalonians as a Reformulation of the Apocalyptic Tradition." Pp. 327–41 in *Society of Biblical Literature 1985 Seminar Papers,* edited by K. H. Richards. Atlanta: Scholars Press, 1985.

_____. *The Tradition that You Received from Us: 2 Thessalonians in the Pauline Tradition.* Ph.D. diss., University of Chicago, 1986.

Hollmann, Georg. "Die Unechtheit des zweiten Thessalonicherbriefs." *Zeitschrift für die neutestamentliche Wissenschaft* 5 (1904): 28–38.

Holtzmann, Heinrich Julius. "Zum zweiten Thessalonicherbrief." *Zeitschrift für die neutestamentliche Wissenschaft* 2 (1901): 97–108.

Horbury, William. "I Thessalonians ii. 3 as Rebutting the Charge of False Prophecy." *Journal of Theological Studies* 33 (1982): 492–508.

Hughes, Frank Witt. "The Rhetoric of 1 Thessalonians." Unpublished paper, 1986.

_____. *Second Thessalonians as a Document of Early Christian Rhetoric.* Ph.D. diss., Garrett-Northwestern Joint Program, 1984.

Hurd, John C., Jr. "Thessalonians, First Letter to the." P. 900 in *Interpreter's Dictionary of the Bible,* edited by K. Crim, supp. vol. Nashville: Abingdon Press, 1976.

_____. "Thessalonians, Second Letter to the." Pp. 900–901 in *Interpreter's Dictionary of the Bible,* edited by K. Crim, supp. vol. Nashville: Abingdon Press, 1976.

Hyldahl, Niels. "Auferstehung Christi—Auferstehung der Toten." Pp. 119–35 in *Die Paulinische Literatur und Theologie: Anlässlich der 50. jährigen Gründungs-Feier der Universität Aarhus,* edited by S. Petersen. Göttingen: Vandenhoeck & Ruprecht, 1980.

_____. "Jesus og joderne ifolge 1 Tess 2:14–16." *Svensk exegetisk Årsbok* 37–38 (1972–73): 238–54.

Jewett, Robert. "Enthusiastic Radicalism and the Thessalonian Correspondence." Pp. 181–232 in *Book of Seminar Papers,* vol. 1. The Society of Biblical Literature, One Hundred Eighth Annual Meeting, 1–5 September, 1972.

Judge, Edwin A. "The Decrees of Caesar at Thessalonica." *Reformed Theological Review* 30 (1971): 1–7.

Kaye, Bruce N. "Eschatology and Ethics in 1 and 2 Thessalonians." *Novum Testamentum* 17 (1975): 47–57.

Kern, Friedrich Heinrich. "Ueber 2. Thess 2, 1–12. Nebst Andeutungen über den Ursprung des zweiten Briefs an die Thessalonicher." *Tübinger Zeitschrift für Theologie* 2 (1839): 145–214.

Klijn, Albertus F. J. "1 Thessalonians 4,13–18 and its Background in Apocalyptic Literature." Pp. 67–73 in *Paul and Paulinism: Essays in Honor of C. K. Barrett,* edited by M. D. Hooker and S. G. Wilson. London: SPCK, 1982.

Koester, Helmut. "Apostel und Gemeinde in den Briefen an die Thessalonicher." Pp. 287–98 in *Kirche: Festschrift für Günther Bornkamm zum 75. Geburtstag,* edited by D. Lührmann and G. Strecker. Tübingen: Mohr-Siebeck, 1980.

_____. "I Thessalonians—Experiment in Christian Writing." Pp. 33–44 in *Continuity and discontinuity in Church History: Essays Presented to George Huntston Williams on the Occasion of his 65th Birthday*, edited by F. F. Church and T. George. Leiden: E. J. Brill, 1979.

Krentz, Edgar. "A Stone That Will Not Fit: The Non-Pauline Authorship of II Thessalonians." Seminar Paper for the Society of Biblical Literature Annual Meeting, Dallas, 1983.

Krodel, Gerhard. *2 Thessalonians*. Proclamation Commentaries: *Ephesians, Colossians, 2 Thessalonians, The Pastoral Epistles*. Philadelphia: Fortress Press, 1978.

Kümmel, Werner Georg. "Das literarische und geschichtliche Problem des ersten Thessalonicherbriefes." Pp. 213–27 in *Neotestamentica et Patristica: Oscar Cullmann zum 60. Geburtstag*. Leiden: E. J. Brill, 1962.

Lang, Friedrich. "Σαίνω." Pp. 54–56 in *Theologisches Wörterbuch zum Neuen Testament*, edited by G. Friedrich, vol. 7. Stuttgart: Kohlhammer, 1964.

Laub, Franz. *Eschatologische Verkündigung und Lebensgestaltung nach Paulus: Eine Untersuchung zum Wirken des Apostels beim Aufbau der Gemeinde in Thessalonike*. Regensburg: Pustet, 1973.

_____. "Paulus als Gemeindegründer (1 Thess)." Pp. 17–38 in *Kirche im Werden: Studien zum Thema Amt und Gemeinde im Neuen Testament*, edited by H. Hainz. Munich: Schöningh, 1976.

Lifschitz, B. and Schiby, J. "Une synagogue samaritaine à Thessalonique." *Revue biblique* 75 (1968): 368–78.

Lightfoot, Joseph Barber. "The Church of Thessalonica." Pp. 253–69 in J. B. Lightfoot, *Biblical Essays*. London: Macmillan, 1893.

Lindemann, Andreas. "Zum Abfassungszweck des Zweiten Thessalonicher briefes." *Zeitschrift für die neutestamentliche Wissenschaft* 68 (1977): 34–47.

Lipsius, Richard Adelbert. "Ueber Zweck und Veranlassung des ersten Thessalonicherbrief." *Theologische Studien und Kritiken* 27 (1854): 905–34.

Lueken, Wilhelm. *Der erste Brief an die Thessalonicher*. Die Schriften des Neuen Testaments neu übersetzt und für die Gegenward erklärt 2. Göttingen: Vandenhoeck & Ruprecht, 1917.

_____. *Der zweite Brief an die Thessalonicher*. Die Schriften des Neuen Testaments neu übersetzt und für die Gegenward erklärt 2. Göttingen: Vandenhoeck & Ruprecht, 1917.

Lünemann, Gottlieb. *Critical and Exegetical Handbook to the Epistles of St. Paul to the Thessalonians*, trans. P. J. Gloag. Edinburgh: T. & T. Clark, 1880.

Lütgert, Wilhelm. "Die Volkommenen im Philipperbrief und die Enthusiasten in Thessalonich." *Beiträge zur Förderung christlicher Theologie* 13 (1909): 547–654.

Makaronas, Charles I. "Via Egnatia and Thessalonike." Pp. 380–88 in *Studies Presented to David Moore Robinson on His Seventieth Birthday*, edited by G. E. Mylonas, vol. 1. St. Louis: Washington University Press, 1951.

Malherbe, Abraham J. "Exhortation in First Thessalonians." *Novum Testamentum* 25 (1983): 238–56.

_____. "'Gentle as a Nurse': The Cynic Background to 1 Thess ii." *Novum Testamentum* 12 (1970): 203–17.

Manson, Thomas W. "St. Paul in Greece: The Letters to the Thessalonians." *Bulletin of the John Rylands University Library in Manchester* 35 (1953): 438–47.

Marshall, I. Howard. *1 and 2 Thessalonians*. Grand Rapids: Wm. B. Eerdmans, 1983.

Martin, Ralph P. *New Testament Foundations: A Guide for Christian Students*. Vol. 2: *The Acts, the Letters, the Apocalypse*. Grand Rapids: Wm. B. Eerdmans, 1978.

Marxsen, Willi. "Auslegung von I Thess 4, 14–18." *Zeitschrift für Theologie und Kirche* 66 (1969): 22–37.

_____. *Der erste Brief an die Thessalonicher*. Zurich: Theologischer Verlag, 1979.

——. *Der zweite Thessalonicherbrief.* Zurich: Theologischer Verlag, 1982.

Masson, Charles. *Les Deux Épitres de Saint Paul aux Thessaloniciens.* Neuchatel and Paris: Delachaux & Niestle, 1957.

——. "Sur I Thessaloniciens V, 23. Notes d'anthropologie paulinienne." *Revue de Theologie et de Philosophie* 38 (1945): 97–102.

Maurer, Christian. "σκεῦος." Pp. 358–67 in *Theological Dictionary of the New Testament,* edited by G. Friedrich, vol. 7. Trans. G. W. Bromiley. Grand Rapids: Wm. B. Eerdmans, 1971.

Mearns, Christopher L. "Early Eschatological Development in Paul: The Evidence of I and II Thessalonians." *New Testament Studies* 27 (1980–81): 137–57.

Michaelis, Wilhelm. "Der zweite Thessalonicherbrief kein Philipperbrief." *Theologische Zeitschrift* 1 (1945): 282–86.

Michel, Otto. "Fragen zu 1 Thessalonicher 2:14–16: Anti-Jüdische Polemik bei Paulus." Pp. 50–59 in *Antijudaismus im Neuen Testament? Exegetische und systematische Beiträge,* edited by W. P. Eckert et al. Munich: Kaiser-Verlag, 1967.

Milligan, George. "The Authenticity of the Second Epistle to the Thessalonians." *Expositor,* Series 6.9 (1904): 430–50.

——. *St. Paul's Epistles to the Thessalonians: The Greek Text with Introduction and Notes.* London: Macmillan, 1908.

Moffatt, James. *The First and Second Epistles of Paul the Apostle to the Thessalonians.* The Expositor's Greek New Testament 4. New York and London: Hodder & Stoughton, 1897.

Moore, Arthur L. *1 and 2 Thessalonians.* Camden, NJ: Nelson, 1969.

Morris, Leon. *The First and Second Epistles to the Thessalonians.* Grand Rapids: Wm. B. Eerdmans, 1959.

——. "KAI APAX KAI DIS." *Novum Testamentum* 1 (1956): 205–8.

Munck, Johannes. "1 Thess i. 9–10 and the Missionary Preaching of Paul: Textual Exegesis and Hermeneutic Reflexions." *New Testament Studies* 9 (1962–63): 95–110.

Neil, William. *The Epistle of Paul to the Thessalonians.* Naperville: Alec R. Allenson, 1957.

Nepper-Christensen, Poul. "Das verborgene Herrenwort: Eine Untersuchung über I Thess 4,13–18." *Studia theologica* 19 (1965): 136–54.

Oberhummer, E. "Thessalonike." Cols. 143–63 in *Paulys Real-Encyclopädie der classischen Altertumswissenschaft,* edited by W. Kroll and K. Mittelhaus, series 2, vol. 6. Stuttgart: Metzler, 1937.

Oepke, Albrecht. *Die Briefe an die Thessalonicher.* Das Neue Testament Deutsch 8. Reprint of the 1933 edition. Göttingen: Vandenhoeck & Ruprecht, 1970.

Okeke, G. E. "The Fate of the Unbelieving Jews." *New Testament Studies* 27 (1980–81): 127–36.

Orchard, J. B. "Thessalonians and the Synoptic Gospels." *Biblica* 19 (1938): 19–42.

Palmer, Darryl W. "Thanksgiving, Self-Defence, and Exhortation in 1 Thessalonians 1–3." *Colloquium* 14 (1981): 23–31.

Pax, Elpidius. "Beobachtungen zur Konvertitensprache im ersten Thessalonicherbrief." *Studii Biblici Franciscani Liber Annus* 21 (1971): 220–62.

——. "Konvertitenprobleme im ersten Thessalonicherbrief." *Bibel und Leben* 13 (1972): 24–37.

Pearson, Birger A. "1 Thessalonians 2:13–16: A Deutero-Pauline Interpolation." *Harvard Theological Review* 64 (1971): 79–94.

Perdelwitz, Richard. "Zu σαίνεσθαι ἐν ταῖς θλίψεσιν ταύταις, I Thess. 3,3." *Theologische Studien und Kritiken* 86 (1912): 613–15.

Peterson, Robert J. *The Structure and Purpose of Second Thessalonians.* Ph.D. diss., Harvard University, 1967.

Plevnik, Joseph. "The Parousia as Implication of Christ's Resurrection: An Exegesis of 1

Thes 4:13–18." Pp. 199–277 in *Word and Spirit: Essays in Honor of David Martin Stanley*, edited by J. Plevnik. Willowdale, Ontario: Regis, 1975.

———. "The Taking Up of the Faithful and the Resurrection of the Dead in 1 Thessalonians 4:13–18." *Catholic Biblical Quarterly* 46 (1984): 274–83.

———. "1 Thess. 5,1–11: Its Authenticity, Intention and Message." *Biblica* 60 (1979): 71–90.

Plummer, Alfred. *A Commentary on St. Paul's First Epistle to the Thessalonians.* London: Roxburghe, 1918.

———. *A Commentary on St. Paul's Second Epistle to the Thessalonians.* London: Roxburghe, 1918.

Reese, James M. *1 and 2 Thessalonians.* Wilmington: Michael Glazier, 1979.

Refshauge, Ebba. "Literaerkritiske overvejelser: Til de to Thessalonikerbreve." *Dansk teologisk tidsskrift* 34 (1971): 1–19.

Reicke, Bo. "Thessalonicherbriefe." Cols. 851–53 in *Religion in Geschichte und Gegenwart*, edited by K. Galling et al., 3d ed., vol. 6. Tübingen: Mohr-Siebeck, 1962.

Rigaux, Béda. *Saint Paul: Les Épîtres aux Thessaloniciens.* Paris: J. Gabalda; Gembloux: J. Duculot, 1956.

———. "Tradition et rédaction dans I Th. V. 1–10." *New Testament Studies* 21 (1974–75): 318–40.

Roosen, A. *De Brieven van Paulus aan de Tessalonicenzen.* Romen: Roermond, 1971.

Rossano, Piero. "Note archeologiche sulla antica Tessalonica." *Revista Biblica* 6 (1958): 242–47.

Saunders, Ernest W. *1 Thessalonians, 2 Thessalonians, Philippians, Philemon.* Atlanta: John Knox Press, 1981.

Schippers, R. "The Pre-Synoptic Tradition in 1 Thessalonians II 13–16." *Novum Testamentum* 8 (1966): 223–34.

Schlier, Heinrich. *Der Apostel und seine Gemeinde. Auslegung des ersten Briefes an die Thessalonicher.* Freiburg, Basel and Vienna: Herder, 1972.

Schmidt, Daryl. "1 Thess 1:13–16: Linguistic Evidence for an Interpolation." *Journal of Biblical Literature* 102 (1983): 269–79.

Schmidt, Johann Ernst Christian. "Vermuthungen über den beyden Briefe an die Thessalonicher." Pp. 380–86 in *Bibliothek für Kritik und Exegese des Neuen Testaments und ältesten Christengeschichte* 2.3. Hadamar: Gelehrtenbuchhandlung, 1801.

Schmidt, Paul Wilhelm. *Der erste Thessalonicherbrief, neu erklärt, nebst einem Excurs über den zweiten gleichnamigen Brief.* Berlin: Reimer, 1885.

Schmithals, Walter. "The Historical Situation of the Thessalonian Epistles." Pp. 128–318 in *Paul and the Gnostics*, trans. J. E. Steely. Nashville: Abingdon Press, 1972.

———. "Die Thessalonicherbriefe als Briefkompositionen." Pp. 295–315 in *Zeit und Geschichte: Dankesgabe an Rudolf Bultmann zum 80. Geburtstag*, edited by E. Dinkler. Tübingen: Mohr-Siebeck, 1964.

Schnelle, Udo. "Der erste Thessalonicherbrief und die Entstehung der paulinischen Anthropologie," *New Testament Studies* 32 (1986): 207–24.

Schürmann, Heinz. *The First Epistle to the Thessalonians*, trans. W. Glen-Doepel. New York: Herder & Herder, 1969.

Schweizer, Eduard. "Πνεῦμα, πνεματικός." Pp. 387–449 in *Theologisches Wörterbuch zum Neuen Testament*, edited by G. Friedrich, vol. 6. Stuttgart: Kohlhammer, 1959.

———. "Zur Trichotomie von I Thess. 5,23 und der Unterscheidung des πνευματικόν vom ψυχικόν in I Kor. 2, 14; 15, 44; Jak 3, 15; Jud 19." *Theologische Zeitschrift* 9 (1953): 76–77.

———. "Der zweite Thessalonicherbrief ein Philipperbrief?" *Theologische Zeitschrift* 1 (1954): 90–105.

Spicq, Ceslas. "Les Thesaloniciens 'inquiets' etaient ils des paresseux?" *Studia theologia* 10 (1956): 1–13.

Stempvoort, P. A. van. "Eine stilistische Lösung einer alten Schwierigkeit in I Thess. V, 23." *New Testament Studies* 7 (1960–61): 262–65.

Stephenson, Allen M. G . "On the Meaning of ἐνέστηκεν ἡ ἡμέρα τοῦ κυρίου in 2 Thessalonians 2,2." Pp. 442–51 in *Studia Evangelica* 4, edited by F. L. Cross. TU 102. Berlin: A. Töpelmann, 1968.

Stepien, J. "Autentyczność listów do Tessaloniczan" ["The Authenticity of the Thessalonian Letters"] *Collectanea Theologica* 34 (1963): 91–182.

———. "Pawlowy charakter nauki dogmatycznej i moralnej listów do Tessaloniczan" ["The Pauline Character of the Dogmatic and Moral Teachings in the Thessalonian Letters"] *Ruch Biblijny i Liturgiczny* 13 (1960): 243–68.

———. "Problem wzajemnego stosunku literarckiego listów do Tessaloniczan i próby jego rozwiazanią" ["The Problem of the Mutual Literary Relations between the Thessalonian Letters and the Attempted Solutions Thereof"] *Ruch Biblijny i Liturgiczny* 13 (1960): 414–35.

Thieme, Karl. "Die Struktur des ersten Thessalonicherbriefes." Pp. 450–58 in *Abraham Unser Vater: Juden und Christen im Gespräch über die Bibel: Festschrift für Otto Michel zum 60. Geburtstag,* edited by O. Betz, M. Hengel and P. Schmidt. Leiden: E. J. Brill, 1963.

Thompson, Edward. "The Sequence of the Two Epistles to the Thessalonians." *Expository Times* 56 (1945): 306–7.

Thurston, R. W. "The Relationship between the Thessalonian Epistles." *Expository Times* 85 (1973–74): 52–56.

Trilling, Wolfgang. "Literarische Paulusimitation im 2. Thessalonicherbrief." Pp. 146–56 in *Paulus in den neutestamentlichen Spätschriften: Zur Paulusrezeption im Neuen Testament,* edited by K. Kertelge. Freiburg, Basel and Wien: Herder, 1981.

———. *Untersuchungen zum zweiten Thessalonicherbrief.* Leipzig: St. Benno, 1972.

———. *Der zweite Brief an die Thessalonicher.* Zurich: Benzinger; Neukirchen: Neukirchener-Verlag, 1980.

Ubbink, J. T. "ὡς δι᾽ ἡμῶν (2 Thess 2,2)—een exegetisch-isagogische puzzle." *Norsk teologisk tidsskrift* 7 (1952–53): 269–95.

Unger, Merril F. "Historical Research and the Church at Thessalonica." *Bibliotheca Sacra* 119 (1962): 38–44.

Unnik, Willem C. van. "'Den Geist löschet nicht aus' (I Thessalonicher v 19)." *Novum Testamentum* 10 (1968): 255–69.

Vacalopoulos, Apostolos E. *A History of Thessaloniki,* trans. T. F. Carney. Thessalonica: Institute for Balkan Studies, 1963.

Veloso, Mario. "Contenido antropologico de 1 Tesalonicenses 5,23." *Revista Biblica* 41 (1979): 129–40.

Vickers, Michael J. "Hellenistic Thessaloniki." *Journal of Hellenic Studies* 92 (1972): 156–70.

———. "Towards Reconstruction of the Town Planning of Roman Thessaloniki." Pp. 239–51 in *Ancient Macedonia* 1, edited by B. Laourdas and C. Makaronas. Thessaloniki: Institute for Balkan Studies, 1970.

Ware, Phil. "The Coming of the Lord: Eschatology and I Thessalonians." *Restoration Quarterly* 1–2 (1979): 109–20.

West, J. C. "The Order of 1 and 2 Thessalonians." *Journal of Theological Studies* 15 (1914): 66–74.

Whiteley, Denys E. H. *Thessalonians in the Revised Standard Version, With Introduction and Commentary.* New York and London: Oxford University Press, 1969.

Wrede, William. *Die Echtheit des zweiten Thessalonicherbrief untersucht.* Leipzig: Henrichs, 1903.

Wrzol, Josef. *Die Echtheit des zweiten Thessalonicherbriefs.* Freiburg: Herder, 1916.

———. "Sprechen 2 Thess. 2,3 und 3,17 gegen paulinischen Ursprung des Briefes?" *Weidenauer Studien* 1 (1906): 271–89.

2. Rhetorical and Linguistic Studies

Allo, Ernest Bernard. "Le défaut d'éloquence et de 'style oral' de Saint Paul." *Revue des Sciences Philosophiques et Théologiques* 23 (1934): 29–39.

Arens, Edmund. *Kommunikative Handlungen: Die paradigmatische Bedeutung der Gleichnisse Jesu für eine Handlungstheorie.* Düsseldorf: Patmos-Verlag, 1982.

Aristotle. *The "Art" of Rhetoric,* trans. J. H. Freese. Cambridge, MA: Harvard University Press, 1926.

Berger, Klaus. "Die impliziten Gegner: Zur Methode des Erschliessen von 'Gegnern' in neutestamentlichen Texten." Pp. 373–400 in *Kirche: Festschrift für Günther Bornkamm zum 75. Geburtstag,* edited by D. Lührmann and G. Strecker. Tübingen: Mohr-Siebeck, 1980.

Betz, Hans Dieter. *Der Apostle Paulus und die sokratische Tradition: Eine exegetische Untersuchung zu seiner "Apologie" 2 Kor 10–13.* Tübingen: Mohr-Siebeck, 1972.

_____. *2 Corinthians 8 and 9: A Commentary on Two Administrative Letters of the Apostle Paul.* Philadelphia: Fortress Press, 1985.

_____. *Galatians: A Commentary on Paul's Letter to the Churches in Galatia.* Philadelphia: Fortress Press, 1979.

_____. "The Literary Composition and Function of Paul's Letter to the Galatians," *New Testament Studies* 21 (1975): 353–79.

Bitzer, Lloyd F. "The Rhetorical Situation." *Philosophy and Rhetoric* 1 (1968): 1–14.

Brandt, William J. *The Rhetoric of Argumentation.* Rev. ed. New York: Irvington Publishers Inc., 1984.

Brock, Bernard L., and Robert L. Scott, eds. *Methods of Rhetorical Criticism: A Twentieth-Century Perspective.* 2d ed. Detroit: Wayne State University Press, 1980.

Bühler, Karl. *Die Axiomatik der Sprachwissenschaften,* Introduction and Commentary by E. Stöcker. 2d ed. Frankfurt: Kostermamm, 1976.

_____. *Sprachtheorie: Die Darstellungsfunktion der Sprache.* Reprint of 1934 1st ed. Stuttgart: Uni-Taschenbücher, 1982.

Bultmann, Rudolf. *Der Stil der paulinischen Predigt und die kynisch-stoische Diatribe.* Göttingen: Vandenhoeck und Ruprecht, 1910.

Bünker, Michael. *Briefformular and rhetorische Disposition im 1. Korintherbrief.* Göttingen: Vandenhoeck & Ruprecht, 1984.

Cicero. *De inventione. De optimo genere oratorum. De topica,* trans. H. M. Hubbell. Cambridge, MA: Harvard University Press, 1949.

_____. *De oratore. De fato. Paradoxa stoicorum. De partitione oratoria,* trans. E. W. Sutton and H. Rackham. 2 vols. Cambridge, MA: Harvard University Press, 1942.

_____. *Letters to Atticus,* trans. E. O. Winstedt. 3 vols. Cambridge, MA: Harvard University Press, 1912–18.

_____. *Letters to his Friends,* trans. W. G. Williams. 3 vols. Cambridge, MA: Harvard University Press, 1958–60.

Clark, Donald L. *Rhetoric in Greco-Roman Education.* New York: Columbia University Press, 1957.

Dijk, Teun A. van. *Text and Context: Explorations in the Semantics and Pragmatics of Discourse.* New York: Longman, 1977.

Fillmore, Charles J. "Pragmatics and the Description of Discourse." Pp. 83–104 in *Pragmatik/Pragmatics 2. Zur Grundlegung einer expliziten Pragmatik,* edited by S. J. Schmidt. Munich: Fink, 1976.

Forbes, Christopher. "Paul's Boasting and Hellenistic Rhetoric." *New Testament Studies* 32 (1986): 1–30.

Gülich, Elisabeth and Wolfgang Raible. *Linguistische Textmodelle: Grundlagen und Möglichkeiten.* Munich: Fink, 1977.

Hellholm, David. *Das Visionenbuch des Hermas als Apokalypse: Formgeschichtliche und texttheoretische Studien zu einer literarischen Gattung* 1. *Methodologische Vorüberlegungen und makrostrukturelle Textanalyse.* Lund: C. W. K. Gleerup, 1980.

Hess-Lüttich, Ernest W. B. *Soziale Interaktion und literarischer Dialog* 1. *Grundlagen der Dialoglinguistik.* Berlin: Schmidt, 1981.

Innis, Robert E. *Karl Bühler: Semiotic Foundations of Language Theory.* New York and London: Plenum, 1982.

Judge, Edwin A. "The Early Christians as a Scholastic Community." *Journal of Religious History* 1 (1960): 4–15, 125–37.

_____. "St. Paul and Classical Society." *Jahrbuch für Antike und Christentum* 15 (1972): 21–36.

Kennedy, George A. *The Art of Persuasion in Greece.* Princeton: Princeton University Press, 1963.

_____. *The Art of Rhetoric in the Roman World.* Princeton: Princeton University Press, 1972.

_____. *Classical Rhetoric and Its Christian and Secular Tradition from Ancient to Modern Times.* Chapel Hill: University of North Carolina Press, 1980.

_____. *New Testament Interpretation through Rhetorical Criticism.* Chapel Hill: University of North Carolina Press, 1984.

_____. *Quintilian.* New York: Twyne, 1969.

Koenig, Eduard. *Stilistik, Rhetorik, Poetik in Bezug auf die biblische Literatur.* Leipzig: Weicher, 1900.

Koskenniemi, Heikki. *Studien zur Idee und Phraseologie des Briefes bis 400 n. Chr.* Helsinki: Suomalaien Tiedeakatemie, 1956.

Kroll, Wilhelm. "Rhetorik." Cols. 1039–1138 in *Paulys Real-Encyclopädie der classischen Altertumswissenschaft,* edited by W. Kroll and D. Mittelhaus, series 2, vol. 7. Stuttgart: Metzler, 1940.

Lausberg, Heinrich. *Elemente der literarischen Rhetorik: Eine Einfürung für Studierende der klassischen, romanischen, englischen und deutschen Philologie.* 3d. ed. Munich: Hueber, 1967.

_____. *Handbuch der literarischen Rhetorik.* 2d ed. Munich: Hueber, 1973.

Mainberger, Gonsalv K. "Der Leib der Rhetorik." *Linguistica Biblica* 51 (1982): 71–86.

_____. "Rhetorik oder die Technologie des Scheins: Zeichenlesen unter Anleitung von Aristoteles." *Linguistica Biblica* 51 (1982): 7–22.

Malherbe, Abraham J. "Ancient Epistolary Theorists." *Ohio Journal of Religious Studies* 5.2 (1977): 3–77.

Marrou, Henri I. *A History of Education in Antiquity,* trans. from 3d ed. by G. Lamb. New York: New American Library, 1964.

Martin, Josef. *Antike Rhetorik: Technik und Methode.* Munich: C. H. Beck, 1974.

Morgenthaler, Erwin. *Kommunikationsorientierte Textgrammatik: Ein Versuch, die kommunikative Kompetenz zur Textbildung und -reception aus natürlichem Sprachvorkommen zu erschliessen.* Düsseldorf: Schwann, 1980.

Morris, Charles W. *Signs, Language and Behavior.* New York: Braziller, 1955.

_____. *Writings on the Social Theory of Signs.* The Hague: Mouton, 1972.

Norden, Eduard. *Die antike Kunstprosa vom VI. Jahrhunderts vor Christus bis in die Zeit der Renaissance.* 2 vols. 5th ed. Stuttgart: B. G. Teubner, 1958.

Perelman, Chaim, and L. Olbrechts-Tyteca. *The New Rhetoric: A Treatise on Argumentation,* trans. J. Wilkinson and P. Weaver. Notre Dame, IN: Notre Dame University Press, 1969.

Plett, Heinrich F. *Einführung in die rhetorische Textanalyse.* 2d ed. Hamburg: Buske, 1975.

_____. *Textwissenschaft und Textanalyse: Semiotik, Linguistik, Rhetorik.* 2d ed. Heidelberg: Quelle and Meyer, 1979.

Pride, John B. "Sociololinguistics." Pp. 1607–28 in *Current Trends in Linguistice,* edited by T. A. Sebeok, vol. 12. The Hague: Mouton, 1974.

Quintilian. *Institutio Oratoria,* trans. H. E. Butler. 4 vols. Cambridge, MA: Harvard University Press, 1953–58.

———. *Rhetorica ad Herennium,* trans. H. Caplan. Cambridge, MA: Harvard University Press, 1954.

Schmidt, Siegfried J. *Foundations for the Empirical Study of Literature: The Components of a Basic Theory,* trans. R. de Beaugrande. Hamburg: Buske, 1982.

———. "Some Problems of Communication Text Theories." Pp. 47–60 in *Current Trends in Textlinguistics,* edited by W. U. Dresser. Berlin: Walter de Gruyter, 1978.

Schubart, Wilhelm. *Einführung in die Papyruskunde.* Berlin: Weidmann, 1918.

Siegert, Folker. *Argumentation bei Paulus gezeigt an Römer 9–11.* Tübingen: Mohr-Siebeck, 1985.

Stalnaker, Robert C. "Pragmatics." *Synthese* 22 (1970): 272–89.

Weiss, Johannes. "Beiträge zur Paulinischen Rhetorik." Pp. 165–247 in *Theologische Studien: Herrn Professor D. Bernhard Weiss zu seinem 70 Geburtstage dargebracht,* edited by C. R. Gregory et al. Göttingen: Vandenhoeck & Ruprecht, 1897.

Wilder, Amos N. *Early Christian Rhetoric: The Language of the Gospel.* Cambridge, MA: Harvard University Press, 1971.

Wilke, Christian Gottlob. *Die neutestamentliche Rhetorik: ein Seitenstück zur Grammatik des neutestamentlichen Sprachidioms.* Dresden and Leipzig: Arnold, 1843.

Wuellner, Wilhelm. "Greek Rhetoric and Pauline Argumentation." Pp. 177–88 in *Early Christian Literature and the Classical Intellectual Tradition: In honorem Robert M. Grant,* edited by W. R. Schoedel and R. L. Wilken. Theologie historique 53. Paris: Beauchesne, 1979.

———. "Paul's Rhetoric of Argumentation in Romans." *Catholic Biblical Quarterly* 38 (1976): 330–51; reprinted pp. 152–74 in *The Romans Debate,* edited by K. P. Donfried. Minneapolis: Augsburg Publishing House, 1977.

Wunderlich, Dieter. *Foundations of Linguistics,* trans. R. Lass. Cambridge, MA: Harvard University Press, 1979.

———. *Studien zur Sprechakttheorie.* Frankfurt: Suhrkamp, 1976.

3. Social-Scientific Studies

Aberle, David. "A Note on Relative Deprivation Theory as Applied to Millenarian and Other Cult Movements." Pp. 537–41 in *Reader in Comparative Religion: An Anthropological Approach,* edited by W. A. Lessa and E. Z. Vogt. New York: Harper & Row, 1964.

Adas, Michael. *Prophets of Rebellion: Millenarian Protest Movements Against the European Colonial Order.* Chapel Hill: University of North Carolina Press, 1979.

Allen, Graham. "A Theory of Millenialism: The Irvingite Movement as an Illustration." *British Journal of Sociology* 25 (1974): 296–311.

Barkun, Michael. *Disaster and the Millennium.* New Haven: Yale University Press, 1974.

Beckford, James A. *The Trumpet of Prophecy: A Sociological Study of Jehovah's Witnesses.* New York: Wiley, 1975.

Burridge, Kenelm. *New Heaven, New Earth: A Study of Millenarian Activities.* Oxford: Basil Blackwell, 1969.

Carney, Thomas F. *The Shape of the Past: Models and Antiquity.* Lawrence, KS: Coronado Press, 1975.

Cohn, Norman. "Medieval Millenarism: Its Bearing on the Comparative Study of Millenarian Movements." Pp. 31–43 in *Millennial Dreams in Action: Studies in Revolutionary Religious Movements,* edited by S. L. Thrupp. New York: Schocken Books, Inc., 1962.

———. *The Pursuit of the Millennium: Revolutionary Messianism in Medieval and Reformation Europe and Its Bearing on Modern Totalitarian Movements.* 2d ed. New York: Harper & Brothers, 1961.

Dickey, Samuel. "Some Economic and Social Conditions of Asia Minor Affecting the Expansion of Christianity." Pp. 393–416 in *Studies in Early Christianity,* edited by S. J. Case. New York: Century, 1928.

Douglas, Mary. *Natural Symbols: Explorations in Cosmology.* 2d ed. London: Barrie & Jenkins, 1973.

———. "Social Preconditions of Enthusiasm and Heterodoxy." Pp. 69–80 in *Forms of Symbolic Action,* edited by R. F. Spencer. Seattle: University of Washington Press, 1969.

Eliade, Mircea. "'Cargo Cults' and Cosmic Regeneration." Pp. 139–43 in *Millennial Dreams in Action: Studies in Revolutionary Religious Movements,* edited by S. L. Thrupp. New York: Schocken Books, Inc., 1970.

Festinger, Leon, Henry W. Riecken, and Stanley Schachter. *When Prophecy Fails: A Social and Psychological Study of a Modern Group that Predicted the Destruction of the World.* New York: Harper & Row, 1964.

Funk, Aloys. *Status und Rollen in den Paulusbriefen: Eine inhaltsanalytische Untersuchung zu Religionssoziologie.* Innsbruck: Tyrolia, 1981.

Gager, John G. *Kingdom and Community: The Social World of Early Christianity.* Englewood Cliffs: Prentice-Hall, 1975.

Gerlach, Luther P. and Virginia H. Hine. *People, Power, Change: Movements of Social Transformation.* Indianapolis: Bobs-Merrill, 1970.

Glock, Charles Y. "The Role of Deprivation in the Origin and Evolution of Religious Groups." Pp. 24–36 in *Religion and Social Control,* edited by R. Lee and M. E. Marty. New York: Oxford University Press, 1964.

Gurr, Ted Robert. *Why Men Rebel.* Princeton: Princeton University Press, 1970.

Harrison, John F. C. *The Second Coming: Popular Millenarianism 1780–1850.* New Brunswick: Rutgers University Press, 1979.

Hobsbawm, Eric J. *Primitive Rebels: Studies in Archaic Forms of Social Movement in the 19th and 20th Centuries.* 3d ed. Manchester: Manchester University Press, 1971.

Holmberg, Bengt. *Paul and Power: The Structure of Authority in the Primitive Church as Reflected in the Pauline Epistles.* Philadelphia: Fortress Press, 1980.

Isenberg, Sheldon R. "Millenarism in Greco-Roman Palestine." *Religion* 4 (1974): 26–46.

Kaminsky, Howard. "The Free Spirit in the Hussite Revolution." Pp. 166–86 in *Millennial Dreams in Action: Studies in Revolutionary Religious Movements,* edited by S. L. Thrupp. New York: Schocken Books, Inc., 1970.

Keller, Bonnie B. "Millenarianism and Resistance: The Xhosa Cattle Killing." *Journal of Asian and African Studies* 13 (1978): 95–111.

Lanternari, Vittorio. *The Religions of the Oppressed: A Study of Modern Messianic Cults,* trans. L. Sergio. New York: Mentor, 1965.

Lienesch, M. "The Role of Political Millennialism in Early American Nationalism." *Western Political Quarterly* 36 (1983): 445–65.

Lofland, John. *Doomsday Cult: A Study of Conversion, Proselytization, and Maintenance of Faith.* Englewood Cliffs: Prentice-Hall, 1966.

Lofland, John and Rodney Stark. "Becoming a World Saver: A Theory of Conversion to a Deviant Perspective." *Annales/Année sociologique Sér. C. Sociologie religieuse* 30 (1965): 862–75.

Mandel, Arthur. *The Militant Messiah, or The Flight from the Ghetto: The Story of Jacob Frank and the Frankist Movement.* Atlantic Highlands: Humanities Press International, 1979.

Meeks, Wayne A. *The First Urban Christians: The Social World of the Apostle Paul.* New Haven: Yale University Press, 1983.

_____. "Social Functions of Apocalyptic Language in Pauline Christianity." Pp. 689–94 in *Apocalypticism in the Mediterranean World and the Near East: Proceedings of the International Colloquium on Apocalypticism, Uppsala, August 12–17, 1979,* edited by D. Hellholm. Tübingen: Mohr-Siebeck, 1983.

O'Dea, Thomas F. and Renato Poblete. "Anomie and the Quest for Community: The Formation of Sects among the Puerto Ricans of New York." Pp. 180–98 in *Sociology and the Study of Religion: Theory, Research, Interpretation,* edited by T. F. O'Dea. New York: Basic Books, 1970.

Oommen, T. K. "Charisma, Social Structure, and Social Change." *Comparative Studies in Society and History* 10 (1967): 85–99.

Pereira de Queiros, Maria Isaura. "Messianic Myths and Movements." *Diogenes* 90 (1975): 78–99.

Petersen, Norman R. *Rediscovering Paul: Philemon and the Sociology of Paul's Narrative World.* Philadelphia: Fortress Press, 1985.

Sandeen, Ernest R. "The 'Little Tradition' and the Form of Modern Millenarianism." *The Annual Review of the Social Sciences of Religion* 4 (1980): 165–81.

_____. "Millennialism." Pp. 104–18 in *The Rise of Adventism,* edited by E. S. Gaustad. New York: Harper & Row, 1974.

_____. *The Roots of Fundamentalism: British and American Millenarianism, 1800–1930.* Chicago: University of Chicago Press, 1970.

Segal, Robert A. "Eliade's Theory of Millenarianism." *Religious Studies* 14 (1978): 159–73.

Sharot, Stephen. *Messianism, Mysticism, and Magic: A Sociological Analysis of Jewish Religious Movements.* Chapel Hill: University of North Carolina Press, 1982.

Shepperson, George. "The Comparative Study of Millenarian Movements." Pp. 44–52 in *Millennial Dreams in Action: Studies in Revolutionary Religious Movements,* edited by S. L. Thrupp. New York: Schocken Books, Inc., 1970.

Stark, Werner. *The Sociology of Religion.* 4 vols. London: Routledge & Kegan Paul, 1966–72.

Talmon, Yonina. "Millenarian Movements." *Archives européennes de sociologie* 7 (1966): 159–200.

_____. "Millenarism." Pp. 349–62 in *International Encyclopedia of the Social Sciences,* edited by D. L .Sills, vol. 10. New York: Free Press, 1968.

_____. "Pursuit of the Millennium: The Relation between Religious and Social Change." *Archives européennes de sociologie* 3 (1962): 125–48.

Theissen, Gerd. *The Social Setting of Pauline Christianity: Essays on Corinth,* trans. and edited by J. H. Schütz. Philadelphia: Fortress Press, 1982.

Thrupp, Sylvia L., ed. *Millennial Dreams in Action: Studies in Revolutionary Religious Movements.* New York: Schocken Books, Inc., 1970.

Wallace, Anthony F. C. "Mazeway Disintegration: The Individual's Perception of Socio-Cultural Disorganization." *Human Organization* 16 (Summer 1957): 23–27.

_____. "Mazeway Resynthesis: A Bio-Cultural Theory of Religious Inspiration." *Transactions of the New York Academy of Sciences* 18 (1956): 626–38.

_____. "Revitalization Movements." *American Anthropologists* 58 (1956): 264–81.

Wallis, Roy. *Salvation and Protest: Studies of Social and Religious Movements.* London: Pinter, 1979.

Wilson, Bryan R. *Magic and the Millennium: A Sociological Study of Religious Movements of Protest Among Tribal and Third World Peoples.* New York: Harper & Row, 1973.

_____. *Religion in Sociological Perspective*. Oxford: Oxford University Press, 1982.
Worsley, Peter. *The Trumpet Shall Sound: A Study of 'Cargo' Cults in Melanesia*. London: MacGibbon & Lee, 1957.
Zygmunt, Joseph F. "Prophetic Failure and Chiliastic Identity: The Case of Jehovah's Witnesses." *American Journal of Sociology* 75 (1970): 926–48.

4. MISCELLANEOUS HISTORICAL, CULTURAL
AND GRAMMATICAL STUDIES

Anrich, Gustav. *Das antike Mysterienwesen in seinem Einfluss auf das Christentum*. Göttingen: Vandenhoeck & Ruprecht, 1894.
Aune, David E. *The Cultic Setting of Realized Eschatology in Early Christianity*. Leiden: E. J. Brill, 1972.
_____. *Prophecy in Early Christianity and the Ancient Mediterranean World*. Grand Rapids: Wm. B. Eerdmans, 1983.
Baltensweiler, Heinrich. *Die Ehe im Neuen Testament: Exegetische Untersuchungen über Ehe, Ehelosigkeit und Ehescheidung*. Zurich: Zwingli, 1967.
Bammel, Ernst. "The Trial before Pilate." Pp. 415–51 in *Jesus and the Politics of His Day*, edited by E. Bammel and C. F. D. Moule. Cambridge, MA: Harvard University Press, 1984.
Bauer, Walter, William F. Arndt, F. Wilbur Gingrich and Frederick W. Danker. *A Greek-English Lexicon of the New Testament and Other Early Christian Literature*. 2d ed. Chicago: University of Chicago Press, 1979.
Baumgarten, Jörg. *Paulus und die Apokalyptik*. Neukirchen-Vluyn: Neukirchener-Verlag, 1975.
Baur, Ferdinand Christian. *Paul, the Apostle of Jesus Christ, his Life and Work, his Epistles and his Doctrine: A Contribution to the Critical History of Primitive Christianity*, trans. A. Menzies. 2 vols. London: Williams and Norgate, 1876.
Beck, Norman A. *Mature Christianity: The Recognition and Repudiation of the Anti-Jewish Polemic in the New Testament*. London and Toronto: Associated University Press, 1985.
Becker, Jürgen. *Auferstehung der Toten in Urchristentum*. Stuttgart: Katholische Bibelwerk, 1976.
Beker, J. Christiaan. *Paul's Apocalyptic Gospel*. Philadelphia: Fortress Press, 1982.
_____. *Paul the Apostle: The Triumph of God in Life and Thought*. Philadelphia: Fortress Press, 1980.
Betz, Hans Dieter. "Eine Christus-Aretalogie bei Paulus (2 Kor 12, 7–10)." *Zeitschrift für Theologie und Kirche* 66 (1969): 288–305.
_____. "Gottmensch. II. Griechisch-römische Antike und Urchristentum." Cols. 234–312 in *Reallexikon für Antike und Christentum*, edited by T. Klauser et al., vol. 12. Stuttgart: Hiersemann Verlag, 1983.
_____. "Jesus as Divine Man." Pp. 114–33 in *Jesus and the Historian: Written in Honor of Ernest Cadman Colwell*, edited by F. T. Trotter. Philadelphia: The Westminster Press, 1968.
_____. *Lukian von Samosata und das Neue Testament: Religionsgeschichtliche und paränetische Parallelen*. TU 76. Berlin: Akademie-Verlag, 1961.
Bieler, Ludwig. θΕΙΟΣ ANHP: *Das Bild des göttlichen Menschen in Spätantike und Frühchristentum*. Vienna: Höfels, 1935.
Bjerkelund, Carl. J. *Parakalô: Form, Funktion und Sinn der parakalô-Sätze in den paulinischen Briefen*. Oslo: Universitets-vorlaget, 1967.

Blaiklock, E. M. *Cities of the New Testament.* London: Pickering & Inglis, 1965.

Bornkamm, Günther. "Die Vorgeschichte des sogenannten Zweiten Korintherbriefes." Pp. 7–36 in *Sitzungsberichte der Heidelberger Akademie der Wissenschaften, Phil.-hist. Klasse.* 2d Abhandlung, 1961; reprinted with addendum, pp. 162–94 in Bornkamm, *Geschichte und Glaube II, Gesammelte Aufsätze IV.* Munich: Kaiser, 1971.

Brandenburger, Egon. *Adam und Christus: Exegetisch-religionsgeschichtliche Untersuchung zu Römer 5, 12–21.* Neukirchen: Neukirchener-Verlag, 1962.

Brandon, Samuel G. F. *Jesus and the Zealots.* Manchester: University Press, 1967.

Broer, Ingo. "'Antisemitismus' und Judenpolemik im Neuen Testament. Ein Beitrag zum besseren Verständnis von 1 Thess 2:14–16." *Biblische Notizen* 29 (1983): 59–91.

Brox, Norbert. *Falsche Verfasserangaben: Zur Erklärung der frühchristlichen Pseudepigraphie.* Stuttgart: Katholisches Bibelwerk, 1975.

Buck, Charles, and Greer Taylor. *Saint Paul: A Study in the Development of His Thought.* New York: Charles Scribners', 1969.

Burkert, Walter. *Greek Religion,* trans. J. Raffan. Cambridge, MA: Harvard University Press, 1985.

Burkitt, Francis C. *Christian Beginnings: Three Lectures.* London: University of London Press, 1924.

Burton, Edgar DeWitt. "The Politarchs." *American Journal of Theology* 2 (1898): 598–632.

Clemen, Carl C. *Die Einheitlichkeit der paulinischen Briefe an der Hand der bisher mit Bezug auf sie aufgestellten Interpolations- und Compilationshypothesen geprüft.* Göttingen: Vandenhoeck und Ruprecht, 1894.

Cole, Susan Guettel. *Theoi Megaloi: The Cult of the Great Gods at Samothrace.* Leiden: E. J. Brill, 1984.

Conzelmann, Hans. *Die Apostelgeschichte.* Tübingen: Mohr-Siebeck, 1963.

Corley, Bruce., ed. *Colloquy on New Testament Studies: A Time for Reappraisal and Fresh Approaches.* Macon: Mercer University Press, 1983.

Cullmann, Oscar. *Christ and Time: The Primitive Christian Conception of Time and History,* trans. F. V. Filson. Philadelphia: The Westminster Press, 1964.

Danker, Frederick W. *Benefactor: Epigraphic Study of a Graeco-Roman and New Testament Semantic Field.* St. Louis: Clayton, 1982.

Davies, Paul E. "The Macedonian Scene of Paul's Journeys." *Biblical Archeologist* 26 (1963): 91–106.

Doty, William G. *Letters in Primitive Christianity.* Philadelphia: Fortress Press, 1973.

Elliger, Winfried. *Paulus in Griechenland: Philippi, Thessaloniki, Athen Korinth.* Stuttgart: Katholisches Bibelwerk, 1978.

Ellis, E. Earle. "Paul and His Co-Workers." *New Testament Studies* 17 (1970–71): 437–52; reprinted, pp. 3–22 in E. Earle Ellis, *Prophecy and Hermeneutic in Early Christianity: New Testament Essays.* Grand Rapids: Wm. B. Eerdmans, 1978.

Farnell, Lewis P. *Greek Hero Cults and Ideas of Immortality.* Oxford: The Clarendon Press, 1921.

Finegan, Jack. *Handbook of Biblical Chronology.* Princeton: Princeton University Press, 1964.

Firmicus Maternus, Julius. *L'Erreur des Religions Païennes,* translation and commentary by R. Turcan. Paris: Societe D'Edition 'Les Belles Lettres,' 1982.

Frey, P. Jean-Baptiste. *Corpus of Jewish Inscriptions: Jewish Inscriptions from the Third Century B.C. to the Seventh Century A.D.* Vol 1: *Europe.* Reprint of 1936 ed., "Prolegomenon" by B. Lifschitz. New York: Ktav Publishing House, Inc., 1975.

Friedrich, Gerhard. "Die Gegner des Paulus im 2. Korintherbrief." Pp. 181–215 in *Abraham Unser Vater: Festschrift für Otto Michel zum 60. Geburtstag,* edited by O. Betz, M. Hengel and P. Schmidt. Leiden: E. J. Brill, 1963.

Funk, Robert W. *Language, Hermeneutic, and Word of God.* New York: Harper & Row, 1966.

Gager, John G. *The Origins of Antisemitism: Attitudes toward Judaism in Pagan and Christian Antiquity.* New York: Oxford University Press, 1983.

Gaston, Lloyd H. *No Stone on Another: Studies in the Significance of the Fall of Jerusalem in the Synoptic Gospels.* Leiden: E. J. Brill, 1970.

Gelzer, Heinrich K. G. "Die Genesis der Byzantischen Themenverfassung." Amsterdam: Hakkert, 1966; reprint of *Abhandlungen der philosophisch-historische Klasse der Sächsischen Gesellschaft* 18:5, 1899.

Georgi, Dieter. *Die Gegner des Paulus im 2. Korintherbrief.* Neukirchen: Neukirchener-Verlag, 1964.

――――. "Second Letter to the Corinthians." Pp. 184–85 in *Interpreter's Dictionary of the Bible,* edited by K. Crim, supp. vol. Nashville: Abingdon Press, 1976.

Glotz, Gustave. *Ancient Greece at Work: An Economic History of Greece from the Homeric Period to the Roman Conquest.* New York: Alfred A. Knopf, 1926.

Goguel, Maurice. *Introduction au Nouveau Testament.* 4 vols. Paris: Leroux, 1925.

Goppelt, Leonhard. *Jesus, Paul and Judaism: An Introduction to New Testament Theology,* trans. E. Schroeder. New York: Nelson, 1964.

Gren, Erik. *Kleinasien und der Ostbalkan in der wirtschaftlichen Entwicklung des römischen Kaiserzeit.* Uppsala: Lundequist, 1941.

Grotius, Hugo. *Operum Theologicorum.* Amsterdam: Blaev, 1679.

Gundry, Robert H. *A Survey of the New Testament.* Rev. ed. Grand Rapids: Zondervan, 1981.

Guthrie, Donald. *New Testament Introduction: The Pauline Epistles.* London: Tyndale, 1961.

Habicht, Christian. *Gottmenschentum und griechischen Städte.* 2d ed. Munich: C. H. Beck, 1970.

Hadas, Moses and Morton Smith. *Heroes and Gods: Spiritual Biographies in Antiquity.* New York: Harper & Row, 1965.

Haenchen, Ernst. *The Acts of the Apostles,* trans. from the 1965 14th ed. by B. Noble and G. Shinn. Philadelphia: The Westminster Press, 1971.

Harder, Günther. *Paulus und das Gebet.* Gütersloh: C. Bertelsmann, 1936.

Hare, Douglas R. A. *The Theme of Jewish Persecution of Christians in the Gospel According to St. Matthew.* Cambridge, MA: Harvard University Press, 1967.

Harris, James Rendel. *The Cult of the Heavenly Twins.* Cambridge, MA: Harvard University Press, 1906.

Hauck, Friedrich. "Arbeit." Cols. 585–90 in *Reallexikon für Antike und Christentum,* edited by T. Klauser et al., vol. 1. Stuttgart: Hiersemann Verlag, 1950.

――――. "Erwerb." Cols. 436–43 in *Reallexikon für Antike und Christentum,* edited by T. Klauser et al., vol. 6. Stuttgart: Hiersemann Verlag, 1966.

――――. "ὅσιος, κτλ." Pp. 488–91 in *Theologisches Wörterbuch zum Neuen Testament,* edited by G. Friedrich, vol. 5. Stuttgart: Kohlhammer, 1954.

Hellholm, David, ed. *Apocalypticism in the Mediterranean World and in the Near East.* Tübingen: Mohr-Siebeck, 1983.

Hemberg, Bengt. *Die Kabiren.* Uppsala: Almquist & Wiksells, 1950.

Hill, David. *New Testament Prophecy.* Atlanta: John Knox Press, 1979.

Hock, Ronald F. *The Social Context of Paul's Ministry: Tentmaking and Apostleship.* Philadelphia: Fortress Press, 1980.

Holladay, Carl R. *THEIOS ANER in Hellenistic-Judaism: A Critique of the Use of This Category in New Testament Christology.* Missoula, MT: Scholars Press, 1977.

Holsten, Carl C. J. *Das Evangelium des Paulus.* 2 vols. Berlin: G. Reimer, 1898.

Horsley, G. H. R. *New Documents Illustrating Early Christianity.* 3 vols. 1976–83.

Hübner, Hans. "Review of Gerd Lüdemann." *Paulus, der Heidenapostel, Theologische Literaturzeitung* 107 (1982): cols. 741–44.

Hurd, John C., Jr. "Chronology, Pauline." Pp. 166–67 in *Interpreter's Dictionary of the Bible*, edited by K. Crim, supp. vol. Nashville: Abingdon Press, 1976.

———. "Introduction." Pp. 265–70 in *Colloquy on New Testament Studies: A Time for Reappraisal and Fresh Approaches*, edited by B. Corley Macon: Mercer University Press, 1983.

———. "Pauline Chronology and Pauline Theology." Pp. 225–48 in *Christian History and Interpertation: Studies Presented to John Knox*, edited by W. R. Farmer, C. F. D. Moule and R. R. Niebuhr. Cambridge, MA: Harvard University Press, 1967.

———. "The Sequence of Paul's Letters." *Canadian Journal of Theology* 14 (1968): 189–200.

Jewett, Robert. "The Agitators and the Galatian Congregation." *New Testament Studies* 17 (1970–71): 198–212.

———. *A Chronology of Paul's Life*. Philadelphia: Fortress Press, 1979.

———. "Conflicting Movements in the Early Church as Reflected in Philippians." *Novum Testamentum* 12 (1970): 363–90.

———. "The Form and Function of the Homiletic Benediction." *Anglican Theological Review* 51 (1969): 18–34.

———. *Paul's Anthropological Terms: A Study of Their Use in Conflict Settings*. Leiden: E. J. Brill, 1971.

———. "The Redaction of I Corinthians and the Trajectory of the Pauline School." *Journal of the American Academy of Religion* Supplement 44.4 (1978): 389–444.

———. "The Sexual Liberation of the Apostle Paul." *Journal of the American Academy of Religion* Supplement 47.1 (1979): 55–87.

Johnson, Sherman. "Notes and Comments." *Anglican Theological Review* 23 (1941): 173–76.

Jonas, Hans. *The Gnostic Religion: The Message of the Alien God and the Beginnings of Christianity*. 2d ed. Boston: Beacon Press, 1963.

Judge, Edwin A. *The Social Pattern of Christian Groups in the First Century*. London: Tyndale, 1960.

Jülicher, Adolf. *Einleitung in das Neue Testament*. Tübingen: Mohr, 1901.

Kahrstedt, Ulrich. *Kulturgeschichte der römischen Kaiserzeit*. 2d ed. Bern: Francke, 1958.

Kallas, James. *The Satanward View*. Philadelphia: Fortress Press, 1961.

Kalleres, Jean N. *Les anciens Macédoniens. Étude linguistique et historique* 2.1. Collection de l'Institut francais d'Athenes 81. Athens, 1976.

Kee, Alistair. "The Imperial Cult: the Unmasking of an Ideology." *The Scottish Journal of Religious Studies* 6 (1985): 112–28.

Kee, Howard Clark. "Aretology and Gospel." *Journal of Biblical Literature* 92 (1973): 402–22.

———. "Divine Man." P. 243 in *Interpreter's Dictionary of the Bible*, edited by K. Crim, supp. vol. Nashville: Abingdon Press, 1976.

———. *Understanding the New Testament*. 4th ed. Englewood Cliffs: Prentice-Hall, 1983.

Kern, Otto. "Kabeiros und Kabeiroi." Cols 1399–1450 in *Paulys Real-Encyclopädie der classichen Altumswissenschaft*, edited by W. Kroll, vol. 10. Stuttgart: Metzler, 1919.

Knopf, Rudolf. *Das nachapostolische Zeitalter: Geschichte der Christlichen Gemeinden vom Beginn der Flavierdynastie bis zum Ende Hadrians*. Tübingen: Mohr, 1905.

Knox, John. *Chapters in a Life of Paul*. New York and Nashville: Abingdon Press, 1950.

———. "Chapters in a Life of Paul—A Response to Robert Jewett and Gerd Luedemann." Pp. 339–64 in *Colloquy on New Testament Studies: A Time for Reappraisal and Fresh Approaches*, edited by B. Corley. Macon: Mercer University Press, 1983.

Knox, Wilfred L. "The 'Divine Hero' Christology in the New Testament." *Harvard Theological Review* 41 (1948): 229–49.

Koenig, John. "From Mystery to Ministry: Paul as Interpreter of Charismatic Gifts." *Union Seminary Quarterly Review* 33 (1978): 167–74.

Koester, Helmut. *Introduction to the New Testament,* trans. H. Koester from the 1980 ed. 2 vols. Philadelphia: Fortress Press, 1982.

Koester, Helmut, and James M. Robinson. *Trajectories through Early Christianity.* Philadelphia: Fortress Press, 1970.

Kühner, Raphael and Bernhard Gerth. *Ausführliche Grammatik der griechischen Sprache.* Reprint of the 1898 3d ed. 2 vols. Darmstadt: Wissenschaftliche Buchgesellschaft, 1963.

Kümmel, Werner Georg. *Introduction to the New Testament,* trans. A. T. Mattill. New York and Nashville: Abingdon Press, 1966.

Lake, Kirsopp. *The Earlier Epistles of St. Paul: Their Motive and Origin.* London: Rivingstons, 1911.

Lampe, Geoffrey W. H. "A. D. 70 in Christian Reflection." Pp. 153–71 in *Jesus and the Politics of His Day,* edited by E. Bammel and C. F. D. Moule. Cambridge, MA: Harvard University Press, 1984.

Larson, J. A. O. "Roman Greece." Pp. 259–498 in *An Economic Survey of Ancient Rome,* edited by T. Frank, vol. 4. Baltimore: Johns Hopkins Press, 1933.

Lehmann, Phyllis Williams and Denys Spittle. *Samothrace: The Temenos.* Princeton: Princeton University Press, 1982.

Liefeld, Walter L. "The Hellenistic 'Divine Man' and the Figure of Jesus in the Gospels." *Journal of the Evangelical Theological Society* 16 (1973): 195–205.

Lohfink, Gerhard. *Die Himmelfahrt Jesu: Untersuchungen zu den Himmelfahrts- und Erhöhungstexten bei Lukas.* Munich: Kösel-Verlag, 1971.

Loisy, Alfred F. *Les Livres du Nouveau Testament.* Paris: Noury, 1922.

Lövestam, Evald. "Über die neutestamentliche Aufforderung der Nüchertnheit." *Studia theologica* 12 (1958): 80–102.

Luedemann, Gerd. *Paul, Apostle to the Gentiles: Studies in Chronology,* trans. E. S. Jones. Philadelphia: Fortress Press, 1984.

Lührmann, Dieter. *Das Offenbarungsverständnis bei Paulus und in paulinischen Gemeinden.* Neukirchen: Neukirchener-Verlag, 1965.

Lütgert, Wilhelm. "Freiheitspredigt und Schwarmgeister in Korinth." *Beiträge zur Förderung christlicher Theologie* 12 (1908): 129–279.

———. "Gesetz und Geist: Eine Untersuchung zur Vorgeschichte des Galaterbriefes." *Beiträge zur Förderung christlicher Theologie* 22 (1917): 473–576.

———. "Der Römerbrief als historiches Problem." *Beiträge zur Förderung christlicher Theologie* 17 (1913): 31–140.

Luz, Ulrich. *Das Geschichtsverständnis des Paulus.* Munich: Kaiser, 1968.

MacMullen, Ramsay. *Paganism in the Roman Empire.* New Haven: Yale University Press, 1981.

———. *Roman Social Relations 50 B.C. to A.D. 284.* New Haven: Yale University Press, 1974.

Marxsen, Willi. *Introduction to the New Testament: An Approach to its Problems,* trans. G. Busewell. Philadelphia: Fortress Press, 1968.

Mattern, Lieselotte. *Das Verständnis des Gerichts bei Paulus.* Zurich and Stuttgart: Zwingli, 1966.

Michaelis, Wilhelm. *Einleitung in das Neue Testament: Die Entstehung, Sammlung und Ueberlieferung der Schriften des Neuen Testaments.* 13th ed. Bern: Haller, 1961.

Moffatt, James. *Introduction to the Literature of the New Testament.* 3d ed. Edinburgh: T. & T. Clark, 1918.

Momigliano, Arnaldo. *Claudius: The Emperor and His Achievement,* trans. W. D. Hogarth. Oxford: The Clarendon Press, 1934.

Moore, Arthur L. *The Parousia in the New Testament.* Leiden: E. J. Brill, 1966.

Morgan, M. Gwyn. "Metellus Macedonicus and the Province Macedonia." *Historia* 18 (1969): 422–46.

Morgenthaler, Robert. *Statistik des neutestamentlichen Wortschatzes*. Zurich: Gotthelf, 1958.

Moulton, James H. *A Grammar of New Testament Greek*. 3d ed. 3 vols. Edinburgh: T. & T. Clark, 1949.

Müller, Christian. *Gottes Gerechtigkeit und Gottes Volk: Eine Untersuchung zu Römer 9–11*. Göttingen: Vandenhoeck & Ruprecht, 1964.

Munck, Johannes. *Christ and Israel: An Interpretation of Romans 9–11*, trans. I. Nixon. Philadelphia: Fortress Press, 1967.

_____. *Paul and the Salvation of Mankind*, trans. F. Clarke. Richmond: John Knox Press, 1959.

Munro, Winsome. *Authority in Peter and Paul: The Identification of a Pastoral Stratum in the Pauline Corpus and 1 Peter*. Cambridge, MA: Harvard University Press, 1983.

Murphy-O'Connor, Jerome. "Pauline Missions Before the Jerusalem Conference." *Revue biblique* 89 (1982): 71–91.

_____. *St. Paul's Corinth: Texts and Archaeology*. Wilmington: Michael Glazier, 1983.

Nilsson, Martin P. *Greek Piety*, trans. H. J. Rose. New York: W. W. Norton & Co., 1969.

_____. *Greek Popular Religion*. New York: Columbia University Press, 1940.

Nock, Arthur Darby. "A Cabiric Rite." *American Journal of Archaeology* 45 (1941): 576–81.

_____. *Conversion: The Old and the New in Religion from Alexander the Great to Augustine of Hippo*. Oxford: The Clarendon Press, 1933.

_____. *Early Gentile Christianity and its Hellenistic Background*. New York: Harper & Row, 1964.

Nörr, Dieter. "Zur Herrschaftsstruktur des römischen Reiches: Die Städte des Ostens und das Imperium." Pp. 3–20 in *Aufstieg und Niedergang der Römischen Welt* 2.7.1, edited by H. Temporini and W. Haase. Berlin: Walter de Gruyter, 1979.

O'Brien, Peter Thomas. *Introductory Thanksgivings in the Letters of Paul*. Leiden: E. J. Brill, 1977.

Ollrog, Wolf-Henning. *Paulus und seine Mitarbeiter: Untersuchungen zu Theorie und Praxis der paulinischen Mission*. Neukirchen: Erziehungsverein, 1979.

Oostendorp, Derk W. *Another Jesus: A Gospel of Jewish-Christian Superiority in II Corinthians*. Kampen: Kok, 1967.

Pagels, Elaine. *The Gnostic Paul*. Philadelphia: Fortress Press, 1975.

Papazoglu, Fanoula. "Quelques aspects de l'histoire de la province Macédoine." Pp. 302–69 in *Aufstieg und Niedergang der Römischen Welt* 2.7.1, edited by H. Temporini and W. Haase. Berlin: Walter de Gruyter, 1979.

Pervo, Richard I. *Profit with Delight: The Literary Genre of the Book of Acts*. Philadelphia: Fortress Press, forthcoming.

Pieper, Josef. *Enthusiasm and Divine Madness: On the Platonic Dialogue Phaedrus*, trans. R. and C. Winston. New York: Harcourt, Brace & World, 1964.

Reicke, Bo. *Diakonie, Festfreude und Zelos, in Verbindung mit der altchristlichen Agapenfeier*. Uppsala Universitets Arsskrift 5. Uppsala: Lundesquistska, 1951.

_____. "Judaeo-Christianity and the Jewish Establishment, A.D. 33–66." Pp. 145–52 in *Jesus and the Politics of His Day*, edited by E. Bammel and C. F. D. Moule. Cambridge, MA: Harvard University Press, 1984.

Reitzenstein, Richard. *Die hellenistischen Mysterienreligionen*. 3d ed. Leipzig: B. G. Teubner, 1956.

Robinson, John A. T. *Jesus and His Coming: The Emergence of a Doctrine*. New York and Nashville: Abingdon Press, 1957.

Roetzel, Calvin J. *The Letters of Paul: Conversations in Context*. Atlanta: John Knox Press, 1975.

Roloff, Jürgen. *Die Apostelgeschichte*. Göttingen: Vandenhoeck & Ruprecht, 1981.

Rostovtzeff, Mikhail I. *The Social and Economic History of the Roman Empire.* 2d ed. Oxford: The Clarendon Press, 1957.

Rowland, Christopher. *The Open Heaven: A Study of Apocalyptic in Judaism and Early Christianity.* New York: The Crossroad Publishing Co., 1982.

Rudolph, Kurt. *Gnosis: The Nature and History of an Ancient Religion,* edited by P. W. Coxon, K. H. Kuhn and R. M. Wilson. Edinburgh: T. & T. Clark, 1983.

Russell, David S. *Apocalyptic: Ancient and Modern.* London: SCM 1978.

Schade, Hans-Heinrich. *Apokalyptische Christologie bei Paulus: Studien zum Zusammenhang von Christologie und Eschatologie in den Paulusbriefen.* Göttingen: Vandenhoeck & Ruprecht, 1981.

Schenke, Hans-Martin. "Auferstehungsglaube und Gnosis." *Zeitschrift für die neutestamentliche Wissenschaft* 59 (1968): 123–26.

Schille, Gottfried. *Die Apostelgeschichte des Lukas.* Berlin: Evangelische Verlagsanstalt, 1983.

Schmithals, Walter. *Gnosticism in Corinth,* trans. J. E. Steeley. Nashville: Abingdon Press, 1971.

———. *Paulus und die Gnostiker: Untersuchungen zu den kleinen Paulusbriefen.* Hamburg-Bergstedt, 1965; English trans. J. E. Steely, *Paul and the Gnostics.* Nashville: Abingdon Press, 1972.

———. "Zur Abfassung und ältesten Sammlung der paulinischen Hauptbriefe." *Zeitschrift für die neutestamentliche Wissenschaft* 51 (1960): 225–45.

Schneider, Gerhard. *Die Apostelgeschichte.* 2 vols. Freiburg: Herder, 1980–82.

Scholem, Gershom. *The Messianic Idea in Judaism and Other Essays on Jewish Spirituality.* New York: Schocken Books, Inc., 1971.

———. *Sabbatai Sevi: The Mystical Messiah 1626–76.* Princeton: Princeton University Press, 1973.

Schrenk, Gottlob. "βάρος, κτλ," Pp. 551–54 in *Theologisches Wörterbuch zum Neuen Testament,* edited by G. Kittel et al., vol. 1. Stuttgart: Kohlhammer, 1933.

Schubert, Paul. *Form and Function of the Pauline Thanksgiving.* Berlin: A. Töpelmann, 1939.

Schulz, Siegfried. "Die Decke des Moses: Untersuchungen zu einer vorpaulinischen Ueberlieferung in 2 Kr. 3, 7–18." *Zeitschrift für die neutestamentliche Wissenschaft* 49 (1958): 1–30.

Scott, Robert. *The Pauline Epistles: A Critical Study.* Edinburgh: T. & T. Clark, 1909.

Scramuzza, Vincent M. *The Emperor Claudius.* Cambridge, MA: Harvard University Press, 1940.

Smalley, Stephen. "The Delay of the Parousia." *Journal of Biblical Literature* 83 (1964): 49–52.

Smallwood, E. Mary. *The Jews Under Roman Rule.* Leiden: E. J. Brill, 1976.

Snyder, Graydon F. "Sayings on the Delay of the End." *Biblical Research* 20 (1975): 19–35.

Spicq, Ceslas. *Notes de Lexicographie Neo-Testamentaire.* 3 vols. Göttingen: Vandenhoeck & Ruprecht, 1978.

Spivey, Robert A. and D. Moody Smith. *Anatomy of the New Testament: A Guide to Its Structure and Meaning.* 2d ed. New York: Macmillan, 1974.

Stanley, David M. "Become Imitators of Me: The Pauline Conception of Apostolic Tradition." Pp. 291–309 in *Studia Biblica et Orientalia.* Analecta Biblica 11. Rome: Biblical Institute Press, 1959.

Stepien, J. "Eschatologia św. Pawla" ["The Eschatology of Saint Paul"]. *Studia Theologica Varsaviensia* 1 (1963): 32–171.

Stern, Menahem. "The Jewish Diaspora." Pp. 117–83 in *The Jewish People in the First Century: Historical Geography, Political History, Social, Cultural and Religious Life and Institutions,* edited by S. Safrai et al., vol. 1. Philadelphia: Fortress Press, 1974.

Strobel, Adolf. *Untersuchungen zum eschatologischen Verzögerungsproblem: Auf Grund der Spätjüdisch-urchristlichen Geschichte von Habakuk 2, 2ff.* Leiden: E. J. Brill, 1961.

Suggs, M. Jack. "Concerning the Date of Paul's Macedonian Ministry." *Novum Testamentum* 4 (1960): 60–68.

Thrall, Margaret E. "Super-apostles, Servants of Christ, and Servants of Satan." *Journal for the Study of the New Testament* 6 (1980): 42–57.

Tiede, David L. *The Charismatic Figure as Miracle Worker.* Missoula, MT: Scholars Press, 1972.

Vielhauer, Philipp. *Geschichte der urchristlichen Literatur: Einleitung in das Neue Testament, die Apokryphen und die Apostolischen Väter.* 2d ed. Berlin and New York: Walter de Gruyter, 1978.

Weinreich, Otto. "Antikes Gottmenschtum." *Neue Jahrbücher* (1926): 633–51.

Weiss, Johannes. *The History of Primitive Christianity,* trans. F. C. Grant et al., 3 vols. New York: Wilson Erickson, 1937.

Wilckens, Ulrich. *Weisheit und Torheit: Eine exegetisch religionsgeschichtliche Untersuchung zu I Kor. 1 und 2.* Tübingen: Mohr-Siebeck, 1959.

Witt, Rex E. "The Egyptian Cults in Ancient Macedonia." Pp. 324–33 in *Ancient Macedonia,* edited by B. Laourdas and C. Makaronas, vol. 1. Thessaloniki: Institute for Balkan Studies, 1970.

———. "The Kabeiroi in Ancient Macedonia." Pp. 67–80 in *Ancient Macedonia,* vol. 2. Thessaloniki: Institute for Balkan Studies, 1977.

Zahn, Theodor. *Introduction to the New Testament,* trans. J. M. Trout et al. from 3d ed., 3 vols. Edinburgh: T. & T. Clark, 1909.

Charts

Chart 1

Outlines of 1 Thessalonians Using Thematic Analysis

Walter F. Adeney

1:1–10	2:1–12	2:13–16	2:17–20	3:1–10	3:11–13
salutation thanksgivings & congratulations	apostle's ministry at Thessalonica	thanksgiving again	visit frustrated	mission of Timothy	hope to visit Thessalonica

Ernest Best

1:1–10	2:1–12	2:13–16	2:17–3:13
address & thanksgiving	initial behavior of apostles	renew thanks	Paul's relationship after departure

F. F. Bruce

1:1–10	2:1–12	2:13–16	2:17–3:13
address & thanksgiving	apostolic defense	further thanks	plans for a second visit

Wilhelm Bornemann

1:1–10	2:1–16	2:17–3:13
address & thanksgiving	early relation between Paul & the church	recent relation between Paul & the church

Karl Paul Donfried

1:1–10	2:1–12	2:13–16	2:17–3:13
greeting & thanksgiving	apostolic behavior	reception of the gospel	apostle's continuing concern for the church

James Everett Frame

1:1	1:2–3:10		3:11–13
super-scription	thanksgiving (subcategory of a. "The Apologia," 1:2–3:13)		prayer

Gerhard Friedrich

1:1–2:13 greeting, section 1 "Rehearsal of the Beginnings," 1:2–3:13

1:2–10	2:1–12	2:13–16	2:17–3:13
thanks for good behavior of church	purity of apostolic mission in Thessalonica	conversion under persecution	recent relation of apostle to congregation

Donald Guthrie

1:1–10	2:1–12	2:17–3:13
greeting & thanksgiving prayer	Paul's mission work in Thessalonica	Paul's present relationship to the Thessalonians

Chart 1   217

Adeney

4:1-8	4:9-12	4:13-18	5:1-3	5:4-11	5:12-22	5:23-28
exhortation to purity	love and quiet work	blessed dead	coming of Christ	call for sobriety	various practical admonitions	final commendations & benediction

Best

4:1-5:22	5:23-28
admonition	close

Bruce

4:1-5:22	5:23-28
exhortation	close

Bornemann

4:1-12	4:13-5:10	5:11-28
marks of discipleship	return of Christ	closing admonitions

Donfried

4:1-12	4:13-5:11	5:12-24	5:25-28
ethical exhortations	instructions about the parousia	exhortations about life in the church	closing

Frame

4:1-5:22	5:23-28
exhortations (subcategory of b. "The Weak, the Idlers, the Faint-hearted, etc.," 4:1-5:17)	prayer requests benediction

Friedrich

section 2 "exhortations," 4:1-5:24   5:25-28

4:1-12	4:13-18	5:1-11	5:12-24	
sanctification in marriage, 4:1-8 brotherly love, 4:9 admonition to work, 4:10-12	comfort concerning the deceased	warning about wakefulness	warnings about congregational life	closing

Guthrie

4:1-12	4:13-5:11	5:12-22	5:23-28
practical exhortation	the parousia	further practical exhortations	conclusion

Willi Marxsen

1:1–10	2:1–16	2:17–3:13
prescript &	apology of	the apostle and
thanksgiving	Paul's gospel	his congregation

I. Howard Marshall

1:1–10	2:1–12	2:13–16	2:17–3:13
greeting &	behavior of	reception	Paul's continued concern
opening	apostles in	of message	for the church
thanksgiving	Thessalonica		

George Milligan

1:1–2:13 address & greeting, 1:1; historical & personal, 1:2–3:13

1:2–10	2:1–12	2:13–16	2:17–3:10	3:11–13
thanksgiving	character	renewed	relation of apostles	prayer
for good state	of apostolic	thanksgiving	to church	
of church	ministry			

Leon Morris

1:1–4	1:5–2:16	2:17–3:13
greeting &	reminiscences	relationship of Paul
prayer of		to the Thessalonians
thanksgiving		

Beda Rigaux

1:1–3:13 Salutation, 1st part: rapport between missionaries & Thessalonians

1:2–10	2:1–16	2:17–3:13
foundation:	foundation:	after the departure
1st scene	2nd scene	of the apostles

A. Roosen

1:1–10	2:1–3:13 historical-apologetic section	
address &	2:1–16	2:17–3:13
introductory	during the founding mission	after the founding mission
thanksgiving		

Heinz Schürmann

opening, 1:1	2:1–16	2:17–3:11	3:12–13
thanksgiving, 1:2–3	looking back to the	concern for the	final
election	beginnings of	constancy of	blessing
& call of the	the community	the community	
Thessalonians, 1:4–10			

Robert A. Spivey & D. Moody Smith, Jr.

salutation, personal & related matters, 1:1–3:13

1:1–10	2:1–16	2:17–3:10	3:11–13
address &	Paul's missionary work	Timothy's	prayer
thanksgiving		misson	

Chart 1 219

Marxsen

4:1–12 behavior as faith lived out	4:13–5:11 faith as hope lived out	5:12–22 individual exhortations	5:23–28 conclusion

Marshall

4:1–12 exhortation to to ethical progress	4:13–5:11 instruction & exhortation about the parousia	5:12–24 instructions for life in the church	5:25–28 closing

Milligan

hortatory and doctrinal, 4:1–5:24   5:25–28

4:1–12 lessons in Christian morals	4:13–18 teaching on those asleep	5:1–11 teaching about the advent of Christ	5:12–22 precepts about church life & holy living	5:23–24 prayer	concluding benediction

Morris

4:1–12 exhortation to Christian living	4:13–5:11 problems with the parousia	5:12–22 general exhortations	5:23–28 conclusion

Rigaux

2nd part: directives and exhortations, 4:1–5:24   5:25–28

4:1–8 appeal for chastity	4:9–12 love	4:13–18 parousia	5:1–11 recommendations on vigilance	5:12–24 exhortations on the life of the community	prayer & salutation

Roosen

dogmatic-paraenetic section, 4:1–5:24   5:25–28

4:1–12 appeal for purity and love	4:13–18 the dead	5:1–11 doctrine of the parousia	5:12–24 diverse exhortations	conclusion

Schürmann

4:1–12 life pleasing to god, 4:1–3a warning on pagan vices, 4:3b–8 love, 4:9–12	4:13–18 salvation for the dead	5:1–11 demands of the hour	5:12–24 Christian life in community, 5:12–22 summing up in a final exhortation, 5:23–24	5:25–28 close of the letter

Spivey & Smith

exhortation & encouragement, benediction, 4:1–5:28

4:1–12 general instructions	4:13–5:11 the return of Jesus	5:12–27 final instructions	5:28 benediction

CHART 2

Outlines of 1 Thessalonians Using Epistolary Analysis

John A. Bailey

1:1–10	2:1–3:13	4:1–5:28
letter opening	letter body	letter close
prescript, 1:1	a. thanksgiving in the middle, 2:13	a. paraenesis, 4:1–5:22
thanksgiving, 1:2–10	b. benediction at the end, 3:11–13	b. peace wish, 5:23–24
		c. greetings, 5:26
		d. benediction, 5:28

Hendrikus Boers

1:1–10	2:1–12	2:13–16	2:17–3:13	4:1–5:22	5:23–28
prescript &	apostolic	unassigned	apostolic	exhortation	conclusion
thanksgiving	apology		parousia		

William G. Doty

1:1–2:16	2:1–3:13	4:1–5:22	5:23–28
opening,	the body	paraenesis	closing
thanksgiving,	a. formal opening, 2:1–4		
& blessing	b. eschatological conclusion, 2:5–16		
	c. travelogue, 2:17–3:13		

John C. Hurd, Jr.

1:1–10	2:1–16	2:17–3:13	4:1–5:22	5:23–24
greeting &	body, with	apostolic	paraenesis	blessing
thanksgiving	renewed thanksgiving	visitation		5:25–28
				autograph coda

Robert J. Peterson

1:1–10	contents part 1, 2:1–3:13	contents part 2, 4:1–5:24	5:25–28
salutation	relation to church, 2:1–12	exhortation, 4:1–8	benediction
& proem	thanksgiving, 2:13–16	love of the brethren, 4:9–11	
	report of Timothy, 2:17–3:6	general exhortations, 4:12–22	
	continuation of thanksgiving, 3:7–10		
	benediction, 3:11–13		

Calvin J. Roetzel

1:1–10	2:1–3:8	3:9–13	4:1–5:22	5:23–28
salutation &	body of letter	unassigned	ethical instruction	closing
thanksgiving	(also possibly 3:11–13)		and exhortation	
(also 2:13 & 3:9–10)				

Chart 3 221

Chart 3

Comparison with Other Rhetorical Analyses of 1 Thessalonians

Frank Witt Hughes

1:1–10	2:1–3:10	3:11–13	4:1–5:5	5:4–11	5:12–22	5:23–28
exordium prescript & thanksgiving	narratio	partitio	probatio	peroratio	exhortation	conclusion

Robert Jewett

1:1–5	1:6–3:13		4:1–5:22		5:23–28
exordium	narratio of grounds for thanksgiving		probatio		peroratio
	a. imitation, 1:6–10		a. marriage ethic, 4:1–8		
	b. apostolic example, 2:1–12		b. communal ethic, 4:9–12		
	c. Judean example, 2:13–16		c. dead in Christ, 4:13–18		
	d. visit, 2:17–3:10		d. eschaton, 5:1–11		
	e. transitus, 3:11–13		e. congregational life, 5:12–22		

George A. Kennedy

1:1–10	2:1–8	2:9–3:13	4:1–5:22		5:23–28
address & proem	refutation of charges	narration in ethical & pathetical terms	headings: general proposition, injunctions		epilogue & closure

Helmut Koester

1:1	1:2–3:13		4:1–5:11	5:12–28
prescript	proem in the form of thanksgiving with 3 major sections:		instructions and admonitions	not specifically identified

	1:1–10	2:1–12	2:17–3:13
	past relation	apology of past behavior	discussion of present situation

CHART 4

Outlines of 2 Thessalonians Using Thematic Analysis

John W. Bailey

1:1–12	2:1–17	3:1–16	3:16–18
address, greeting & thanksgiving	the revelation of the man of lawlessness	closing appeals, instruction & prayer	closing greeting & thanksgiving

Ernest Best

1:1–12	2:1–12	2:13–17	3:1–5	3:6–15	3:16–18
address, thanksgiving, encouragement & prayer	the end	assurance of salvation	mutual prayer	idle brothers	conclusion

F. F. Bruce

1:1–12	2:1–12	2:13–17	3:1–5	3:6–15	3:17–18
prescript, thanksgiving, encouragement & prayer	rise and fall of the man of lawlessness	further thanksgiving, encouragement & prayer	further prayer	exhortation	closing

Karl Paul Donfried

1:1–12	2:1–17	3:1–16	3:17–18
greeting & thanksgiving	instructions about the man of lawlessness	exhortations	letter closing

Hans-Andreas Egenolf

1:1–2	1:3–12	2:1–12	2:13–3:5	3:6–16	3:17–18
letterhead	explanation of the situation	warning about the return of Christ	the right spirit of faith	idleness & laziness in the church	closing

George G. Findlay

1:1–4	1:5–12	2:1–12	2:13–3:5	3:6–16	3:17–18
salutation & thanksgiving	approaching judgment	revelation of the lawless one	words of comfort and prayer	the case of the idlers	conclusion

James Everett Frame

1:1–2	1:3–2:17	3:1–17	3:18
super-scription	encouraging the faint-hearted thanksgiving & prayer, 1:3–12 exhortation, 2:1–12 thanksgiving, command & prayer, 2:13–17	warning the idlers finally, 3:1–5 command and exhortation, 3:6–15 prayer, 3:16 salutation, 3:17	benediction

Gerhard Friedrich

1:1–12	2:1–12	2:13–17	3:1–5	3:6–16	3:17–18
greeting, thanks assurance & intercession	the signs preceding the parousia	certainty of salvation	request for intercession	church discipline	signature

Chart 4   223

Donald Guthrie

1:1–4	1:5–10	1:11–12	2:1–12	2:13–17	3:1–15	3:16–18
greeting & thanksgiving	judgment of God	prayer	the parousia	further thanksgiving	exhortations	conclusion

Willi Marxsen

1:1–12			2:1–12	2:13–3:5	3:6–12	3:13–16	3:17–18
prescript thanksgiving & teaching on judgment at the parousia			the place of the present in the apocalyptic plan of events	different exhortations	the disorderly	summary of exhortation	closing

I. Howard Marshall

1:1–12	2:1–17	3:1–16	3:17–18
greeting & opening thanksgiving	instruction: the coming of the day of the Lord	exhortation: prayer for Paul's mission, 3:1–5 the danger of idleness, 3:6–16	concluding greeting

George Milligan

1:1–2	1:3–2:17	3:1–16	3:17–18
address & greeting	historical & doctrinal thanksgiving & prayer, 1:3–12 teaching on parousia, 2:1–12 renewed thanksgiving, 2:13–15 prayer, 2:16–17	consolatory & hortatory requested prayer, 3:1–2 confidence, 3:3–5 exhortations, 3:6–15 prayer, 3:16	salutation & benediction

Alfred Plummer

1:1–12	2:1–17	3:1–16	3:17–18
salutation historical & doctrinal 1:3–12	doctrinal & hortatory doctrine of the Lord's coming, 2:1–12 thanksgiving, 2:13–15 prayer, 2:16–17	cheering & commanding request, prayer, 3:1–5 reproof & instruction, 3:6–15 prayer, 3:16	salutation & benediction

Beda Rigaux

1:1–12	2:1–3:5	3:6–15	3:16–18
address & first part: exhortations & encouragements	second part: the parousia and the signs a. parousia not yet present because signs are lacking, 2:1–12 b. salvation assurance to the brothers, 2:13–3:5	third part: admonition vs. unruly brothers	salutation & benediction

Wolfgang Trilling

1:1–12	2:1–14	2:15–3:16	3:17–18
opening greeting & introduction (proömium)	the Day of the Lord, 2:1–12 thanks for election, 2:13–14	exhortative portion: exhortations, prayerful wishes regulations	letter closing

Chart 5

Outlines of 2 Thessalonians Using Epistolary Analysis

John A. Bailey

1:1–12	2:1–16	2:17	3:1–18
letter opening	letter body	unassigned	letter close
a. prescript, 1:1f.	a. thanksgiving in		a. paraenesis, 3:1–15
b. thanksgiving, 1:3–12	the middle, 2:13		b. peace wish, 3:16
	b. benediction		c. greetings, 3:17
	at the end, 2:16		d. benediction, 3:18

John C. Hurd, Jr.

1:1–2	1:3–12	2:1–12	2:13–17	3:1–15	3:16–18
greeting	thanksgiving	body	renewal of	moral introduction	closing
			thanksgiving		

Gerhard Krodel

1:1–12	2:1–12	2:13–3:5	3:6–15	3:16–18
prescript &	eschatological	thanksgiving,	admonitions	closing
thanksgiving	exhortation	admonition & benediction	a. idlers	
		1st cycle, 2:13–16	b. general	
		2nd cycle, 3:1–5	admonition	

Robert J. Peterson

1:1–2	1:3–12	2:1–17	3:1–16	3:17–18
salutation	proem	contents part I	contents part II	conclusion
	prayer, 1:3–5	eschatological argument, 2:1–12	general exhortation, 3:1–5	
	proof, 1:6–10	thanksgiving continuation, 2:13–14	exhortation to idlers, 3:6–15	
	continuation of	exhortation, 2:15	benediction, 3:16	
	thanksgiving, 1:11–12	benediction, 2:16–17		

Chart 6   225

CHART 6

Outlines of 2 Thessalonians Using Rhetorical Analysis

Glenn Holland

1:1-2	1:3-4	1:5-12	2:1-17	3:1-13	3:14-15	3:16-18
epistolary prescript	exordium	narratio a. scene, 1:5-10 b. prayer, 1:11-12	probatio a. topic of doctrinal exhortation, 2:1-3a b. proof of falsehood, 2:3b-12 c. description of thanksgiving, 2:13-14 d. conclusion, 2:15-17	exhortatio a. prayer request, 3:1-5 exhortation against unruly, 3:6-13	peroratio	epistolary postscript

---

Frank Witt Hughes

1:1-12		2:1-2	2:3-17	3:1-15	3:16-18
epistolary prescript & exordium: thanksgiving, 1:3-10		partitio	probatio 1st proof, 2:3-12 2nd proof, 2:13-17	exhortatio	epistolary postscript

---

Robert Jewett

1:1-12	2:1-2	2:3-3:5	3:6-15	3:16-18
exordium a. epistolary prescript, 1:1-2 b. thanksgiving, 1:3-10 c. intercessory prayer, 1:11-12	partitio	probatio 1st proof, 2:3-12 2nd proof 2:13-3:5	exhortatio a. discipline, 3:6 b. ethical grounding, 3:7-10 c. on the disorderly, 3:11-13 d. on exclusion, 3:14-15	peroratio a. homiletic benediction, 3:16 b. postscript 3:17 c. final greeting, 3:18

PASSAGES

New Testament

Acts   49–52, 55, 57, 59, 114
  9:26–29   55
  10:25–26   155
  14:11f.   155
  17   114–15, 117–20
  17:1–9   115–17
  17:1–10   115
  17:2   114
  17:4   22, 117, 120
  17:5   114–16
  17:6   114–16
  17:6–7   115
  17:7   114, 117, 125
  17:10–13   22
  17:14   50
  17:14–15   25
  17:15   52
  18   58
  18:1   53
  18:2   58
  18:5   25, 50, 60
  18:22   50–51, 55
  19:22   51
  20:4   118–19
  21–23   55

Romans   12, 38
  1–2   8
  1–3   12
  1:18–25   40
  1:24   151
  6:19   151
  9–11   9, 12, 38, 40
  15:25–32   55
  16   12
  16:5   24

1 and 2 Corinthians   12, 36, 38, 51, 57

1 Corinthians
  2:8   38
  4:2   80
  5   12
  9:14   152
  13   12
  16:4   55
  16:15   24

2 Corinthians   149, 155–56
  1:1–2:13   43
  2:14–17   154
  3:1–3   154
  3:5   154
  4:2   153
  4:5   154
  5:10   100
  6:3–10   15
  7:5–8:24   43
  8:1–9:4   39
  8:2–4   120
  10–13   12
  10:1   153
  10:12   154
  10:18   154
  11:12–13   153
  11:13   153
  11:20   152
  11:20–21   153
  11:24–31   15
  11:32–33   59
  11:7–9   152–53
  12:1–13   154
  12:11   153–54
  12:16   153
  12:21   151
  13:3–7   154
  13:11   80

Galatians   12–13, 26, 38, 54–56, 142
  1:17–22   54
  1:18–19   55

Galatians
  1:18–2:1   59
  2:1–10   55
  2:2   54
  2:4   54
  2:6   54
  2:11–15   54
  2:14–16   54
  3:1–4:31   54
  5:12   38
  5:19   151
  6:11   185
  6:12   39

Ephesians   16
  4:19   151
  5:3   151

Philippians   12, 56
  3:1   80
  3:2   40
  4:8   80
  4:16   116–17

Colossians   16
  3:5   151
  4:10–11   118

1 Thessalonians
  1:1   60, 70, 216, 218, 220–21
  1:1–10   216, 218, 220–21
  1:1–4   218
  1:1–5   72, 221
  1:1–2:12   33, 43
  1:1–2:13   216, 218
  1:1–2:16   220
  1:1–3:13   218
  1:2   33, 42
  1:2–3   69–70
  1:2–4   69
  1:2–5   72, 76
  1:2–5:14   70
  1:2–7   41
  1:2–10   41–42, 69, 216, 218, 220
  1:2–2:12   40
  1:2–2:16   69
  1:2–3:10   216
  1:2–3:13   34, 69–70, 216, 218, 221
  1:3   34, 76, 143
  1:4   76, 97
  1:5   13, 29, 76–77, 100, 102, 148
  1:5–6   100
  1:5–7   45
  1:5–10   13, 35

  1:5–2:12   34
  1:5–2:16   218
  1:6   9, 13, 28, 43, 77, 93–94, 100
  1:6–9   41
  1:6–10   73, 76–77, 168, 221
  1:6–3:13   72–73, 77, 221
  1:7–8   53
  1:8   50
  1:9   77, 118, 148
  1:9–10   14, 29, 77
  1:10   26, 33, 68, 76, 145, 171, 189
  2   40, 49, 92, 150–51
  2:1   69, 77, 102
  2:1–2   43
  2:1–4   220
  2:1–8   9, 221
  2:1–9   13
  2:1–12   29, 30, 35, 69, 73, 77, 102, 148–
    49, 153, 156, 169–70, 216, 218, 220–21
  2:1–16   45, 76, 216, 218, 220
  2:1–3:8   220
  2:1–3:10   221
  2:1–3:13   218, 220
  2:1–3:18   220
  2:2   13, 28, 117, 154, 189
  2:3   151–52
  2:4   13, 154
  2:5   152
  2:5–16   220
  2:6   152
  2:6–7   152
  2:7   152
  2:8   154
  2:8–9   13
  2:9   143, 152
  2:9–12   9, 13, 76–77, 120
  2:9–3:13   221
  2:10   77, 151–52
  2:10–12   38
  2:12   35, 38
  2:13   13, 33, 38, 43–44, 69, 220
  2:13–16   33, 35–42, 45–46, 50, 69, 73,
    189, 216, 218, 220
  2:13–17   77
  2:13–4:2   33
  2:14   28, 39, 50, 93–94, 116
  2:14–16   40–41, 54–55
  2:14–17   13
  2:15   38
  2:15–17   14
  2:16   37–38, 40–41, 57, 117, 189
  2:17   29, 35, 38, 116–17
  2:17–20   43, 74, 216
  2:17–3:2   44

1 Thessalonians
2:17–3:4   43
2:17–3:6   220
2:17–3:10   40, 74, 77, 218, 221
2:17–3:11   218
2:17–3:13   69, 216, 218, 220–21
2:18   35, 52, 186–87
2:18–19   187
2:19   77
3   137
3:1   25–26, 43
3:1–2   43
3:1–5   74, 93
3:1–6   76
3:1–10   29, 216
3:2   13, 53, 60, 143
3:2–3   29, 116
3:3   24, 93
3:3–4   28, 34
3:4   35, 94
3:5   43, 143, 187
3:5–10   43
3:5–11   44
3:6   43, 53
3:6–10   34, 43, 74, 77
3:7–10   220
3:8   29
3:9–10   220
3:9–13   42, 220
3:10   69, 187
3:11   34, 42, 77
3:11–12   220
3:11–13   14, 34, 43–44, 69, 74, 77–78,
       188, 216, 218, 220–21
3:12   34, 77
3:12–13   218
3:13   34, 68–69, 76, 77, 145, 151
3:13–16   221
3:14   181
3:14–15   36
4   22, 96, 137
4–5   58–59, 92
4:1   34, 80, 105, 127
4:1–2   9, 13
4:1–8   54, 75–77, 105, 106, 108, 138, 148,
       173, 217, 219, 220–21
4:1–12   45, 217, 219
4:1–5:5   221
4:1–5:11   221
4:1–5:22   75, 78, 217, 220–21
4:1–5:24   70, 217, 219, 220
4:1–5:28   219, 220
4:2   105
4:3   35

4:3–5:28   33
4:3–8   78, 127
4:6   105, 106
4:6–8   9
4:7   151
4:8   77, 105
4:9   13, 78, 217
4:9–10   43, 44
4:9–11   220
4:9–12   25, 75–77, 143, 217, 219, 221
4:9–5:11   25
4:10–12   78, 217
4:11   120
4:11–12   104, 152
4:12–22   220
4:13   77, 78, 95, 190
4:13–14   43–44
4:13–17   44
4:13–18   5, 25–26, 41–42, 50, 75–76, 94–
       96, 148, 217, 219, 221
4:13–5:3   78
4:13–5:9   14
4:13–5:10   217
4:13–5:11   9, 43, 76, 148, 191, 217, 219
4:14   26
4:15   42, 95, 99, 148–49, 182
4:16–17   25
4:17   182
4:18   78
5:1   13, 25, 78, 96
5:1–2   9, 97
5:1–3   78, 149, 217
5:1–5   43–44, 187
5:1–11   5–7, 25, 33, 36, 41–42, 45, 75,
       96–97, 148, 151, 217, 219, 221
5:1–22   44
5:2   97, 99, 188
5:3   149
5:4–10   78
5:4–11   78, 217, 221
5:5   145
5:5–7   127
5:6   78
5:6–10   190
5:6–8   97, 100
5:9–11   43–44
5:10   42, 190
5:11   78
5:11–28   217
5:12   78, 104, 143
5:12–13   23, 103, 148, 170, 175
5:12–15   45
5:12–18   76
5:12–22   75–76, 80, 217, 219, 221

1 Thessalonians
  5:12–24 217, 219
  5:12–27 219
  5:12–28 221
  5:13 143
  5:14 23, 36, 97, 104
  5:16–22 43
  5:19–22 44, 77, 101, 108, 127
  5:21 101
  5:21–22 45
  5:22 104
  5:23 44, 107, 175–76, 188
  5:23–24 14, 70, 72, 219–20
  5:23–26 43
  5:23–28 70, 76, 217, 219, 220–21
  5:24 70
  5:25–28 43, 70, 216–17, 219, 220
  5:26 220
  5:27 21, 23, 28, 70, 185
  5:28 43, 219–20
  5:30 28

2 Thessalonians
  1:1 60
  1:1–2 222–25
  1:1–4 222–23
  1:1–12 33, 79, 82, 222–25
  1:3 22, 79, 81–82
  1:3–4 79, 225
  1:3–5 224
  1:3–10 79, 225
  1:3–12 15, 79, 82, 222–24
  1:3–2:17 222–23
  1:4 60, 79, 189
  1:4–7 28
  1:4–10 7
  1:5 86
  1:5–10 13, 79, 81, 223, 225
  1:5–12 5, 79, 222, 225
  1:6–8 7, 9
  1:6–10 224
  1:7 8, 145
  1:8 13, 26
  1:8–10 28, 86
  1:9–10 9
  1:11 79
  1:11–12 79, 143, 223–24
  2 25, 57
  2:1 35, 52, 79
  2:1–2 43, 83, 86, 181, 225
  2:1–3 225
  2:1–12 5, 7, 9, 33, 81, 222–24
  2:1–14 223
  2:1–16 224

  2:1–17 222–25
  2:1–3:5 223
  2:2 6–8, 14–15, 17, 22, 24, 27, 52, 58, 87,
      97–101, 148, 176–78, 181–85, 189
  2:3–12 6, 24, 83, 86, 187, 225
  2:3–17 225
  2:3–3:5 83, 225
  2:4 6
  2:5 52, 97
  2:5–12 36
  2:6 187
  2:6–7 58
  2:7–9 54
  2:10–12 35
  2:11 151
  2:13 9, 22, 24, 35, 81–82, 224
  2:13–14 9, 33, 43–44, 79, 224–25
  2:13–15 223
  2:13–16 224
  2:13–17 79–80, 222–25
  2:13–3:5 80–84, 86, 222–25
  2:14 35
  2:15 5, 9, 13, 17, 22, 27, 29, 35, 45, 80,
      86, 182, 183, 186, 224
  2:15–17 225
  2:15–3:5 33
  2:15–3:16 223
  2:16 34, 224
  2:16–17 34, 43–44, 82, 86, 223–24
  2:17 52, 143, 224
  3 45
  3:1 50, 52, 79–80
  3:1–2 50–51, 86, 223
  3:1–5 80, 222–24
  3:1–13 80, 225
  3:1–15 223–25
  3:1–16 222–24
  3:1–17 222
  3:1–18 224
  3:2 5
  3:3–4 80
  3:3–5 223
  3:4 45
  3:5 82, 86
  3:6 23, 36, 52, 80, 85–86, 177, 225
  3:6–10 45, 105
  3:6–12 13, 120, 223
  3:6–13 7, 152, 225
  3:6–15 8, 25, 45, 81–82, 85, 86, 104–5,
      137, 176, 222, 222–25
  3:6–16 33, 143, 222–23
  3:7–10 85–86, 225
  3:10 52
  3:11 104, 143

2 Thessalonians
   3:11–13   85, 225
   3:11–15   43, 45
   3:12   177
   3:13–14   5
   3:13–16   223
   3:14–15   85, 225
   3:14–16   225
   3:15   87
   3:16   81–82, 87, 222–24
   3:16–17   81, 224
   3:16–18   85, 87, 222–25
   3:17   3, 5–7, 9–10, 15, 17, 22, 24, 27, 182–
      85, 222, 224–25
   3:17–18   33, 43, 222–25
   3:18   87, 222, 224–25

Philemon   12, 16
   24   118

2 Tim
   2:18   6, 148
James
   1:18   24

Old Testament and Pseudepigrapha

Genesis
   1–3   149

1 Enoch
   10:19   122

Syrian Baruch
   29:5   122

Miscellaneous

Acta apostolorum apocrypha I   155
Aristotle
   Rhetoric 2. 1355–56   65
Cicero   119
   De Oratore 2. 115   65
   De Oratore 2. 183–85   65
   pro Flacco 37   67
Clement of Alexandria
   Protrepticus II 19:1–4   128
Firmicus Maternus XI   128, 207
Irenaeus
   Against Heresies 5,33–36   122
Josephus
   Ant. xx, 112   38
   Bell. ii, 224–27   38

Orphica
   Arg 2   129
   Hymn 39, lines 5–6   129
Plato
   Phaedrus   144
Strabo, 7. Fragment 21   119

Index

SUBJECTS

Achaia 53, 123
Adam 173
Aegean Sea 60
Agrippa 37
Alexander the Great 123
Anomie 163
Antioch 54, 146
Antony 124
Aphrodite 127
Apocalyptic 4, 13–14, 122, 145, 147, 168, 171, 188
  Christ 128, 165, 168–69, 176
  Confusion 5, 22, 86–87, 138–39, 147, 156
  Drama 80
  Ethos 13, 28, 78, 141, 147, 171
  Judgement 41
  Proclamation xiii, xv, 14, 77, 101, 122–23, 125, 139, 146
  Theology xv, 5, 7, 9, 13–14, 22, 25, 28, 41–42, 77, 79, 80, 82, 86, 96, 98–99, 131, 139, 141, 149, 155, 161–62, 165, 168, 187–89
  Woes 87
Archeology 113–15, 118, 120, 126
Aretas IV 59
  Escape from 56
Aristarchus 118
Aristotle 72
Asclepius 127
Asia 50, 121
Assumption into paradise 96
Athens 24, 26, 50–53, 56, 60, 74
Augustus 126, 131
Average congregation model 140–42

Bacchus 128
Barnabas 54, 155
Beroea 26, 50, 52
  Church in 22
  Letter to 22
Bohemia 173

Cabirus 127–32, 165–67, 169–70, 173
Caesar 124–26
Caligula 24, 57, 145
Celsus 154
Charismatic leader 170, 175
Christology 26
Cicero 67
Claudius 37, 58
  Edict of 56, 58
Comanches 171
Corinth 24, 26, 49–53, 56, 58–60, 127, 142, 154
  Paul's arrival in 56, 60
  Congregation in 51, 101
  Congregational situation 95
  Ministry in 53
  Situation in 148, 150, 153–54, 176
Cornelius 155
Corybantes 129
Cynic influence 150
Cyprus 125
Cyrene 125

Day of the Lord xiii, 97, 99, 137, 143, 146, 171, 177, 184, 186, 188–89, 191
Death of Christians xiii, 25–26, 41, 50, 76, 94–96, 137, 138, 143, 145–48, 155, 171, 176–78
Demeter 127
Demetrius 129
Democratic ideals 122–24, 131, 166
Dio Chrysostom 150
Dionysus 126
Divine man model 149–57
Divinization 130, 149, 156, 170, 176–77
Doukhobors 168

Ecstasy xiii, 100–103, 107, 137, 140, 143–46, 153–56, 161, 166, 169–70, 172, 174–77 184, 189
Elijah 173

232

Enoch 173
Enthusiasm 95, 101–4, 106, 135, 142–47, 149, 176
Enthusiastic model 142–49
Ephesus 49, 51, 155
  Ministry in 51
Eschatology 145, 147
  Deferred 145
  Future 97–98, 145
  Imminent 187–89
  Realized 95, 97–98, 139, 144–47, 176–77, 188
Exhortation 12, 34–35, 73–76, 78–80, 82, 84–85, 87, 221–25
Exordium 77, 79, 82, 86–87, 225

First Jerusalem journey 55
First missionary journey 55
Forgery hypothesis 4–10, 14–16, 27, 181–84, 191
Fourth Jerusalem journey 55
Frank 175

Gallio inscription 53, 56
Gnostic model 147–49
Gnosticism 6, 9, 15, 51, 95, 98, 103, 108, 135, 148–50, 176

House church 117, 120–21
Hutterites 168

Impractical congregation model 138–40
Ishatai 171
Isis 126
Islam 162

Jason 114–17, 119–20, 125, 132, 170
Jehovah's Witnesses 168
Jerome 121
Jerusalem 54
  Conference 51, 54–56, 58–59
  Destruction of 37, 39
  Offering 51
  Riot in A. D. 48 37, 57
  Temple 6, 39
Jewish Christians 13, 39
Jewish-Roman War 37, 39, 57
Josephus 37
Judea 50
  Christians 73–74
  Churches in 54–55, 60
  Famine 37, 57

Judaism 162
  Hellenistic 156
  Proselytes 137
Judaizer crisis 54–55, 60

Lawlessness 54, 222
  Man of 24, 54, 57, 83, 222
Letter 224
  Benediction 34, 44–45, 70, 72, 74, 76–77, 80–82, 84–86, 107, 185, 188–89, 216, 218, 220, 224
  Body 68–70, 220, 224
  Closing 70, 76, 216, 219–20, 222–24
  Greetings 72, 76, 85, 182, 185, 216, 218, 220, 222–24
  Opening 70, 218–19, 220, 223–24
  Postscript 70, 85, 185, 225
  Prescript 70, 72, 79, 82, 218, 220–25
  Salutation 72, 82, 216, 218, 220, 222–23
  Signature 3, 6, 9–10, 24, 70, 87, 182–85
  Superscript 72
  Thanksgiving 33–34, 36, 38–39, 41–45, 63, 68–74, 76, 79, 82, 84, 86, 91, 100, 102, 137, 141, 168, 222–25
Libertinism 106, 148–49, 152, 161, 190
Linguistics 65
Lystra 155

Macedonia 50, 56, 58, 119–21, 123, 126, 128
Marriage 105–6, 127, 151
Melanesia 174
Messiah 169
Messianism 122, 126, 132, 150, 161–65
Millenarism 162–63, 166, 168, 173, 175–77, 186, 191
  Comparative analysis 163
  Definition 161
  Ideology 168, 174, 187
  Model xv, 161–78
  Symbols 161, 165, 168
Millenarian movements 163, 168–70, 172–76
  Brazilian 167
  Cargo cults 172, 174
  Characteristic features 161
  Christian 162
  Cologne Beghards 172
  Frankist 175
  Irvingites 163
  Jewish 164–65, 175
  Modern 165
  Old Believers 173
  Palestinian 164
  Rise of 163–65, 167

Sabbatian   172
Taborites   173
Thessalonian   167, 171–72, 176, 181
Xhosa   173
Millenarian practices   165, 172–76
Millenarian radicalism   xiii, xv, 176–78, 181,
    190–91
Millennium   xiii, 171, 173–74, 177, 181
Millerites   168
Monetary compensation   144, 151–52, 153,
    178

Narratio   72–73, 77, 79, 91, 93, 100, 102,
    105, 221, 225
Nizhny Novgorod   173

Octavian   123–24
Paphlagonia   125
Papias   122
Paraenesis   224
Parousia   4, 5–6, 8, 17, 25–26, 34–35, 38, 41–
    42, 55, 57, 74, 77, 79, 83–84, 86–87,
    94–100, 104–5, 107, 140, 143, 143,
    145–48, 151, 172, 175–76, 178, 186 89,
    191, 222–23
Partitio   77–78, 225
Pastoral Epistles   44–45
Patrons   103, 117, 120
Paul
    Apostolic commission   9, 146, 148, 152–
        54
    Apostolic leadership   35, 38, 69, 71, 73–
        74, 77, 86, 169, 221
    Behavior   34, 49, 73, 92, 152–54
    Criticism of   170
    Example   151
    Handworker   116, 120
    Imprisonment   155
    Labor   152
Pauline letter corpus   22, 34, 182
Peroratio   76, 78, 81, 85–87, 107, 221, 225
Persecution   xiii, 7, 28, 50, 54, 60, 74, 76, 79,
    83, 86, 91, 93–94, 99, 116, 137, 146–47,
    155, 171, 176–78, 188
Peter   54, 146, 155
Philippi   56, 117, 124
    Arrival in   56
    Financial support from   116
    Poverty   120
Politarchs   114, 123, 131–32, 170
Polycarp   6, 23
Probatio   75, 78, 83, 86, 102, 221, 225
Proem   76, 220–21, 223–24

Prophecy   99–101, 135, 144–45, 150, 169,
    171, 173, 184
Propositio   83, 86
Pseudo-Demetrius   67, 71
Pseudo-Libanius   67, 71, 81

Quintilian   203

Relative deprivation   xiv, 163–64, 166
Resurrection   26, 94–96, 143, 148
Revivalistic model   136–38
Rhetoric
    Classical   63–66, 76
    Deliberative   71, 82, 87
    Demonstrative   71–72, 82, 91, 171
    Genre   67, 71
    New   64–66
Rome   121, 124, 126, 132, 169
    Expulsion of Jews from   37

Sabbatai Zvi   173
Samothrace   129, 130–31
Satan   74, 187
Second Jerusalem journey   55
Second missionary journey   49, 51–53, 55
Secundus   119
Serapis   126
Sexual ethic   45, 105–6, 108, 127, 129, 137–
    38, 140, 145–46, 151, 156, 172–73,
    175–77
Simon Magus   155
Silas   33, 50, 52–53, 60, 82
Sociolinguistics   65–66
Spirit   100–02, 105–8, 136, 143–44, 146–47,
    149, 154 8–69, 175–77, 184

Therme   119
Thebes   130
Thessalonica
    Affliction in   93, 99, 140
    Cabiric cult   xiv, 127, 129, 130, 131, 149,
        156, 165, 169–70, 172, 174, 176
    Civic cult   xiv, 124–26, 131–32, 165–66
    Conversion   100
    Criticism of leaders   103–4, 137–38, 146,
        170, 175, 177
    Cultural situation   113
    Departure from   138
    Despair   95–96, 155
    Disorderly   7, 22–23, 36, 44, 75, 80, 82,
        85–86, 92, 99–100, 103–5, 137, 139–40,
        143–44, 146, 151, 152, 156, 170, 172–
        77, 192
    Economy   120–21

Excavation   114–15, 128
Founding mission   29, 35, 50, 52, 58–59,
    77, 95, 115–16, 185
Gentile-Christians   21, 118–19
Gnostic missionaries   148
Greek population   xiv, 119, 125–26, 166–
    67
Handworkers   xiv, 165–66
Immigrants   121
Jewish agitation   116–17, 150
Jewish Christians   21, 118–19
Jewish population   119–20
Latin population   119, 126, 167
Minority population   119
Mystery religions   126–27, 131
Paul's departure from   117
Political status   123
Roman influence   121, 123, 125
Samaritan synagogue   120
Slaves   120
Temples   124, 126
Women   120
Working class   120
Theudas   37–38, 57
Third Jerusalem journey   55
Third missionary journey   49, 51, 148
Timothy   25–26, 28–29, 33, 43, 50–53, 60,
    74, 82, 91–93, 96, 105, 216
Transitus   74, 77, 221

Utopianism   122, 169, 174

Via Egnatia   121
Virgil   126

Work ethic   173–74, 176–77

Zeus   126–27

Index

MODERN AUTHORS

Aberle, D.   163, 166, 203
Adas, M.   163, 203
Adeney, W. F.   69–70, 193, 216–217
Allen, G.   163, 203
Allo, E. B.   64, 201
Anrich, G.   127, 130, 206
Arens, E.   64, 201
Askwith, E. H.   4, 185, 193
Aune, D. E.   100–101, 189, 206
Aus, R. D.   58, 99, 193

Bailey, J. A.   15, 69, 193
Bailey, J. W.   70, 78–79, 193, 220, 222, 224
Baltensweiler, H.   22, 106, 193, 206
Bammel, E.   38, 206
Barkun, M.   163, 174, 203
Bassler, J. M.   13, 171, 193
Bauer, W.   52, 93, 107, 149, 206
Baumgarten, J.   100, 168, 206
Baur, F. C.   4, 193, 206
Beare, F. W.   92, 193
Beauvery, R.   106, 193
Beck, N. A.   41, 206
Becker, J.   95, 206
Beckford, J. A.   163, 203
Beker, J. C.   12, 100, 168, 206
Berger, K.   92, 201
Best, E.   22, 30, 51–53, 55, 57, 69, 78–80,
     92–93, 98, 101, 104–5, 107, 113, 115,
     118, 120, 140–41, 147, 183 84, 187,
     190, 193, 216–17, 222
Betz, H. D.   64, 153–56, 201, 206
Betz, O.   187, 193
Bieler, L.   153–55, 206
Bitzer, L. F.   65, 201
Bjerkelund, C. J.   34, 206
Black, D. A.   97, 103, 193
Blaiklock, E. M.   115, 121, 207
Blake, B.   96, 193
Boers, H.   40, 69–70, 193, 220
Bornemann, W.   4, 11, 70, 104, 139, 184,
     193, 216–17

Bornkamm, G.   36, 207
Brandenburger, E.   108, 207
Brandon, S. G. F.   39, 207
Brandt, W. J.   65, 201
Braun, H.   7, 194
Brock, B. L.   63–64, 201
Broer, I.   40, 207
Brox, N.   182, 207
Bruce, F. F.   27, 38, 52–53, 55, 69, 79–80,
     94, 98, 100, 104, 113–15, 118, 141, 145,
     149, 184–86, 190, 194, 216 17, 222
Buck, C.   26, 57, 58, 207
Bühler, K.   65, 201
Bultmann, R.   64, 201
Bünker, M.   64, 201
Burkert, W.   127, 128, 144–45, 207
Burkeen, W. H.   194, 194
Burkitt, F. C.   22, 207
Burridge, K.   171–72, 203
Burton, E. D.   113, 123, 207

Carney, T. A.   135, 203
Cavallin, H. C.   194
Chadwick, H.   93, 194
Clark, D. L.   67, 201
Clemen, C. C.   37, 114, 142, 194, 207
Cohn, N.   162, 204
Cole, S. G.   128, 130, 207
Collins, R. F.   33, 37, 40, 42, 94, 97, 100,
     102, 106–7, 113, 115, 123, 194
Conzelmann, H.   116, 207
Coppens, J.   40, 194
Corley, B.   207
Cullmann, O.   102, 187, 194, 207

Danker, F. W.   124, 207
Davies, P. E.   121, 207
Day, P.   8, 194
Delling, G.   22, 152, 194
Demke, C.   44–46, 194
Denis, A. M.   34, 50, 150, 187, 194
Dewailly, L. M.   91, 194

Dibelius, M. 17, 23, 98, 102, 107, 152, 184, 194
Dickey, S. 122–23, 204
Dijk, T. A. van 66, 201
Dobschütz, E. von 6, 11,-12, 27, 41, 52, 60, 98, 105, 115, 118 19, 123, 138–40, 150, 152, 184, 186–87, 189, 194
Donfried, K. P. 41, 69, 70, 78, 80, 113, 125, 127, 130, 195, 216–17, 222
Doty, W. G. 67, 69–70, 207, 220
Douglas, M. 164, 166, 204

Eckart, K. G. 34, 42–43, 45–46, 195
Edgar, T. R. 190, 195
Edson, C. 113–14, 123–24, 126–29, 131, 195
Egenolf, H. A. 78, 80, 195, 222
Eliade, M. 174, 204
Elliger, W. 115, 119, 121, 123, 126–27, 207
Ellis, E. E. 23, 207
Evans, R. M. 113, 115, 118–21, 123–24, 126–27, 131, 195

Farnell, L. P. 130, 207
Faw, C. E. 92, 195
Festinger, L. 164, 204
Fillmore, C. J. 66, 201
Findlay, G. G. 70, 78–80, 141, 195, 222
Finegan, J. 53, 207
Forbes, C. 68, 201
Frame, J. E. 11, 60, 68–70, 80, 94, 103–4, 107, 115, 118, 136–37, 150, 184, 190, 195, 216–17, 222
Frey, P. J. B. 119, 207
Friedrich, G. 15, 41–42, 45, 53, 69–70, 78, 80, 98–99, 101, 103, 105–6, 115, 144–46, 153, 195, 207, 216–17, 222
Fuchs, E. 41, 195
Funk, A. 24, 103, 204
Funk, R. W. 38 , 208

Gager, J. G. 40, 162, 204, 208
Gaston, L. H. 37, 208
Gelzer, H. 129, 208
Georgi, D. 144, 149, 152–56, 208
Gerlach, L. P. 176, 204
Gerth, B. 97, 210
Giblin, C. H. 98, 195
Gillman, J. 98, 195
Glock, C. Y. 163, 166–67, 204
Glotz, G. 120, 208
Goguel, M. 22–23, 37, 208
Goppelt, L. 39, 208
Graafen, J. 7, 195
Gregson, R. 25–26, 195

Gren, E. 121, 208
Grimm, C. L. W. 4, 195
Grotius, H. 3, 24, 26, 208
Gülich, E. 65, 202
Gundry, R. H. 53, 208
Gurr, T. R. 163, 204
Guthrie, D. 53, 70, 79–80, 92, 208, 216–17, 223

Habicht, C. 153, 208
Hadas, M. 156, 208
Hadorn, W. 49–51, 195
Haenchen, E. 52, 115–17, 208
Harder, G. 82, 208
Hare, D. R. A. 39, 208
Harnack, A. von 21–23, 196
Harnisch, W. 95–97, 148–49, 196
Harris, J. R. 128, 208
Harrison, J. F. C. 162, 204
Hauck, F. 144, 151–52, 208
Hellholm, D. 28, 65, 168, 202, 208
Hemberg, B. 127–30, 208
Hendrix, H. L. 114, 124, 126, 128, 196
Hess-Lüttich, E. W. B. 66, 202
Hilgenfeld, A. 4, 196
Hill, D. 101, 208
Hine, V. H. 176, 204
Hobsbawm, E. J. 162, 171, 204
Hock, R. F. 120, 208
Holladay, C. R. 156, 208
Holland, G. S. 15, 68, 79–80, 99–100, 104, 196, 225
Hollmann, G. 5, 7, 196
Holmberg, B. 103, 204
Holsten, C. C. 4, 208
Holtzmann, H. J. 4–5, 192, 196
Horbury, W. 150, 196
Horsley, G. H. R. 123, 208
Hübner, H. 59, 208
Hughes, F. W. 3, 15–16, 24, 63, 68, 77–80, 86, 196, 221, 225
Hurd, J. C., Jr. 24, 57, 58, 69–70, 79, 196, 209, 220, 224
Hyldahl, N. 40, 96, 196

Innis, R. E. 65, 202
Isenberg, S. R. 164, 204

Jewett, R. 12, 34, 36, 38–39, 51, 53, 56–59, 106–8, 146–47, 149, 155, 188–89, 196, 209, 221, 225
Johnson, S. 37, 209
Jonas, H. 108, 209

Judge, E. A.   64, 103, 113, 125, 202, 209
Jülicher, A.   4, 209

Kahrstedt, U.   153–54, 209
Kallas, J.   187, 209
Kalleres, J. N.   119, 126, 209
Kaminsky, H.   172–73, 204
Kaye, B. N.   141, 196
Kee, A.   125, 209
Kee, H. C.   53, 156, 209
Keller, B. B.   173, 204
Kennedy, G. A.   63, 65, 68, 71, 77–78, 107,
    202, 221
Kern, F. H.   3, 196
Kern, O.   128, 209
Klijn, A. F. J.   96, 196
Knopf, R.   37, 209
Knox, J.   49, 51, 55–59, 209
Knox, W. L.   156, 209
Koenig, E.   64, 202
Koenig, J.   100, 209
Koester, H.   15, 63, 67–68, 76, 78, 92, 102,
    115, 196, 210
Koskenniemi, H.   29, 185, 202
Krentz, E.   15, 16, 197
Krodel, G.   14, 79–80, 189, 197, 224
Kroll, W.   67, 202
Kühner, R.   97, 210
Kümmel, W. G. 8, 42, 210

Lake, K.   22, 210
Lampe, G. W. H.   37, 210
Lang, F.   93, 197
Lanternari, V.   163, 166, 204
Larson, J. A. O.   121, 210
Laub, F.   14, 15, 94, 97–98, 103, 144, 197
Lausberg, H.   63, 107, 202
Lehmann, P. W.   130, 210
Liefeld, W. L.   156, 210
Lienesch, M.   163, 204
Lifschitz, B.   120, 197
Lightfoot, J. B.   91, 103, 113–14, 128, 139,
    197
Lindemann, A.   15, 197
Lipsius, R. A.   4, 197
Lofland, J.   163, 204
Lohfink, G.   96, 210
Loisy, A. F.   37, 210
Lövestam, E.   97, 101, 210
Luedemann, G.   51, 58–59, 95, 210
Lueken, W.   70, 197
Lührmann, D. 13, 210
Lünemann, G. 4, 100, 120, 139, 197

Lütgert, W. 9, 103, 106, 142–48, 197, 210
Luz, U.   95, 210

MacMullen, R.   120, 124, 130, 210
Mainberger, G. K.   63, 202
Makaronas, C. I.   121, 197
Malherbe, A. J.   67, 102, 106, 150, 197, 202
Mandel, A.   175, 205
Manson, T. W.   24–26, 197
Marrou, H. I.   67, 202
Marshall. I. H.   11, 13, 15, 24, 42, 51–53, 55,
    69–70, 72, 78, 80, 93, 97, 99, 100–104,
    113, 115, 118, 141, 184, 190, 197, 218–
    19, 223
Martin, J.   63, 202
Martin, R. P.   53, 63, 197
Marxsen. W.   8–10, 15, 38, 53, 55, 69, 72,
    79–80, 93–96, 98 99, 101–4, 113, 115,
    118, 146, 181–82, 188–89, 197, 210,
    218–19, 223
Masson, C.   7, 98, 101, 107, 113, 115, 118,
    150, 152, 197–98
Mattern, L.   97, 210
Maurer, C.   106, 198
Mearns, C. L.   145, 147, 188, 198
Meeks, W. A.   24, 28, 103, 121, 169, 175,
    205
Merk, O.   123, 195
Michaelis, W.   8, 23, 49–51, 198, 210
Michel, O.   40, 198
Milligan, G.   4, 69–71, 80, 98, 104, 115, 141,
    183, 198, 218–19, 223
Moffatt, J.   4, 37, 72, 104, 152, 198, 210
Momigliano, A.   58, 210
Moore, A. L.   6, 97, 139, 210
Morgan, M. G.   123, 210
Morgenthaler, E.   66, 202
Morgenthaler, R.   11, 66, 211
Morris, C. W.   66, 202
Morris, L.   69, 186, 198, 218–19
Moulton, J. H.   97, 211
Müller, C.   9, 211
Munck, J.   9, 187–88, 198, 211
Munro, W.   44–46, 211
Murphy-O'Connor, J.   58–59, 120, 211

Neil, W.   22, 53, 91, 94, 98, 101, 107, 150,
    152, 177, 198
Nepper-Christensen, P. 94, 198
Nilsson, M. P.   124, 130, 211
Nock, A. D.   129–30, 153–54, 211
Nörr, D.   124, 211
Norden, E.   64, 202

O'Brien, P. T. 69, 211
Oberhummer, E. 115, 198
O'Dea, T. F. 163, 205
Oepke, A. 101, 118, 184, 198
Okeke, G. E. 40, 198
Olbrechts-Tyteca, L. 63, 65–66, 202
Ollrog, W. H. 24, 103, 211
Oommen, T. K. 170, 205
Oostendorp, D. W. 156, 211
Orchard, J. B. 37, 198

Pagels, E. 108, 211
Palmer, D. W. 69, 150, 198
Papazoglu, F. 121, 123, 211
Pax, E. 137–38, 198
Pearson, B. A. 37–41, 45, 198
Perdelwitz, R. 93, 198
Pereira de Queiros, M. I. 167, 169, 205
Perelman, C. 63, 65–66, 202
Pervo, R. I. 117, 120, 211
Petersen, N. R. 64, 205
Peterson, R. J. 8, 70–71, 79, 198, 220, 224
Pieper, J. 144–45, 211
Plett, H. F. 66, 202–3
Plevnik, J. 42, 96–97, 198–99
Plummer, A. A. 69–70, 101, 150, 199, 223
Poblete, R. 163, 205
Pride, J. B. 66, 203

Raible, W. 65, 202
Reese, J. M. 51, 55, 91, 101–2, 105, 107, 115, 145, 147, 190, 199
Refshauge, E. 43–46, 199
Reicke, B. 8, 39, 144–45, 199, 211
Reitzenstein, R. 155, 211
Riecken, H. W. 164, 204
Rigaux, B. 3, 8, 11, 22, 24, 42, 69–70, 79–80, 104, 106, 107, 113–14, 118, 149, 199, 218–19, 223
Robinson, J. A. T. 6, 211
Robinson, J. M. 15, 210
Roetzel, C. J. 69–70, 211, 220
Roloff, J. 116, 211
Roosen, A. 199, 218–19
Rossano, P. 115, 199
Rostovtzeff, M. 121, 212
Rowland, C. 168, 212
Rudolph, K. 108, 212
Russell, D. S. 168, 212

Sandeen, E. R. 162, 205
Saunders, E. W. 145, 199
Schachter, S. 164, 204

Schade, H. H. 59, 212
Schenke, H. M. 99, 212
Schiby, J. 120, 197
Schille, G. 116, 119, 212
Schippers, R. 37, 199
Schlier, H. 69, 141, 199
Schmidt, D. 40–41, 199
Schmidt, J. E. C. 3, 199
Schmidt, P. W. 141, 182, 199
Schmidt, S. J. 66, 203
Schmithals, W. 33–36, 44, 46, 49, 51, 92, 95, 97, 101, 102, 106, 108, 147–50, 199, 212
Schneider, G. 117, 119, 212
Schnelle, U. 199
Scholem, G. 163, 172–73, 212
Schrenk, G. 152, 212
Schubart, W. 67, 203
Schubert, P. 34, 42–43, 69, 212
Schulz, S. 153, 212
Schürmann, H. 69–70, 199, 218–19
Schweizer, E. 23, 108, 199
Scott, R. 33, 212
Scott, R. L. 63–64, 201
Scramuzza, V. M. 58, 212
Segal, R. A. 174, 204
Sharot, S. 163–65, 175, 205
Shepperson, G. 163, 205
Siegert, F. 64, 203
Smalley, S. 97, 212
Smallwood, E. M. 58, 212
Smith, D. M. 53, 69–70, 212, 218–19
Smith, M. 156, 208
Snyder, G. F. 187, 212
Spicq, C. 104–5, 107, 199, 212
Spittle, D. 130, 210
Spivey, R. A. 53, 69–70, 212, 218–19
Stalnaker, R. C. 66, 203
Stanley, D. M. 9, 212
Stark, R. 163, 173, 205
Stark, W. 126, 205
Stempvoort, P. A. van 107, 199
Stephenson, A. M. G. 98, 199
Stepien, J. 7, 200, 212
Stern, M. 120, 212
Strobel, A. 6, 8, 213
Suggs, M. J. 58, 213

Talmon, Y. 161–63, 173–75, 205
Taylor, G. 26, 57–58, 207
Theissen, G. 103, 205
Thieme, K. 34, 42, 200
Thompson, E. 24, 200

Thrall, M. E.   156, 213
Thrupp, S. L.   163, 205
Thurston, R. W.   24, 200
Tiede, D. L.   156, 213
Trilling, W.   3, 7–8, 10–16, 45, 80, 105, 181–
    83, 200, 223

Ubbink, J. T.   185, 200
Unger, M. F.   115, 200
Unnik, W. C. van   101, 200

Vacalopoulos, A. E.   115, 118, 121, 200
Veloso, M.   107, 200
Vickers, M. J.   114, 119, 200
Vielhauer, P.   15, 115, 213

Wallace, A. F. C.   163, 165, 205–6
Wallis, R.   168, 205
Ware, P.   188, 200
Weinreich, O.   153–54, 213
Weiss, J.   24, 45, 64, 203, 213
West, J. C.   24, 26, 200
Whiteley, D. E. H.   70, 200
Wilckens, U.   108, 213
Wilder, A. N.   64, 203
Wilke, C. G.   64, 203
Wilson, B. R.   164, 171, 205–6
Witt, R. E.   127–30, 213
Worsley, P.   163, 172, 174, 206
Wrede, W.   5–8, 10, 21, 182, 200
Wrzol, J.   7, 200
Wuellner, W.   63–64, 203
Wunderlich, D.   66, 203

Zahn, T.   4, 213
Zygmunt, J. F. 168, 206